FROM CHRISTMAS TO CHRISTMAS

Stories from *Joulusta Jouluun* by Väinö Havas

A Translation from the Finnish by Tyynie S. Kiefer

Pen-and-Ink Artwork by N. Gordon Nelson
Edited by Marilyn and David Cummins

From Christmas To Christmas
Copyright © 1993, 1994
First Printing 1993
Second Printing 1994, with corrections
All rights reserved.

The Cummins Company
2775 Manchester
Ann Arbor, Michigan 48104-6571

Printed and bound by McNaughton & Gunn Inc.
in the United States of America.

ISBN 0-9640069-2-8

TABLE OF CONTENTS

Title	Page
CHRISTMAS	
Father's and Son's Christmas	1
Christmas Sermon	7
The Christmas Gift	9
The Broken Cradle	12
Martha's Christmas Eve	15
Christmas of All Christmases	19
It Surely was a Christmas Angel	21
WINTER	
New Year's Sauna	24
The Trail	25
A Fearful Night for Charles	26
A Miserable Ski Trip	28
"Can You Forgive Me, Son?"	31
Trip to School	34
A Truly New Year	37
Quarrels Break Friendships...	41
...But Love Rebuilds Friendships	43
Hardened Surfaces	46
Pointing the Way	48
John's Heroic Deed	49
"Mother, Repent!"	51
Gethsemane	52
The Hardest Thing	55
Suffering Jesus	57
SPRING AND SUMMER	
Easter Song	58
Spring	60
Spring Teaches From The Highway	62
The Great Catch	63
Reward for Sunday Work	67
The Butting Wooden Cow	69
The Confirmation Gift	73
David's Fish	75
Only Two	78
Sunday Fish	79

SPRING AND SUMMER (continued)

Gifts of Holy Communion	81
Cry Unto Me for Help in Distress	85
Stephen's First Communion	87
Distress Bells	90
First Time/Last Time	92
Falling Into Sin	94
The Rosebush	97
The Church Trip	98
Lessons from the Swallow	101
A Worm-Eaten Apple	103
Strawberry Girl	104
Midsummer Salmon	109
A Hay-Making Week	113
Four Kinds of Soil	116
How Olle Got Services	121
When God Blessed the Seed	124

FALL

The Thole-Pin	126
The Reluctant Outboard Motor	130
The Cucumber Field	132
The Return	136
Little Gertrude's Wreath	140
In Darkness	144
Judgment	146
The Broken Sled	148
Learning Contentment	150
The Hat	153
The Conversion of Peter Juuti	155
Jesus, Little and Poor	158
Little Arthur's Enduring Decision	161

CHRISTMAS AGAIN

A Christmas Roast	163
"I'm Going To Buy Christmas!"	166
The Christmas Fish	169
Sarah Marie Returns Home	172
Christmas Gift for Old Teacher	176
Little Things are Important	179
Appendix: A Little Finnish History	181

ACKNOWLEDGEMENTS

Gordon Nelson created the delightful line drawings which illustrate and illuminate the stories. The Nelsons made available the photograph of Väinö Havas which appears on the next page, from among the papers of Rev. John Nelson, Gordon's father. The picture is almost certainly from a mission trip by Havas to the U.S.

Raymond Tulkki, whose boyhood language was Finnish, encouraged translation of these stories, wrote the notes about the author Väinö Havas and helped us clarify several passages.

Leo Torola was consulted often by Tyynie when she found that translating some part of a story was a challenge.

Maija Laurmaa Kaldjian helped us to improve the accuracy of some sections. Maija grew up and was educated in Finland. In 1957 she came to the U.S. when she was 28, intending to stay just long enough to earn another degree in English at The University of Michigan. Instead she married and has lived here in Michigan since then. Maija's fluency in Finnish and English and her familiarity with life and customs in Finland made her contributions invaluable.

David and Marilyn (Kiefer) Cummins
Editors

VÄINÖ HAVAS

Väinö Rafael Havas was born August 15, 1898, at Lempäälä, Finland. His parents were public school teachers and during his early school years he also thought about becoming a teacher. However, in the spring of 1916 he registered for the study of theology in Helsinki. After several interruptions in his studies he graduated with honor and was shortly ordained to the ministry of the Evangelical Lutheran Church of Finland.

During his university studies Havas turned to the New Awakening (Uusiheräys), one of several schisms within the revival movement which began in northern Sweden through the ministry of Rector Lars Levi Laestadius.[1] Havas sought earnestly for truth revealed in God's word and for a God-given inner peace and personal assurance. After much anguish of soul and spirit he embraced the freeing Gospel of Jesus Christ for the forgiveness of sin, as proclaimed by the conservative (vanhoillis) believers of the Laestadian revival movement.

This conversion experience took place while Havas was Rector of the Merijärvi parish. He had found his spiritual home, had found the Kingdom of God. Havas remained in the fellowship and faith of these believers until his death on the battlefield August 20, 1941.

---

[1] Lars Levi Laestadius, 1800-1861. The name Lars in Swedish Lapland becomes Lauri in Finland; both spellings are frequently encountered.

INTRODUCTION

(THE STORIES BEHIND THE STORIES)

This little book is doubly a labor of love by Väinö Havas and Tyynie Kiefer.

Väinö Havas wrote these sixty-eight stories with love particularly for the young folks of the families among whom he preached and ministered. The stories are mostly unconnected anecdotes which could have happened in the lives of these young people. Each has a clear moral or spiritual message which, as in parables, reinforces or clarifies an aspect of religious faith in our lives with which we already have some knowledge. The stories also reveal the depth and breadth of Havas' interests in gardening, fishing, hunting, skiing and boating in his life devoted to spiritual leadership and teaching. Havas was a gifted writer with insight, imagination and a rich, wide vocabulary. The book in Finnish was published in 1953 by Suomen Rauhanyhdistysten Keskusyhdisys, r.y., Oulu, Finland.

Tyynie Sigrid Salo was born March 10, 1906, in Brainerd, Minnesota, the eighth of Oscar and Selma Salo's twelve children. Oscar and Selma both immigrated to America, he from Finland and she from Norwegian Lapland. They began homesteading a farm near New York Mills, Minnesota, when Tyynie was one year old. Tynnie attended Moorhead State Teacher's College and the University of Minnesota. She left teaching grade school in May of 1931 to marry Paul M. Kiefer.

Tyynie was always interested in her Finnish heritage; Finnish was spoken in her childhood home and church. In 1970, with her husband Paul and two daughters, she spent nearly a month in Finland visiting friends and relatives and places of interest. After the Kiefers retired in 1968, T (to all who knew her) translated into English scores if not hundreds of Finnish sermons and articles, some transcribed from tapes and some from the Finnish-language monthly of the Apostolic Lutheran Church.

After reading several stories in *Joulusta Jouluun,* she exclaimed, "I have never seen anyone write like this before!" So that she could share her exciting discovery, she translated a few stories to the best of her ability and sent copies to family and friends. Some of them, particularly Ingrid Ylisto and Ray Tulkki, encouraged her to do more and she did.

Discussions with her husband Paul often began, "How would you say this?" Eventually T's laborious longhand copy began to find its way into the computer they bought when Paul was eighty, entered with Paul's two-fingered skills. Paul's contribution to this book demands that we call it a joint effort.

Printed copies began to replace typed copies. Marilyn and David Cummins edited several of the stories and sent back copies closer to publishing format, with thoughts about assisting in a wider circulation. Thus encouraged, T set about translating all of the remaining stories. A book which vividly illustrates how faith affects a Christian's daily life became a dream made real which Tyynie was joyfully anticipating when she died April 7, 1993.

About translating and editing:

The stories are consistent with the doctrine and practice of the congregations among which Havas moved. Every attempt was made in translating and editing to preserve all aspects of the author's doctrine. The right and duty of individual believers to preach forgiveness now, in the present time, is essential doctrine which is abundantly evident in the stories. The services mentioned in the stories were in many instances more like meetings or gatherings in homes with singing and with local laymen or visiting ministers speaking.

It is a real challenge to edit these translations, in at least three respects:

1. A translation attempts to move from one vernacular to another; a dictionary equivalent is not always successful.
2. Finnish and English sentence structures are very different and a word-by-word linear translation often appears awkward.
3. A few scenes and circumstances which were familiar and common before 1940 in small-town Finland, generally apart from the larger cities, are not in the experience of many of the readers.[1]

The guidelines for editing were simply to understand as accurately as possible what Havas wrote and then to present this in American English in the current vernacular in reasonably correct sentence structure. This was to be accomplished without adding or subtracting from the original thought and to "sound" as much like the original as possible!

A number of titles including grandfather, grandmother, auntie and uncle were and are commonly used for addressing respected adults in the community and do not necessarily imply relation. Master and mistress were used where we would say the man of the house or the lady of the house; these usages were freely kept in the stories. Steam bath, bath house and sauna are used interchangeably. Some personal names were arbitrarily changed to common English names for familiarity and variety.

Twenty-five poems are sprinkled through the original book. Poetry is so delicate and demands such complete mastery of the language that translation was not attempted. Poetry, with its precise meaning, its rhythmic cadence and its rhyming syllables, is an art form above story translation. Nevertheless, several hymns which are integral to stories were translated.

---

[1] So we felt that the Appendix at the end of this book was quite necessary.

FATHER AND SON'S CHRISTMAS

In the fall of the year 1939, war was spreading over the world and many things were happening which could not be understood by a small boy.[1] One night someone from the police station knocked on the window, waking Father with a start to come and receive a card. He turned quite pale as he read it by the light of a candle, and Mother also looked worried. "Did it come now?" she whispered.

"Yes."

"Did <u>what</u> come?" Henry had been wakened from the very sound sleep that comes just before morning and could no longer be quiet. But Mother urged him to return to bed: "Sleep, sleep peacefully, child."

Henry closed his eyes, but not very tightly, for he was not sleepy any more. He peeped secretly and saw how Father's army uniform had been brought out and his boots oiled. His rucksack was packed with shirts, socks, the mission paper of Zion, his New Testament and a hymnal.

Henry had already seen many happenings which seemed to have more meaning than usual. There was sharing in getting ready for military service, attending church services together, preparing for confirmation school examination. And last night Henry saw his father and mother kneel together beside their bed and embrace one another and preach to each other forgiveness of sins in Jesus' name and precious blood.

Next day Father lifted Henry high over his head and gazed at him with a warmth and intensity that made him cry. Finally he pressed his cheek against Henry's and his chin quivered as he said, "God's peace, my son."

---

[1] See Appendix: *A Little Finnish History.*

Then he rode away on his bicycle. The boy stood by his mother for a long time, looking down the lane and at the yellow leaves over which the bicycle had passed.

That was many weeks ago. The hired man Peter worked alone to plow the frozen fields. Mother was mostly silent as she did the necessary tasks, travelling familiar paths to the kitchen, the barn and from along the fence to the cellar. In the evenings she sat knitting near Henry's bed, making thick wool socks for Father. She also knitted special warm mittens with an opening for the trigger finger.

Henry knew about those mittens. He had learned that his father carried a government rifle in the army with a company of others from his own neighborhood and church. The men served so that Henry and Mother and all other Finns could live in peace in their own homes.

As Christmas approached, Father had written that he would get a furlough, time off for the great holiday. Then came another message on an Army postcard:

Loved ones there at home: John's mother is seriously ill. The only way he can get a furlough is that I must remain here in his place. God bless your 'orphaned' Christmas without a father. Remember that Jesus is with you every day. Pray for me and for all the people of Finland.

From near Kankaalla Isthmus. 18 December 1939. Father.

Mother sighed heavily and was silent for a moment and then snatched their son into her lap quite emotionally and said, "You have a Christian father."

Then began an excited rushed preparation of a Christmas package to send to Father—somewhere. Tyyne Harmala brought gray woolen trousers she had woven. "These were to be for John," she explained, "but of course now they should go to your Sam." Mother got ready multi-colored wool socks she had knitted. Henry bought an enormous slab of chocolate with money he got from his loganberries. Last of all, in the middle of the goodies, they put Henry's Christmas letter. Scrawled in black letters, it was like this:

DEAR FATHER, GOD'S PEACE! I AM A BIT LONESOME FOR YOU. MOTHER IS LONESOME TOO. WE LOVE YOU. BUT MOTHER SAYS SHE WOULD HAVE DONE THE SAME AS YOU. WE PRAY FOR YOU, THAT YOU WOULD HAVE A BLESSED CHRISTMAS. MAY JESUS AND THE GOOD CHRISTMAS ANGELS BE WITH YOU THERE NEAR THE KANKAALLA ISTHMUS. MAY JESUS BLESS MY OWN FATHER, WISHES HENRY.

On Christmas Eve Henry pulled wood for the bathhouse with his sled. It was neat to go to the woodpile stacked against the drying barn and then climb atop the load and slide down a gently sloping hill right to the bathhouse door. On a gray winter evening like this the drying barn was quite a mysterious place and so was the blackened bathhouse by the dock. Familiar smells lingered around them and the dark log walls sent out a feeling of warmth. Chickens had drawn their tracks all over the yard and a weasel had bolted under the floor. It seemed years had gone by since sounds of threshing were heard at the barn.

Henry remembered that last Christmas Eve Father had been the horse pulling the sled loaded with firewood and Henry had been the driver. You could hear the little driver's shouted orders clear up to the farmhouse: "Giddyap, giddyap!"

"Oh Father, Dear Father!" Henry thought and his heart was touched. He sat down on his emptied sled and his eyes followed the smoke from side to side as it pushed its way out of the bathhouse door, into the darkening sky and then toward the house where the pine trees stood.

Father had written as he sat on a stump at Kankaalla, remembering the boy. Henry stared into the shade of the pines where the dusk got denser and the junipers and rocks changed into spooky mounds and shapes. He saw something move there!

Grey men flitted from tree to tree. They glided quietly on their skis behind the pasture fence and sped like a snow flurry toward the house. Their rifles slung on their backs swayed back and forth as snow whirled from the ends of their ski poles. One of them left the group and glided silently right up to Henry. It was Father!

"Greetings from Kankaalla from the top of a stump. I came to bring you a Christmas package. Look! Here is a......"

"Is my driver sleeping here?" asked Mother as she shook Henry by the shoulders. "The little old man must be worn out," she laughed.

"Was it a dream?" he puzzled.

"Was what a dream?"

"Father just visited me and he brought a Christmas package."

"Really! That just means that he remembers us and prays for us where he is, far away."

But Father's Christmas package was not altogether just a dream. After coming in from the bathhouse, Henry sat at the head of the supper table with his face still glowing. The candles burned and the Christmas pudding steamed, when there was a knock at the door.

"A package, a package," someone shouted from outside. The door opened and a parcel flew through it onto the floor.

"Greetings from Sergeant Tuomainen," the voice said, and the door was closed and the sound of steps faded away past the gate. Mother picked up the package and read:

Army mail. Mrs. Hilkka Tuomainen and Henry, Lake Tava, Toppila. To be opened Christmas Eve. Sender: Master Sergeant Samuel Tuomainen.

Mother exclaimed, "Just look! They have made Father a master sergeant! From a sergeant to a master sergeant. That is a Christmas present too!"

The parcel held three smaller packages and a letter. They opened Henry's first. In it was a drum with drumsticks, and burned into the side was "Recruit Henry Tuomainen, Christmas 1939." There was also a beautifully carved and decorated wall placque with a motto burned into it: "Lord protect our country."

Mother's package held a little pail carved from juniper wood, and inside it was a letter written in very tiny print. Mother didn't read it to Henry, but he guessed that it had only good words because her eyes filled with happy tears and her face glowed.

There was also a letter for both of them which went like this:

"My loved ones! May the Christmas peace fill your hearts. I made these keepsakes for you during the long candle-lit hours. While I worked on them I remembered my dear home, my dear wife and my dear child. On this great festival let us be joined in faith and prayer by the child in the manger, even though we are far apart. God's peace! Father."

Another knock sounded at the door and a white envelope landed on the floor. A woman's clear voice called out, "A blessed Christmas!" and then sleigh bells jingled away down the road. When the envelope was opened a green money order and a letter fell out which Mother read:

"To Mrs. Hilkka Tuomainen. Here is a gift for you. The women of Lake Tava send wishes for Christmas peace for an active co-worker and a wife of a capable army man at the front."

Henry felt that Christmas spirit was overflowing in the living room. The candles shone brightly, the fire crackled delightfully at the back, the Christmas pudding was just perfectly delicious.

"May Jesus bless my little recruit," wished Mother as she blew out the candle.

"May Jesus bless the master sergeant's wife," added the boy.

Meanwhile, Father walked the circuit inspecting his patrol. His new woolen clothes warmed his body and the rustle of little Henry's letter in his jacket pocket warmed his heart. Earlier that morning a huge package addressed to the quartermaster was delivered; it was the Christmas package for the whole company.

He climbed a familiar path to a hill on the edge of a vast marsh. Stopping at the ridge, he looked up to the heavens and sighed, "My Heavenly Father, thank you for this Christmas!" All that evening a quiet heavenly rapture filled the bosom of the soldier.

Some of the very young soldiers felt a bit low in spirits. It was the first Christmas out in the world for many of them. Some tried to grasp happiness by acting casual and cracking jokes, but the stories and songs gradually collapsed altogether. Ransu Raapana finally admitted straight out, "I'm a grown man feeling like a little boy and a sob seems to jump from my heart into my throat."

"In our hearts we've become little boys again tonight and possibly that's not a bad thing for our souls," decided Abe Pirska. "What do you think, Sergeant? You are the only married man still here and you have experience and were promoted to be our leader. Tell us. Are we being tested to see if we are grown up? This Christmas is such a children's festival and we are only boys. So let's sing that cute old Christmas song, 'Mother's Babes Are We All,'" Abe suggested with a sardonic smile.

This brought a mischievous twinkle to the eye of Ervin Vuohenkalma, the company's activities director. They started singing and their Christmas festival began and their depressed spirits rose higher and higher. The sergeant led them in the angels' song and read the Christmas gospel story. Then he prayed in a voice that sometimes quivered for "us bad soldier boys," for the faraway homes near Lake Tava and all the rest of the country, praying to Him who guards his own as the shepherds once guarded their flock in the countryside. They ended their Christmas festival by singing "A Mighty Fortress is our God."

"At least the Kingdom of God remains with us," echoed still in the sergeant's heart. "These boys still don't understand these things inside themselves very much, and only a couple of them are believers. They confessed their Lord very weakly and even so God led and helped them wonderfully." He could not help but praise God.

The sergeant's home seemed to come incredibly close to him. Strange, for a man alone there by the hill, to be picturing his home on Christmas Eve. "I see the bathhouse slowly cooling off there by the dock, the lovely gleam of the candles through the living room window. I hear the clink of the cows' chains from the barn, Henry tapping on his drum, my wife clearing dishes from the table. Beloved, beloved! Dear wife, nearer and dearer than ever! Dear little lad, my son, beginning his life! Beloved cottage home, precious home town, dear country."

"Ransu Raapana was right: it just seems that a sob jumps from my heart and sticks in my throat," thought the sergeant meditatively. Then he continued his circuit of the patrol.

"Guard number three. Nothing unusual, sir," he heard.

"A blessed Christmas, boys."

"The same to you, sergeant, sir."

"Did you see how his face shone?" the senior guard asked his companion when the sergeant's steps had faded away into the valley.

"Yes, surely he is a man who believes in God."

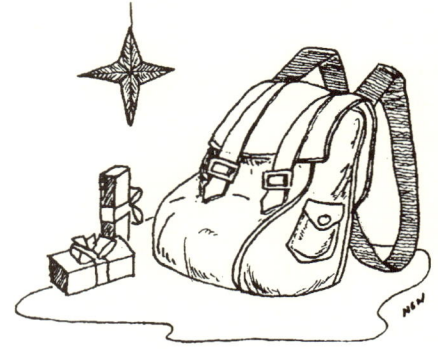

CHRISTMAS SERMON

Charles Väänänen shivered in his cot late on Christmas Eve. Earlier there had been a tree ceremony in the barracks. The chaplain spoke of the sinner's Saviour, the Prince of Peace: "He wants to proclaim peace even to those who serve in the army and who trust in an eternal peace."

Charles was one of the soldiers who hoped for a blessed Christmas. A young music student, he played the Christmas hymn as a solo on his trumpet while tears came to his eyes. The melody lulled him into memories of Christmases at home. Then he recalled those those gray days which followed nights of crying himself to sleep. When his father, Toivola's clear-voiced song leader, was living, his mother did not have to work outside the home. Now she worked as a waitress and served rowdy cafe patrons amidst clouds of smoke and raucous laughter where evil was loose.

Barracks lights were out but the men stayed up late. Bottles and glasses clinked. Shadows moved with unsteady steps between the beds. Somewhere someone stumbled and swore in a way to make one shiver. Someone else sang a bawdy jingle in an uneven voice. Charles Väänänen curled up under his covers like a little ball. His fingers were folded tightly. He tried to say his evening prayer, but the words got muddled in the surrounding clamor.

"Right about now the old ladies and old men out there in the backwoods towns are shuffling to church," someone recalled.

"But now we have the real church services," laughed another. "We even have song leaders for a fifth chapel service, but what about a preacher?"

"Say, we have the cub from Toivola here; he's a great religious fanatic," brought up another.

"Yes, let's make him say a sermon!" came from still another.

Charles Väänänen curled himself still smaller, pulling the covers over his head. Suddenly his bed was upside down and he was dragged out in his underwear and hoisted onto the table amidst its bottles and glasses and his trumpet.

"Now let's have a real Christmas sermon for the enlisted men, holy pastor, a mass, with wine. Let's hear it! Shout it out!" he heard from this one and that.

Charles pleaded with them: "Don't, don't. It is mocking God! Think! It is Christmas!"

"He isn't a man yet, though he is in a school for men," put in one.

Suddenly Charles stood up straight and said, "I am more of a man than all of you put together. If you have the nerve, tease me. Twenty heroes against one miserable student. But I will **not** mock my God!"

"Now, now, don't get angry over a mere trifle, mister corporal, sir!" sarcastically mocked Sergeant Paasonen.

But First Sergeant Niskanen growled, "The boy is right. Let him be."

"The old woman's sickness still stinks in you, too, Sergeant."

"Let it stink! But give the boy peace! Did you hear? Or will you have to be taught a lesson?" His voice was hard. The men retreated to the side.

Charles slipped off the table and climbed back into bed. Gazing through the window, he could see part of the starlit sky. It felt wonderful. His covers were warm and cozy. He clasped his hands together tightly.

"Father, friend of little ones, bless my father, my mother, my sisters and brothers and me, a young lad. Friend of children, bless me, give me peaceful sleep. Send an angel throng for my refuge, my protection. Let me rest under white wings without fear." His evening prayer went on familiarly. His own father had written it and composed the melody.

Now it seemed like years ago at home. The last candle burned on the tree. The little imp was dressed for bed. The gifts were on the pillow, opened. When Father sat at the piano, the melody sprang out at his touch, clear and bright, floating through the dim house. As Mother sat by his side holding the youngest by the hand, Father sang the song of the angels. The candle flame swayed and flickered. Shadows on the wall moved. Were they the wings of the angels?

Someone appeared quietly and sat on the edge of his bed. "What's that you are humming?" asked Sergeant Niskanen in a friendly voice.

"Just my evening prayer," he responded.

"Does it have a tune?"

"Yes."

"Would you sing it for me?"

Charles sang. The clamor of the drunken quieted. A sublime melody hovered over the beds. It rested here and there on the ears of the revellers. It even tried to enter hearts and feelings.

"Mr. Corporal has a voice, and an ear too," whispered Paasonen to his neighbor.

"And faith," was the reply.

But Sergeant Niskanen cried, his broad shoulders shaking. When the song ended, he touched Väänänen's head and said, "Remain in that place, under those white wings, boy. I have not stayed."

"But God does help one return," Charles encouraged .

"Listen, boy, don't flatter me. Say it straight. Do you think I can still have my sins forgiven?"

"Absolutely. Today, believe them forgiven in Jesus' precious blood."

"Attention!" Just then the officer of the day awakened the band members for the Christmas morning church service.

Charles Väänänen sat in the balcony beside the sergeant who played tuba. It seemed to him that a joyous, stirring new feeling rose powerfully from the great horn. Charles played his trumpet so triumphantly and clearly that the Chapel Master looked in wonder. On the benches down below, shy boys from the backwoods towns heard the old familiar hymn, "Angels From the Realms of Glory." It stirred them to the bones and marrow. Christmas in the regiment was possible. Marvelous!

THE CHRISTMAS GIFT

All fall Father and Mother had deep misgivings. Selma, their oldest daughter, was working for strangers during her first year away from home. In the fall--in November--she had left home as a believer. Her parents could not forget her "going-away" services. They had begged forgiveness of one another and the words of blessing had comforted sad hearts. At first Selma called often to her little cabin home. In her homesickness, she sent letters too. But during the summer her visits became less frequent; even letters did not appear. Something cold had crept between her parents and their child. Selma's eyes seemed evasive. Particularly on her last visit, her answers were short and she appeared to be in a great hurry to be off. All this pained her parents and in the evening they talked about it between themselves. Through the night they carried their firstborn in prayer to the Father's heart.

Selma had promised to be home for the Christmas holidays. On Christmas Eve she wrapped two little gift packages for her knapsack. There should have been more, but she had spent lavishly on herself in the fall, so she felt a bit guilty. Last Christmas was different; two months of her salary were saved for family gifts. Her heart had throbbed with joy as she anticipated the delight of her sisters and brothers when they received her gifts. But so what? She was still a child back then! Now, like other people, she had things beyond the necessities, a hat and purse for example.

The snow creaked under her boots. The midwinter sky was a dark red in the south. Bathhouses smoked. Boys hauled Christmas trees on their little sleds. Their cheeks glowed, their eyes shone and their whole beings were brimming over with the spirit and bustle of Christmas. Selma could see her home from Tuomi's hill. It squatted there, grey, in the bend of the woods. Smoke rose in a straight wide ribbon to the freezing sky. Of course there was a fire in the back of the room. The bathhouse door opened and out came a cloud of steam. She saw Mother hurrying across the yard to the barn. Once more Selma felt badly. Last year she had hurried home so she could help her mother with milking but today she poked along the way. Hadn't she had to stop at Ann Mattila's to plan for the St. Stephen's Day dance? Hadn't she toiled enough in a stranger's barn? Shouldn't she be permitted a rest, at least on Christmas?

Peter and Hjalmar dashed out to the porch to meet her. "God's peace, Selma. What's in your knapsack?"

"We'll see this evening," answered their big sister brusquely. The boys looked at each other, amazed.

The cottage was clean. Two candles burned on the table, with an open Bible between them. Father sat beside the table, half dressed, waiting to go to the bathhouse. Seeing Selma he exclaimed, "Ah, finally you have come! God's peace and a blessed Christmas festival!"

Selma mumbled some customary greeting in return and slipped into another room. "It has always been this way at home, too religious and serious," she thought to herself in exasperation. "It would have been better to stay on at Mattila's." The men there were already in a holiday spirit; carefree singing and a swinging polka echoed from the barn.

Mother entered the house with her pails clattering. Selma thought of hurrying to meet her, but instead remained sitting by the window in the dark. The fire sent a flicker of light across the floor and onto the opposite wall. Mother crossed the room obviously disappointed, though she tried to greet Selma cheerfully. "And are you sitting here already, my child? I have thought of you all day. God's peace!" Selma extended her hand without a word. "I see that your faith is no longer in the best of health," sighed Mother and moved on slowly.

"Why pretend?" is what Selma intended to respond, perhaps a little cruely, but she became silent instead.

Father and Mother went bathing with the little ones. Selma went last to the bathhouse, alone. She lounged a long time on the platform with benches and went slowly through the motions of washing. It seemed so depressing to return to the living room. There would be the same old things: the children's little delights, the singing of hymns, the reading, tears and sighs.

Finally Selma sneaked into her bedroom. She dressed entirely in her Sunday clothes and then moved on into the living room where she gave the children their Christmas packages. They were delighted and very pleased. Hesitating at first, they whirled around their big sister and then Katie swung into her lap. Holding Selma around the neck, she thanked her sister for her boots. Mother presented her gift. Selma laid the package beside her without opening it. Father also hunted for something and gave it to Selma, but his package also was left unopened on the bench. Father and Mother received nothing from Selma. Mother began the Christmas hymn.

As Selma's eyes fell on the straw Christmas ornament hanging from the ceiling, she remembered how her parents sang the Christmas hymn to her as a child. She felt as though angel wings hovered like a great blessing over the log walls. Father read about the manger, the child and the shepherds. Then, varying from his usual custom, he read about St. Stephen's death and remarked how close Christmas and St. Stephen's Day are to one another. Joy and suffering go together side by side on the road of life.

But the martyr who died in a rain of rocks was luckier than many of today who celebrate St. Stephen's Day. Stephen saw heaven open before him. But if the young people of this community were to step over death's threshold straight from the St. Stephen's Day partying, the gate of darkness might open before them. The children listened with solemn faces. But Father took Katie on his knee and sang, "There Are Treasures For Children in Heaven Above." The boys and Mother joined in the singing and the faces of the children shone again. When the singing ceased for a while, they moved away to play.

Mother carried the Christmas pudding to the table. Selma barely tasted it. Instead she fed Katie from time to time and prepared the little girl for bed. "Selma bless Katie too," asked the child. The older sister clasped her hands as Katie murmured her evening prayer, the one Selma had learned as a child. She had not prayed it for many months. "Jesus, bless Big Sister," said Katie and fell asleep with her Christmas gifts near her head.

"Katie too," whispered Selma, who felt like crying. She didn't open her gift packages until just before going to bed. Mother had knitted gray woolen stockings again. Father had wrapped a new *Songs of Zion* hymnal in gift wrapping. He wrote on the first page in flourishing letters, "Hold tightly to faith and a good conscience; by rejecting conscience, some persons have made shipwreck of their faith," putting I Timothy 1:19 into his own words for her.

Selma slept very badly that night. On Christmas morning she went to church. During the day she kept busy, helping her mother in silence.

Next day was St. Stephen's Day, December 26. That evening, Ann Mattila waited in vain for Selma to show up at the party. This is why. Selma went to St. Stephen's Day services on Strawberry's lease-farm. Since there was no visiting speaker, Father sat by the Bible. He read again about Stephen and spoke about him. Selma had never heard her father speak so tenderly and yet powerfully. Every word burned her conscience. Father closed: "You who have failed and gone into the ways of the world, you, prodigal child, will not see heaven open before you if you die with your sins on your conscience. The gates of darkness very likely will open before you. But for you, too, on Christmas Eve was born the one who opens heaven, Jesus, your Saviour. Believe again this evening, dear child, as you believed when you were an innocent little child. Believe your sins forgiven in His name and blood."

Selma wept. The old lady from the Strawberry Farm came to Selma. "Has the ungodly world tempted and deceived my godchild?" she asked.

"Yes," sobbed the girl. "Can God still have mercy for me?"

"He has already shown mercy through his Son," assured the godmother, and blessed her. Father also came and blessed her. Mother, her face aglow, rocked back and forth thanking God, "Thank you! Thank you, Father, for the Christmas gift! Let us all thank Him. I have received such a great Christmas gift. Thank you! Thank you, Father!"

THE BROKEN CRADLE

The oldest son of Gus the carpenter slept blissfully. He did not yet appear to be a grown man but it was said that already he mixed with the men in the drinking places. He often sneaked home in the wee hours of the morning and then during the day attempted to avoid his mother's eyes.

Daniel, the second son, was becoming a vigorous young man. There was no one in elementary school who could compete with him in carpentry. He brought many pieces of his woodwork home to his mother; some had been sold. Evenings, Daniel kept busy at home working on wood by the light of the fireplace or at his late father's planing bench where the shavings just flew as he worked.

Christmas time was drawing near. In the Arts and Crafts hour, Daniel brought his towel rack for the teacher to examine. The teacher nodded approvingly and said, "With this you have completed all of the required work, so you may work on whatever you wish." He himself was just completing the base of a cradle. "May I make such a thing for a Christmas gift for my little sister?" Daniel asked diffidently.

"Why not? You may use this one for a pattern."

Soon pieces of dry wood were found, the saw bit happily into the edges of the board and the plane shaved everything smooth. Not a nail was needed, the carefully-made joints fit one another so well! The teacher praised the work many times with a pleased smile. "You have inherited the gifts of your father, who was a beloved brother in faith," he said as he admired the boy's efforts.

Next the shop teacher set out the paints and together they painted the cradle a bluish grey. On the ends, the teacher painted bright red mountain ash clusters. And so school ended. Daniel brought his treasure home secretly in the dusk, taking it to the attic where it would be hidden until the evening before Christmas.

Those last days before Christmas seemed long. Mother was completely busy with cleaning. It wasn't convenient to do carpentry work any more, so Daniel hunted in the woods with a squirrel gun. A couple of squirrels swung from the branches and for their skins Daniel got many bright new coins from the fur trader. His Christmas cash account swelled nicely. He was able to buy coffee and a bag of rice for Mother. And a most beautiful doll from the shelf of the storekeeper appeared in the cradle hiding in the attic!

Yes, Christmas was coming! In the woods one could feel it inside oneself, a good mood, one of anticipation. It was like being in church. On the edge of the clearing twinkled the cheery red cabin home, with smoke from the stove pipe rising straight up into the freezing sky like the smoke of Abel's sacrifice. The barn squatted so fancifully on the side of the hill. Wasn't it like it was on Jesus' Christmas night? There was the manger with straw and the shepherds bowing through the door at the scene inside.

The candles still burned on the table after Christmas eve dinner. Mother washed up the dishes quietly and looked out through the window every now and then. Miina was already asleep. Her cradle was right close to her bed and the doll lying in it, carefully wrapped in Mother's scarf. Daniel was also in bed but still awake. What a fine Christmas! Miina had jumped for joy when she saw the doll and cradle. She flung herself onto Daniel's lap and patted her brother on both cheeks with her little hands. Mother smiled through happy tears.

And then the cradle was rocked. Mother, Daniel and Miina each had to take a turn at rocking the baby and singing familiar songs. Then the doll had to be warmly wrapped and laid with great care back into the cradle. "That's how they swaddled the baby Jesus," Miina said, glancing aside at her mother.

"That's right, my child," said Mother with a laugh. Then seriously she related about the Christmas Jesus in the stable and about the angels and the shepherds. Then the family sang the angels' song together.[1] Mother also told of that song, of how on one Christmas night Martin Luther rocked his little one in the cradle and hummed it then for the very first time.

Big Brother was more like a guest in the house. He joined in the festivities mechanically and was even cold to the hymn. The only thing which brought a bit of a smile to his face was Miina's happy chatter. He often glanced at the clock and eventually slipped out of the room and didn't return. At that point, an uneasiness crept into the room. The candles burned, the Christmas pudding steamed. Miina still talked her baby talk, but Mother began to look out the window now and then and she no longer smiled. The evening now oppressed Daniel, but Miina's playful ways passed the night until just before midnight.

Now Daniel was weary. "Merciful Father, look down from heaven on this little child also," the boy prayed. "Send angels to guard, then nothing will hurt me." Then he fell asleep.

Crash! Daniel awakened suddenly; Miina began crying. Mother searched for matches. From downstairs they could hear groaning: "Ohh...scoundrel...put traps in people's path!"

Mother got the candle lighted. Downstairs, Big Brother clambered to his feet with difficulty. "Cradle...Oh...Miina's cradle!" and burst into fiercer and more uncontrollable groans than before, then staggered to bed.

Daniel reached the main floor. There he stood speechless in front of the broken toy, an awful hatred choking his heart. "I'll take splinters of the cradle and throw them into the scoundrel's face! I'll hit him till the blood squirts!" raced his thoughts. Mother only sat helpless and wan with her hand pressed to her heart.

Then Daniel lifted the doll, which was undamaged, from the floor and into Miina's lap. Together they put the "baby" under the covers beside the girl as she forgot her grief. "The poor thing would soon have frozen," comforted the boy. Then Daniel slowly picked up the pieces of the cradle and gathered them into a corner, after which he crept back up to bed and in bed burst out crying. Through his tears, he heard his mother bemoaning, "Oh, my son, my boy! Oh, that accursed whiskey."

When Big Brother awakened, he had a splitting headache and felt awful generally. The sounds of morning crept into the living room. Sleigh bells jingled as people headed to church. Mother got up, looking pale and as though she had not slept as she lighted the fire on the hearth. It was a difficult scene.

Daniel also rustled around. He picked up the pieces of the broken cradle, felt them and tried to reassemble them, but shook his head. Big Brother suddenly remembered how he stumbled in the night before. Of all things that had to happen! But it might have happened even if he had a clear head. Miina also awakened, shushing her baby: "Miina doesn't have cradle any more. Big Brother broke."

Big Brother rolled over to face the wall. This on Christmas morning! Mother brought him coffee there in bed, looking at him but without a word. He heard Daniel comforting his sister. "In the spring, brother will make a new rocker, just as beautiful."

Outside the window, the children could see beautiful mountain ash clusters just like the ones Daniel's shop teacher was able to paint on the ends of the cradle. Big Brother slipped out the door and wasn't heard from for days. Mother heard that he was visiting the shop teacher and was glad to hear that.

Ann, the teacher's little girl, brought Mother a note on New Year's Eve. Mother read it. She brightened and began preparing for the festival. The children looked on, astonished. New candles were arranged on the table. A white Christmas pudding cooked in the double boiler. New gold-colored straw was carried out to the sauna. Mother smiled and hummed the angels' song as she worked.

Daniel felt Christmas spirit somehow creeping anew from somewhere into each room. He sat by the window, intrigued. Smoke from the sauna rose straight up into the freezing sky like the smoke of Abel's sacrifice. The barn still squatted so fancifully on the side of the hill, as if waiting for the shepherds to gaze upon the newly born Jesus child.

There was a clatter on the porch. Big Brother pushed in with a big wrapped package under his arm. He quickly put the package on the corner of the table and hurried to embrace his mother: "Forgive me, Mother."

"In Jesus' name and blood, your sins are forgiven, son."

Big Brother begged for forgiveness from Daniel and Miina, too. The teacher had come in behind Big Brother, and he watched with big tears on his face.

They opened the package. It held a new cradle, exactly like the broken one. Miina took it and jumped for joy. Soon the little feet stopped jumping and the baby was rocked. Then in her clear little voice, the child started Luther's well-known hymn, "Good news from heaven the angels bring..." Daniel and the teacher joined in, as Mother and Big Brother held each other by the hands and cried.

---

[1] *From Heaven Above* and *Good News From Heaven The Angels Bring* are two translations of a hymn by Luther, tune *Geistliche Lieder*, 1539.

MARTHA'S CHRISTMAS EVE

Grownups are funny. They talk of hard times and all kinds of things which are hard to understand.

Martha's mother said: "This year we won't be getting a Christmas tree and will be giving just a very few gifts. Instead, we should bring Christmas packages to all poor homes." Little Martha was dazed; this surely would be a strange and empty Christmas!

The evening before Christmas Eve, Mother put thinbreads, meat, oats, pearled barley and candles into bags, and into some of them she put the Christmas newsletter. Now the Christmas gift bags were ready.

Mother said: "Tomorrow you can start early with these to our neighbors' cottages." Martha almost had a notion to argue, but didn't have the heart to do that to her own sweetheart of a mother.

So next morning (it was the day of Christmas Eve) Martha loaded the bags onto her sled and trudged down the road while it was frosty and still midwinter dusk. The furthest stop of her trip would be the Kangas cottage, two kilometers along the edge of the woodland pond called Mela.

The tenant farmer's little cottage was not much more than a shack, no bigger than a family's sheepfold, and snow was shoveled against the walls right up to the windows. Evergreen trimmings had been placed around the front of the porch and the floor looked freshly scrubbed.

Inside it was crowded. The big stone oven took almost one fourth of the room. A wide bed stood up close to one wall, and in front of the window was a little table and bench. A pale little girl lay on her bed and a shivering boy warmed his red hands next to the stove.

When Mrs. Kangas entered through the door carrying brushwood from the woods, Martha handed her the gift bag, saying: "Mother sent you this and told me to say 'God's peace'." She showed that she took her errand seriously.

"May the Lord bless your mother and bless you too! As for food, we did not have much hope for a miracle. We've only been able to get a drop when we milked Strawberry, so we've been eating nothing but mashed potatoes for many days," went on the delighted woman. "Can't even send the children on an errand.

Poor Siiri is sick and Emil does not have mittens. He almost froze his hands when he started to collect brush wood with me."

This struck Martha as very sad. "There could be much less happy Christmases than ours," she thought to herself. It seemed wrong that she should have warm mittens to pull on her hands. Suddenly she turned around and faced Emil: "You take these mittens of mine. I have others at home, and I can make it home even with bare hands." And she ran out the door, choking on her sobs. By the time Emil's mother reached the porch after the fleeing girl, Martha's thick hair-braid already swung far down the road.

The morning seemed brighter, and the festive-looking spruce trees stood motionless on either side of the road. A squirrel jumped from branch to branch. The snow crunched under the soles of her shoes and squeaked under the sled runners. The freezing cold attempted to reach her nose and fingers, but Martha scarcely noticed. Real Christmas came to her after all!

Mother didn't scold Martha at all for giving away her mittens, but just turned her head the other way. She herself had been at the neighbors and seen that only one tree was left to supply wood.

It was already late afternoon. "Now go to take this one more, to Kreta Anjala," said Mother. Martha pulled on another pair of mittens and was on her way in a flurry.

Dusk was falling and it was getting colder. Her collar and the border of her cap frosted over altogether. Smoke rose from all the neighbors' saunas and cowbells clanked in the barns. Nikkola's big hired man was emptying his load of hay. When a door opened, the white vapor looked so pretty in the luster of the lamplight. Christmas was coming.

Kreta hurried to answer the knock and open the door. "God's peace, Grandmother! Mother sent Christmas greetings," chirped Martha.

"Christmas peace! Come in and get warm," responded the old lady. In the fireplace the fire crackled. It was always so cozy here, and so easy to enjoy a visit. "The Lord's peace abides there," is what Father had said. Cleanliness shone everywhere. The Bible was open on the table and a flame twinkled atop the candle.

The old lady busied herself opening her bag. She hung the thinbreads on the pole up among the ceiling beams where there had been only one bread before. She put the hulled grain bag on the shelf and put the meat somewhere in the porch.

The only thing left in the bag was a little piece of paper, where Father had written: "You will receive the mission paper of Zion all next year."

"Food for the soul and the body," murmured the old lady. "But I have the best gift here," as she pressed her hand to her breast. "Soon I'll be able to celebrate Christmas in heaven." Then the old lady sat down on the bench right beside Martha. The girl rested her head against the the lady's shoulder and the elder smoothed her hair. I wonder whether anyone else had a Christmas as delightful as Kreta Anjala in her little cottage.

It was almost dark while Martha trudged home. Many stars had been kindled in the heavens. The girl gazed at them and mused: "I wonder which is the Star of the East?"

At home, her first stop was the bathhouse. Coming to the house from sauna, she found the Christmas table already set. Candles burned in a three-branched candelabra, and there were ham and Christmas pudding. Tonight they tasted especially good!

After dinner Father brought in a little basket, with just one package for each. Martha received a long woolen coat, woolen socks and wonderfully beautiful mittens <u>and</u> a piece of paper on which Father had written: "You will receive the children's Zion paper for a year." Martha was just wonderfully happy.

Father read the Christmas gospel and together they sang a Christmas hymn. That night Martha said thoughtfully: "I have never had such a delightful Christmas. It seems to me that I have never received so many gifts!"

Her mother replied: "It <u>is</u> more blessed to give than to receive."

A CHRISTMAS OF CHRISTMASES

Leila was ill. She had lain in her bed for months already. Her face was pale and her eyes large and bright. Her hands lay limp on her covers; she could scarcely lift her head any more. Her breathing had become very slow and deep.

Christmas was coming, for the days were getting very short. There was just a thin strip of dusk between the darkness of the morning and the darkness again of evening. The finch had flown away from the birch tree under the window. Only the greater titmouse still came peeping and tapping on the windowsill.

Christmas! Last Christmas Leila was perfectly well. She could sing Christmas hymns with enthusiasm and vigor at the Christmas services. She could still see bright candle crowns and the pastor uncle's friendly face. Nothing was ever so beautiful. "Is it like this in heaven?" she had asked her father.

Often now she asked Father or Mother: "Can I go to the Christmas services?"

"If the heavenly Father makes you well," was always the answer. Often in the evenings Leila folded her hands and prayed: "Dear Father, make me well enough that I am able to go to the Christmas service on Polle, our horse."

Leila called her mother over to the bedside. Mother had plenty of work, but she seated herself anyway on the edge of the bed and smoothed her sick one's forehead. "Mother, tell me about the Christmas church service."

Mother related this to her: "When Jesus was little, very little, his mother carried him to church. Old believing Simeon was there also.[1] When Simeon took the baby Jesus in his arms, his wrinkled face became radiant and his eyes gleamed. Beaming, he said, "Lord, since you have promised that I should not die till I have seen your Christ, now let your servant go in peace, for I have seen your salvation!" Then, bursting with emotion, he pressed the child to his heart. That was Simeon's Christmas morning service. The true Christmas church service is where Jesus is. And if Jesus is completely your own Saviour, the Christmas church is open."

"Mother, tell me more about that Christmas service. Please."

"There is no need of candles there, for Jesus is the light. All people who get there have brightly shining bodies. Beautiful-sounding organs play there and angels sing praise and thanksgiving. Sickness does not reach there, nor old Adam nor death. Would you like such a church, my child?"

"I would, Mother, but I have experienced the effects of the old Adam within me so many times!"

"Believe all of those sins forgiven," comforted Mother. "Jesus is your Saviour even as he was Simeon's Saviour. Remember when your father took you to church amidst jingling sleigh bells last year? In the same way, the good angel will take you to heaven's Christmas service." Leila smiled.

That night she dreamed that someone knocked on the window. Leila hurried to look. There was a beautiful angel!

"I have come to take you to heaven's Christmas services. Open the window, little Leila." Leila opened it. Breezes of warm summer air came into the house, even though the trees glittered with hoarfrost and snowdrifts covered the meadows. It seemed that thousands of finches and summer swallows twittered. The angel took Leila by the hand and together they lightly sprang to the ground where a gleaming white colt was tied. Behind the colt was a bright silver church sleigh in which they seated themselves. The colt sprang into flight. A summer breeze brushed their faces and more swallows of summer sang somewhere far away where a church of glistening gold was dimly visible. Countless Christmas candles shone from its windows. Under its vaulted roof was an open door.

In the morning, Leila's pale body was put into a white casket. When the Christmas service was over, the minister blessed her grave which was under a window right next to the church wall. Through the window still shone the crown of candles which the sexton was just snuffing out.

---

[1] See Luke 2: 25-32.

IT SURELY WAS A CHRISTMAS ANGEL

Johnny had been thinking about it all autumn. For Christmas, he would bring home the tree from their home woodlot himself. He had already picked one out while gathering cowberries. Uniform and compact, the branches extended out in every direction. It was tall enough that the tip would reach to the ceiling. Father would not have to go slogging his way in the snow when he returned tired from work. The Christmas tree would already be in front of the window!

There was no sign of snow the morning before Christmas day, only frost on the ground and a thin crust of ice on the paths. Early in the morning Johnny sneaked out to the shed, took an ax and a bucksaw and climbed the yard fence into the pasture.

The birches near the fence were like splendid old snowmen. Sharp tinkling crystals showered down from their branches into the cowberry thicket below. Further on, into the spruce and pines, it was still dark and quiet. Johnny's footsteps first boomed on an icy patch and then faded away oddly on a frost-covered mossy patch. A cuckoo flew from tree to tree without a sound. A raven glided over the woods without cawing. It was awe-inspiring.

The Christmas tree should have been right there by the pasture fence. Johnny looked around but not one young spruce was a suitable shape. Branches from the prettiest one were broken off, making it unsightly.

Johnny circled every single tree which was the right size or a little taller. From one side, many appeared to have even branches and be pretty and attractive, but then they would be ugly and unsymmetrical on the other side. Once already Johnny had to sit on a stone for a rest. He was now in the wasteland called heath. Finally Johnny, almost in disgust, picked another spruce and began work to cut it down. He began to saw but the saw blade stuck and he got it loose with a great effort. The blows of his ax hardly made a mark on the spot where he struck. He was panting by now and the back of his shirt was wet. What brought the magpies here to wrangle and chatter? Eventually the spruce did fall.

After resting a bit, Johnny started home with the Christmas tree on his shoulder. His surroundings looked a little strange, but surely he knew the way to press onward. Tuohi's familiar slope was obviously right over there and behind the hill was the fence of their home pasture. They must have waited for him already for breakfast. The bank **did** seem rather high. The young spruce pressed his shoulder. His ax and saw got in the way, but he had to take them both.

The home pasture fence **wasn't** at the bottom of the hill! The woods thinned out and the land became boggy. Ice gleamed between the grassy hummocks. It cracked easily and he made progress by stumbling along. Then there were no trees at all and a swamp opened before him, a sinking unfamiliar swamp. The young man's shoulders ached. He was sweaty. Ice broke under him and one boot slipped into muddy water.

Johnny realized that he had gone astray; he was lost. For some time he stood by the edge of the swamp and contemplated. "Maybe this is the 'Place of the Lost' I've often heard about. It is in the north as we see it from home, so now I must turn south soon."

Father had told him: "The branches are thicker on the south side. Look for the ant hills; they take you south." But it was difficult to be sure from looking at the tree branches. Ant hills seemed a better sign.

He could leave the spruce in the swamp but he **had** to drag the ax and saw with him; he would not dare throw them away. Johnny plodded on, already sweaty from exertion, but familiar land did not appear. He was hungry. Dusk deepened. It was nearly dark when the youth reached the edge of the swamp. The moon's disk rolled slowly up into the heavens. Dwarf trees squatted here and there, spaced apart from each other in the open, looking like lost boys. One of them reached out its arms as though in prayer. Johnny had praying quietly for a long time already, saying over and over: "Good God, help me home. Dear Heavenly Father, bring Johnny home. Dear God..."

His feet were like heavy frozen blocks of wood. He choked back his crying and stumbled ahead in the darkening woods. Suddenly he came up to the wall of a great shed, a barn. It was full of sweet-smelling hay. With difficulty he was able to pry apart the boards of a door enough to let him crawl inside, where he dug into the hay. A bit fearful, he folded his hands and slept at once.

JOHNNY HAD A DREAM. He was with his mother making hay in the lower meadow and his father's mower clacked away somewhere in the distance. Mother carried the hay with a fork, straight into the barn. Johnny had his own little fork, too. Mother tied a little bundle of hay on it and hoisted it on his shoulder. Then they hurried together across the yard to where Mustikka and Mansika were housed. It was already filling up with hay but the manger was still empty.

The sun was hot and Johnny was tired. He only had a small bunch on his shoulder while Mother was burdened down under her huge load. Johnny was no longer able to jump over the last ditch and his bare feet slipped into the cold water. Mother looked on, kindly encouraging, as he strove to get up. At last, they laid their hay bundles into the manger in the barn.

"You are all worn out," Mother said sympathetically. "I'll wrap you up for sleep in the manger!"

Johnny almost laughed. "Do you still treat me like a baby?" On the other hand, it was so good to be like this. Mother wrapped him with a soft white sheet. Heat from the glowing sun rose from the hay and a sweet smell wafted from it. Light flowed in through the barn door.

"Mother, you are good."

"God alone is good. Good night, my child."

Mother closed the door and the place darkened. Only a ray of light showed under the window. The air cooled suddenly; it formed an icy fog curling between the cracks in the logs. Cold nipped the nose and toes. The cows Blueberry and Strawberry were close by; he heard them chewing their cuds. Johnny became scared, but just then the door flew open and warmth from somewhere again flooded the place. Once again the smells of summer filled the area.

Outside the barn they were singing a Christmas hymn. He saw angels. The biggest angel flew quite close to the manger and laid his hand on the boy's forehead: "Johnny. Johnny, it's time to get up."

JOHNNY AWAKENED. Surely someone had poked him in the ribs! The moon peeked though the boards of the door. Another light came between the cracks of the logs.

"Johnny, Johnny!" he heard so plainly. It was Father's voice! The boy could hardly get a word out of his mouth, then at last he shouted, "Father!" as he burst out crying. Soon the shaking boy was held in his father's arms. It was so secure and warm there. It was neat to listen to Father's heart under his coat as he strode home and to see the light of the lantern flashing on the path.

Christmas did come. It was true that they did not try any more to get a tree, but a row of candles burned on the table. Mother never had cooked such truly delicious Christmas pudding. The gift package contained almost everything Johnny could desire. And just think, the American uncle had sent a toy car which buzzed at great speed around the living room floor.

The hymn of the angels seemed amazingly familiar. He could listen to the Christmas gospel without yawning or glancing at the gifts. Johnny imagined that he could see the stable, the beasts of burden, the hay and a bright-eyed little child in the manger.

After the prayer, the boy asked earnestly, "Father, guess who came to the shed to awaken me?"

"You probably heard me calling," guessed Father.

"No, a Christmas angel came and awakened me!"

NEW YEAR'S SAUNA

Father and Willie went to the sauna together on the evening of the last day of the year. They raced into the bathhouse, chasing one another as fast as they could over the hard crusted snow. Inside, it was glistening clean. Three new candles burned on the windowsill. Golden yellow straw was spread on the platform of this new Finnish bath. Bath whisks made from new leafy twigs had been recently steeped in hot water and sent out scented vapor into the hot air. Mother knew how to give a festive air to the bathhouse as well as the home.

Father threw water on the pile of hot stones atop the bathhouse fireplace, making steam. The black stones hissed. Father had a big whisk which gave a loud whack. Smack, smack! Willie's little whisk snap-cracked! That is what it is like when men bathe and this time seemed no less than the real thing. Father again threw on water to make more steam. The candle flames swayed and sent shadows dancing on the ceiling and walls. Smack, splash! Snap-crack. Playfully, Father switched Willie with his whisk. Willie began to lash his father's broad back.

"That way, over here! Lower!" puffed Father and Willie switched him below his shoulder blade. "Okay, that's enough. Come here now so we can wash away the old year's dirt." Father soaped the brush and began to work on the calluses of his toes. In Willie's mind, this particular bathing chore was the least enjoyable. His feet tended to be ticklish. When he rinsed his head, too, soapy water would run into his eyes and fill his ears. But being unruly in this place didn't help. "I have to bring Mother a clean boy, clean as a snow bunting," explained Father.

"The Heavenly Father also desires that you would be a clean boy," he went on seriously. "It is not enough that our bodies are clean. God also requires a clean conscience. It is good that we don't have to carry the sins of this year into the coming year. We can believe them forgiven in the merits of Jesus, in his name and blood. We can ask forgiveness of one another and from our hearts we forgive one another. Willie, will you forgive me for when I have sometimes spoken very harshly to you in a temper?" The boy jumped to the bench, wound an arm around his father's neck and said, "You should forgive **me**. I am the one who has been bad."

"You are forgiven, son, in Jesus' name and blood. But bless me, too, will you not?" Willie stammered: "Father, believe all sins forgiven in Jesus' name and blood."

The candles burned lower. The straw reflected warmth. The sauna cooled to a gentler heat that gave a perfect warmth to the skin. Water dripped onto the floor from the platform that served them for benches. Then they heard the boom of church bells from the far side of the village. The sexton played a sacred hymn for the coming New Year.

"Your body is cleansed with clean water and your soul is sprinkled clean from having a bad conscience!" declared Willie's father happily.

THE TRAIL

It was New Year's Eve. The sun, cold and far away, barely peeped over the edge of the woods. The crust of snow and hoarfrost glittered. Sleigh bells jingled at a village on a village road nearby. A titmouse twittered in the patch of hemlock.

Father and Toni were skiing. They had been struggling up Island Ridge Hill for some time already. They stopped to take a breath with 300 meters still remaining to the summit.

"Just look back, son, at the trail behind us! On one side is a deep stony gully and on the other side an impassable thicket. There is no chance to make a detour either way!" Toni nodded, guessing that his father had something special in mind. His father went on:

"I have been thinking here that a child of God also strives on a kind of narrow ridge toward heaven, toward the light. On one side lurks the deep gully of going along with sin. Over on the other side is the ugly thicket of self satisfaction and hypocrisy."

"Is that what Jesus meant when he taught that the narrow way leads to life?" wondered Toni.

"Exactly!"

A FEARFUL NIGHT FOR CHARLES

So many customers were waiting to have their grain ground that the tenant farmer from Spruce Tree Farm was delayed overnight on his trip to the gristmill. He was concerned and uneasy because the wife he left at home would have a little one very soon to join their son and four daughters.

That evening the wife stumbled and fell off the porch slab onto the frozen ground in the yard. Charles, the oldest child, found her there as she lay moaning in pain. With considerable difficulty, he helped his mother into the house and to bed. "Go, child, and fetch a midwife from the church village! Tell her that your mother is hurt and needs her," Mother whispered and squeezed Charles' hand. "Hurry!" The other children were gathered about the bed, crying.

Charles started off on his skis. It was a struggle because the frozen road was so sparsely covered with snow. Often his skis criss-crossed. The boy slid and fell on an icy patch, got up and once again thrust his ski poles into the ice. Early in the trip someone on a horse met and passed him. After that the road became quite desolate. It was late and now, after some ten kilometers of travel, came this quite uninhabited stretch. It was a boggy or swampy area known as Koppelo's and was well-known for the large grouse which were found there. "Oh, dear God, help me and my mother," whispered the little skier.

The moon rose, casting shadows of the trees across the road. A gust of wind whistled from the marsh, throwing swirling snow at the skier. Occasionally darkness covered the area when a fleecy cloud flew over the moon. The cold became more intense and the wind noticeably more blustery. What looked like a large dog ran across the road.

When Charles slid and fell down the first hill past Koppelo's, that large gray dog rushed at his throat, attacking without warning. "Wolf!" flashed into the boy's mind. In its speed, the wild beast flew right over the fallen boy. Charles jumped to his feet. When the wolf attacked again, Charles struck it with his ski pole with all his might. The blow landed and the beast yelped and backed off. "Dear, good Heavenly Father!" gasped the youth. "Help me! Oh, help my mother!" Over the next hill a sleigh bell jingled.

The wolf attacked again. This time Charles' ski pole missed its mark and Charles fell. The back of his head thumped on the sheet of ice and his sight dimmed.

Charles awakened in a sleigh. The sleigh bells had a lovely ring. The sky was filled with stars. A strange uncle sat in the driver's seat, urging the horse to go faster while another uncle sat with Charles and rubbed his head with snow. "Hurry, hurry, go to the midwife! Mother is hurt!" cried the boy before he again became unconscious.

When Charles woke again, lights shone brilliantly around him. The doctor finished wrapping white gauze around his head and neck. "There, now the lad will surely recover," he assured the men. Then he turned to the two gentlemen with a laugh: "Was it Old Nick who happened to bring you there at night?"

Tears rose in Charles' eyes. "God led them! The Heavenly Father!" He stammered a bit. "I...I prayed and God heard. That same good God will help my mother yet, also." The doctor stopped laughing and one of the other gentlemen remarked, "The lad is right." Charles was taken home with the doctor. The midwife joined them at the roadside and the sleigh pressed on in haste.

When Father got home with his load from the mill in the morning, Mother was in her bed. She was well but weak. In the cradle slept a baby boy, the brother Charles had asked for. Charles slept nearby too, with the bandages still on his head. Although Father smoothed his hair over his forehead, the boy did not waken.

On his way home that same morning, the doctor shot a big gray wolf in an open field in Koppelo's area. It was the last wolf ever seen in those parts.

A MISERABLE SKI TRIP

"Who of the children is going to services?" asked Mother. All remained silent.

"Won't you go, Kaisu?"

"I don't want to. I would rather go skiing," answered the girl sulkily.

"You have time to ski the trails on weekdays," the mother suggested. "This is the Lord's Day. Remember the explanation of the third commandment."

But the boys had already hurried out and Kaisu followed, a bit ashamed. The boys remained near home but Kaisu hurried straight toward the trails used by the big men. She followed them enthusiastically, straining to keep up with the competitors as they dashed past. She wanted to see their last lap so that tomorrow in school she could boast about seeing it.

The trail led from the steep hillside to an inlet and across to the opposite shore and into the woods. There it sought the meanest climbs and the steepest downgrades. This made for alternately difficult climbing followed by dangerous downhill speed.

Dusk sneaked in the bends and darkness stared from the shadows of the forest and from under the dark spruce. A dark red lingered on the horizon and above it twinkled a star. The trail continued on, rising and falling endlessly.

"Is twenty kilometers really this terribly long?" Kaisu was fatigued and thoroughly wet through. Her back felt steamy. Sweat glued locks of hair to her forehead. She had already fallen twice and the second time a branch tore a smarting scratch on her wrist. A subtle uneasiness crept into her heart.

"I was crazy to start. Soon they will return from services and get concerned about me. Mother is like that---tenderhearted."

The path rose dangerously till it finally reached the ridge. The skier stopped, puffing. At last, home was there below, back of the church, back of the village. But first there was a fearful descent ahead. Hills up until now were little children compared to this mother hill. Kaisu's legs trembled as she gasped for breath at the top.

"Oh, why did I start! It would have been safer at the services!"

Dusk now ventured right into the open and the darkness deepened between the trees. The heavens looked back at her with thousands of stars. Lights blinked down in the village, but the only thing the skier heard was her own puffing and the heart pounding under her shirt.

"Go for it! Trust the Lord!" Kaisu had heard the mountain boys exclaiming half in fun, applauding a bold ski-jumper as he took off on his jump. Now God's help was needed indeed, but why should God help such a disobedient child? No matter, she had to go.

Kaisu pushed with both poles so that the snow flew in clouds and the brush snapped. But then on the great hill her speed increased without her trying at all! Great pine trees flashed by, then small ones, then came a slashing pain, a groan and...nothing!

Kaisu awakened in waist-deep snow beside a great rock. Her shoulder hurt terribly as she crawled to the trail. She found one pole but her skis had disappeared. It was a steep descent to the shore. Struggling along painfully and leaning on the pole in her good hand, Kaisu was able to get down and began dragging herself along. With every step, pain jabbed her injured shoulder. Slowly the village lights came closer. She was sweaty but an icy draft swept across the middle of her back and her hands and toes were getting cold. A dog barked somewhere.

"Heavenly Father, help," repeated the girl. "Heavenly Father, help me!" Having heard from the boys about Kaisu's intentions, her father had started off to meet her. When he found her, she was half unconscious and he had to carry her the last kilometer. A doctor was called to the home and with some difficulty was able to reset the dislocated shoulder. Then the thoroughly chilled Kaisu was put to bed and covered warmly.

Gradually Kaisu's body became warmer and the shivering subsided. Kaisu awakened in the morning to see her father and mother sitting before a roaring crackling fireplace. Mother glanced at the bed and noticed the girl opening her eyes.

Mother hurriedly asked, "Kaisu dear, are you still ill?"

"No."

"Do you feel completely well?"

"No."

"How then?"

"I did wrong yesterday to skip services. God punished me. Forgive me!"

"My child, trust in God. The Lord has had mercy on you. Your sins are forgiven in Jesus' name and precious blood."

"Mother, I will always go to church services with you," said Kaisu. She smiled a little and slept again.

"CAN YOU FORGIVE ME, SON?"

An older government official in Finland in charge of law enforcement in a relatively large district tells this story:

My father completed his twentieth year as an elementary school teacher in the same spring in which I was admitted to the fourth year of high school.[1] He and Mother were believing Christians, but while away at school I was powerfully gripped by a different spirit.

My parents noticed it and grieved. Sometimes we had wrangling words. On my part, I became convinced that there were no real true Christians. In my mind the whole business about believing was hypocritical piety. I did not even attempt to hide the new grownup light of mine under a bushel basket. All this is why the first part of my summer vacation became painfully tense.

My father was an enthusiastic fisherman. At least once a week, he went far out with his great rigging of nets and lines. His regular fishing companion was the pleasant Willie Yli. However, just before Midsummer Day, Willie died and now slept in the rest of his Lord. I often had been the third party on those fishing trips; now, for the first time, there were just the two of us, father and son.

Father had always prepared for these trips with a quiet eagerness. While humming old hymns, he gathered his things into the boat. Then he navigated silently, studying the faint shoreline and the glistening water. Like a narrow silver ribbon, it first passed by the narrow channel which led in to the church, then flowed between the points and finally opened out to the great open lake. The same mood continued at the island around the campfire. While Willie had lighted the coffee fire, the old man had squatted before the blaze and neatly baited his hooks. The pressing quiet of the wilderness evening almost brought tears from the fearful boy fishing from the shore.

This time Father was more serious than ever. No doubt he yearned for the Holy Spirit and for the gift of a new, different life and for the friend that he missed. At the same time, I saw a pleased warmth in his eyes when he noticed my interest.

At the narrows near Church Inlet, the wind turned suddenly against us and freshened. I had to row my hardest, even though the old man helped by pulling with the spare paddle.

I was sweaty and exhausted when we arrived at the shore. I cooked coffee and we drank from our full mugs without exchanging a word. Father showed concern when he looked out at the open stretch of the lake where white-maned seahorses galloped at one another's heels. Thundering and rumbling from farther away sounded like an avalanche striking the shore rocks. After Father got our lines, sinkers and floats into place, he suggested: "It might be best if we trade places now."

"Don't be silly, old man! Certainly I am the stronger," I said, trying to firm my resolve.

At the start, we worked along with the wind. The line ran into the water smoothly. Occasionally the crest of a huge wave slopped a little water over the back end of the boat; my father's trousers became wet. Otherwise things went well and without problems. Then we changed course broadside to the waves and the boat tumbled like an eggshell from one white crest to the next. With the worst gusts, we felt thrown forcibly and terrifyingly close to protruding rocks near the shore.

"Pull! Hard toward the ridge, boy!" ordered the captain. Gritting his teeth and panting, he also pulled while water splashed over the sides. Finally we turned back into the wind. Everything below in the boat was creaking as if about to crack. Then we heard waves as high as a cabin smashing on the shore. At times it seemed we didn't make an inch of progress. Gusts of wind were closer and closer together and it seemed that I couldn't take it any longer!

"Boy, boy, the wind is only taking us backward!" Father cried. It only made me angry and resentful.

"You couldn't budge it, either!" I screamed in response.

"Pull on it! Pull on it! We're almost there! We don't have tens of points of land to get past any more!" I rowed frantically just as the angry gale suddenly hurled us right toward the shore.

"A brat is always a brat!" exploded Father on shore. He cut the line and tied a sinker on the end and threw it out into the white capped waves. Snatching one oar, he began to take refuge on the nearby point of land. "So this is how a true believer speaks!" was on the tip of my tongue but I didn't dare to say anything.

When the wind calmed just a bit, we traded places. I was able to lower the last of the line where the point joins the mainland. Then my father, with a great effort, rowed the boat on a straight line through the boiling sea to Campfire Island.

He still looked angry. Deep, tired creases hovered around his mouth. Sweat stood out on his pale forehead like pearls. I had carelessly thrown down the oar by the rower's seat without fastening it and now I stood averting my gaze to the high seas, glancing at the old man now and then.

Midnight came. The wind tore gray tatters in the cloudy sky and shortly the whole sky was enveloped in thicker gray. Soon rain beat upon the rocky shore. We didn't speak a word. Father turned the boat upside-down near the campfire. I thrashed about in the darkness of the woods seeking firewood and fir twigs. We crouched in the protection of the tarred boat, sitting on fallen trees, trying to dry our clothes. The branches burned reluctantly, sputtering smokily.

Finally, Father encouraged me to eat, saying as he threw himself down that he was not hungry. I munched on some bread and butter and drank buttermilk to help it slide down.

"Well, forget it. Let it be. Shall we hear an evening hymn?" asked Father. I almost took malicious pleasure in our discomfort and trouble, although on the other hand I was sorry for something that had mixed feelings of regret striving under my vest.

No hymn was heard. The old man gazed into the wind. I recalled many moments from former fishing trips in the wilderness. I had been covered for sleep on a bed of fir boughs. The older men drank their last cups of coffee and squatted there in the flare of firelight like two black crows. The campfire crackled as now and then the distress signal of sandpipers could be heard from Seagull Island. Then Willie would start the evening hymn:

> Now across the lands, woods and sea
> All thank God.
> Those who were active during the day
> Now rest in the shade.
> You, my soul, alone may speak.
> I go now to rest, but Jesus,
> Help me to rest on your breast.
> And having rested, grant that I arise joyfully
> To praise your gracious name.

For some reason, I began to have feelings of blessing. I imagined that the flickering firelight on the boat, heeled to one side, was the glittering of angel wings and the bright star in the clearing sky was the Heavenly Father's radiant twinkling eye. But Father did not sing or recite, just looked unhappily at the campfire.

I threw myself down on the spruce branches. I sought the evening star but only saw the last glistening drops fall into the fire. Sleep evaded me. Defiance and regret fought strangely under my vest, so hard that I rolled from side to side.

Apparently Father was doing the same. He arose extra often to poke the fire. A couple of times he went stumbling about in the wet and darkness and brought back with him a handful of wet brush.

Finally, he crawled over to me. "Can you forgive me, son, for shouting at you!"

"I do, I do," I stammered in confusion.

"Forgive me in Jesus' name and blood."

"In Jesus' name and blood, sins are forgiven," in a subdued echo. The old man crawled back to his own place, but after a minute I drew up behind his broad back. I, too, received forgiveness. **Then** I slept as I had years earlier, on those first hunting trips.

Since then I have known that living Christianity is not hypocritical piety, but is the struggle of a troubled believing soul on heaven's way. It is surely the truth.

---

[1] All children attended four years of elementary school or public school (*koulu*). For those on an academic track, another eight years of high school (*oppikoulu*) followed. Community college or the university would come after graduation from high school.

TRIP TO SCHOOL

Christmas vacation was over and Paul was to start high school in town. He could have gone there on the train but he decided to make the three-league[1] trip on skis. He was given new skis for Christmas and they simply had to be tried out. After all, had he not tested himself this way twice before? The country boys were sturdy and bold, although they chafed and squirmed at the school benches.

On the morning he was to start, a frosty wind developed. Out in the open, the snow blew and drifted up at the fences. The temperature was a freezing twenty degrees. "It is best if you go on the train," counseled his mother.

Actually, Paul had the same thought when he awoke and glanced outside through the window. But, since he had already bragged a bit to his chums about his intended trip, it would be embarassing to give it up. "Suppose I just try? There are plenty of sheltered spots in the woods on the way," he responded, avoiding his mother's glance.

His averted gaze told of other things, also. Paul had denied his faith in the fall due to the ridicule of fellows around him. During vacation, he had fallen in with a village crowd of party-goers. He went on a hiking trip and even tried dancing on the eve of the Epiphany. Mother found cigarette papers in his jacket pocket on several mornings. Life at home changed and became tense and awkward. Mother grew quiet and looked sad.

On several occasions Father called him into a room lighted only by the twilight of evening. There, in privacy with the two of them alone, Father cautioned him concerning the temptations of the broad road. These words especially touched Paul uncomfortably:

"Remember, Paul, that you have received a poor inheritance from your father. When I was young, I was a miserable man, a wretched slave to sin. I brought sorrow and shame to my parents and would have gone to ruin altogether if God had not awakened my conscience and granted his peace as a gift to my heart. I would never want to see you, son, going down these same roads. Even yet they are shameful memories. I often feel that I should ask all of you children for forgiveness for this, that they have been born into this world with such a spoiled inheritance." Tears slid down his bearded face as he spoke.

Paul supposed that the memory of those moments would never fade away from his mind and never let him descend into the fellowship of those who had no consciences. Some of the time the incident only bothered him somewhat, but at other times it bothered him to the point of being infuriated. But it did have the power of truth and the warmth of love, forces which silenced his opposition.

Father did not forbid Paul to go on the trip by skis. "Well, one who is alive knows his own strength," he said half-jokingly, to comfort Mother. "Exercise is a good antidote for bad practices. But I do hope, son, that you try to know that your conscience is clear."

But Mother begged him as she was saying goodbye: "Please don't choose to go into that weather which God has sent. You might become exhausted on the way!" Paul offered only his hand. No hugs. Mother held his hand, trying to hold back tears. "Then go in the name of the Lord. May God bless you. I will pray for you."

Paul's skis slid easily in places but where the snow had been scoured away by the biting wind they grabbed as though on metal filings. Close to home he had to work hard to make any headway and a cutting wind penetrated his clothes. His nose and cheeks were in danger of frostbite.

On the road through the woods, the trip began to go better. The gale could not reach him and the road was firm. His face felt hot and his back was sweaty. Yet the young skier was not conscious of all this. It just felt great to him. For a shy country boy away from home at school, **this** is what drew him to the lonely trails in the evenings or on long walks in the spring while gray saunas smoked and frogs croaked in the ditches and dark puddles.

Abruptly the woods ended and an expanse of field opened before him. Gusts of wind pounded the frozen snow on his face so that it hurt. Once more the wind had whirled windrows of sand onto the surface of the road to slow his progress. The biting wind numbed his face and tried to freeze his clothes which were damp with his sweat.

Now Paul had to cut across several points of land to the shore of Holly Lake. He stopped to gasp a bit for breath in the lee of a small hill. From a cluster of spruce trees he could already see the town. The electric lights shone dimly through the wintry haze. Smoke from the factory stack was flung over a sea of housetops. An angry current of air blew against the rocky bed of the rapids where splashes of snow shone bright against the dark bare ice.

The snow flew for three kilometers over a gentle rise in a continuous powdery cloud. Paul was alarmed at the thought of skiing into it. His skis didn't want to go where they were pointed. They slid here and there with the gusts of wind until the wind got control and turned the skier sidewise to the island. Many times it knocked the boy down when it ripped his skis crosswise.

Finally Paul took the skis and poles under his arm and started plodding on foot toward the shore of the town. Paul had to rub his frozen nose and cheeks with snow. His hands were terribly cold. His arms were weary from holding the skis and poles against his body. His feet cramped when he had to strain to keep upright on the slippery ice. Nowhere did he see a single traveler. And still the storm increased in fury!

"You should have obeyed your mother!" said his conscience. "You'll at least be sick from this!" Then after a bit: "If you fall down on the ice before you get to the shore and you have secret sins on your conscience...you'd better pray! The prayer of the godless is appalling to the Lord. But Mother does pray on your behalf."

Paul became more and more scared and alarmed. He had already started the last kilometer, but the dimly visible streets that ran along the lakeshore seemed distant and rugged when seen through the whirling snow.

"God help me just this once," cried the panting schoolboy aloud. "I will surely obey you. I will repent. I will become a Christian and a preacher, just as Mother and Father hope!"

Sometimes on a winter day, as the train speeds through fields near Distress Point, a minister of a backwoods congregation sits looking out through the window. He gazes at Holly Lake where snow clouds still fly over its frozen surface. His eyes are wet and he sees in his memory a sturdy little country boy with his skis in his arms trudging toward Wollet Market.

"Yes, yes," he thinks. "One's whole life is such a school trip, striving toward the City of God. Near the finish, progress gets slower and slower. The storms of trials and doubts are strong, and the ice is slippery under one's feet. Lord, strengthen my faith! I want to obey you and continue to be your minister."

---

[1] A league is not mentioned often nowadays; it is approximately 6 1/4 miles or 11 kilometers. Paul's trip to school was almost 19 miles or 33 kilometers.

A TRULY NEW YEAR

Kyllikki was Mummo's own girl. When she was very little, the old lady would not let her out of sight for even a moment. It was interesting to follow those two busy white-haired playmates. The child would sit cross-legged. Mummo would relate endlessly about her childhood years, of the Bible's wondrous heroes and particularly about Kyllikki's parents, who had gone to their heavenly home. Sometimes when they thought that nobody could see them, the old lady crawled like a big barking dog. The little girl would try to provoke her into a fight by treading on her heels, yapping like a little dog. At those times joy was at its height and laughter rang in Tyynela's parlor. Who would have ever guessed that this dignified, respected old widow could be so wonderfully full of fun?

During the summer, the little girl squatted beside one hummock covered with berries, Mummo beside another, and both exclaimed gleefully over their finds. Or sometimes Kyllikki went splashing in the boat harbor with the aged one cautioning her from the rock on the shore: "Darling, be careful, don't go too deep!"

But Kyllikki didn't stay little. After elementary school, she went right on to secondary school in a nearby town and now she was at Tyynela's only on her vacations. She grew to be a slender attractive young lady. She excelled in her studies and soon she was to get a white graduation cap.

Mummo shrank smaller and smaller. The furrows on her face became deeper and deeper even as the sparkle in her eyes became brighter and brighter. She dwelled more on heavenly things. Many hours each day slipped past with her Bible before her. "When one's memory weakens, one needs to read that much more," she explained. She had to sit in front near the speaker, since her hearing was poorer. Her place very seldom was vacant. She often visited with the wife of a believing old forester. They no longer talked much of cactus plants or card games, of Mari Tyynela or Amelia Metsola, as I am sorry to say they often had earlier. Instead they bemoaned the trials on this road to heaven. They sighed over common sorrows and comforted each other with Bible verses. At other times, they recalled how Runtti Jusso had taught them or what Mummo's late believing husband, the dean, had said in this or that sermon.

Secret sighs and prayers rose constantly from the heart of this aged one, both at home and about the village. Often in the wee hours before day-break, when sleep fled earlier and earlier, her quiet prayers rose continually to the heavenly Father. When spring came, a giant beech tree extended its budding branches clear to the window and a house-finch sang, fairly bursting. Thankfulness filled her thoughts.

She tenderly remembered her husband who carried the fire of God with glowing ardor as a chaplain, far into the back woods. Only after blessing his wife and their son would he retire to sleep. She recalled an early spring morning like this one when her little granddaughter Kyllikki, with nothing on but a nightie and a cluster of flowers in her hand, had run to awaken Mummo. She had memories of Christian friends, whose patience and forgiveness seemed beyond comprehension, and of all the people who had been so kind to her.

In the fall, leafless bare branches rattled on the windowpane and the titmouse thumped on the sill. A far-away din could be heard from distant larger villages. It brought back black memories and her soul was in distress before the Lord. She remembered her son, who earned a Master of Arts degree, giving up his faith. Young people who had been sensitive and idealistic destroyed their peace of conscience by yielding to lustful cravings. Instead of repenting, they became caught up in what was popular, the rash denial of their faith.

The hair of the pastor father, now a dean at the school, greyed in those days. In her mother's heart, Mummo lovingly besieged God to have true heavenly love for their son. When their boy went at night to wordly affairs that disgraced the Sabbath with indecent and sensual pleasures, pain brought both spouses to their knees by their beds.

The memories still oppressed her, even though the Heavenly Father had turned everything for the best. God had led the son to ask his dying father for forgiveness and blessing; persuaded him to wed the girl he had seduced; even gave little Kyllikki a tender father. The son with the M.A. confessed his Lord and carried His cross as a teacher in a Christian community college.

But it was not long before he was wrenched away to be with his late father. By grace, his shy and loving wife soon followed him. Mummo was left with Kyllikki.

Now Mummo sorrowed over her granddaughter: "May the good God help and have mercy." Kyllikki had fought the fight all her life in her precious faith. Frank and sensitive, she had been shielded in the calm of Tyynela. But the long winter in new surroundings at school alienated the young girl from her Mummo and the light of living Christianity. Instinctively, Mummo felt how dirty logs of secrecy were forming a separating wall, log by log, between her and her child. The girl's look clouded. Not even playful tussles with her namesake could hide her trouble from her grandma's eyes. Mummo had heard that the Torchbearer literary movement was the choice of Tyynela's student, and that within that circle were egotism and paganism and wordly practices and burning restlessness.

Christmas vacation began with strained tension. Kyllikki's laughter echoed at Tyynela's, but it was hard and unnatural. The aged one could not join in. Pale, bent and silent, she kept busy in the kitchen. With shaking hands, she hung slightly red-cheeked apples from the home orchard on the Christmas tree. Tear-drops fell near Kyllikki's Christmas gift package. In the evening Mummo sat alone. Often it was daybreak before she heard her beloved child slipping into her room from the cold. Mummo no longer was able to speak to her son's daughter, so she cried all the more unto the Lord.

It was after midnight following St. Stephen's day[1] when Kyllikki returned from her sleigh-ride. Her dance partner for the evening nodded at the reins. The moon shone at its brightest. The runners squeaked as it grew colder, and the hoarfrosted woods wormed past like powerful white ghosts. The girl, wrapped in her fur coat, fretted over the slow pace of the ride. Life seemed oppressing. The taste of tobacco lingered in her mouth. An emotional memory from her childhood days forced itself into her thoughts.

Father was suddenly stricken in the night with a fatal illness. Mother awakened Kyllikki, on a frosty morning just like this, and carried the child, shaking with cold, to the bedside of the stricken one. Father stared straight ahead and mumbled something Kyllikki couldn't understand. "Fall to your knees, girl," whispered Mother as she groaned: "Good God, heal Father...no!...Heavenly Father, thy will be done!"

A light glimmered from Mummo's window . Mari's shadow moved against the curtain. Kyllikki hardly said goodbye to her sleepy escort before she slipped through the door with a painful premonition. Mummo had become gravely ill. The doctor had diagnosed that it would be unlikely that the aged one would survive the high fever, explained Mari. Kyllikki became frightened to the depths of her soul. Impulsively in her chest the prayer arose, "God help and have mercy!"

Mummo uttered only, "Where have you been, my child?"

That question followed the girl everywhere. The old servant saw the girl, pale and staring absentmindedly, wandering to the shed and along the fence, stealing from room to room. Her hands performed their duties, but her thoughts stood still, stopped on the words of the aged one, "Where were you, my child?"

Mari wanted to cry. Aunt Metsola and the old speaker brother came later in the day from Tuunala. The old ladies held each other's hands, the sister from Tuunala sitting furthest from the bed. "I'm going to get to go!" said the sick one. "Go home," added her believing sister. The dying one looked radiant. Then Mummo noticed Kyllikki at the door and her face fell. "Pray...for...the child..." A cramping pain shook her body and her statement was left incomplete.

Old Mari longed sorrowfully for the mistress of the home, but the young woman's state touched her heart even more deeply. On St. Sylvester's eve,[2] she said timidly, "If only Kyllikki would cry." Kyllikki suddenly turned and fled angrily to her room, slamming the door shut.

"She's hard. So was her father, but she has signs of breaking down. The devil holds on furiously as he is about to depart," thought her family's faithful servant. "If only she can stand it, poor thing. It is difficult when these proud relatives and learned people meet what is mightier than themselves...Truly we must pray for the child." And earnest prayers arose from the breast of the aged Mari all that night. Finally such agony overcame her that she had to fall on her knees beside her bed.

Metsola's old wife in Tuunala took the words of the deceased as a holy commission. Kyllikki was constantly on her heart. On New Year's Eve the elderly couple in the rear room did not sleep . The aged wife lighted a candle and lay with her hands crossed at her breast. If someone carefully followed her lip movements, they could have made out the words: "Father...help...Kyllikki...God...your grace sufficient."

"Why don't **you** sleep?" asked the old lady of her husband. "I was given night work to do by the dean's widow," he replied.

"What's that?"

"I am to pray for Miss Kyllikki. If only I knew how!"

"The Lord will give you words," comforted his wife, "and I too want to help you."

St. Sylvester's night was truly remarkable.

Kyllikki got out her New Testament. Apprehensively and painfully, she fumbled over its pages. Her eyes stared at its letters but the sentences were strange and so remote. Only one thought stayed with her: "Seek ye first the Kingdom of God and His righteousness." Her ears rang. She felt how the Tyynela farm stood in the middle of a dreadful, terrifying expanse in the pale moonlight. In the emptiness of the house, Kyllikki shivered alone and without help, a soul with great transgressions---alone with death.

In the Torchbearers' book-reading meetings at school, they had often experienced fearful and painful emotions. Now the horrors were real! "Oh good God, I'll lose my mind. I can't stand it! Was that someone at the door?" Anguish and terror shook her body. Mari, quivering on her knees in prayer, was startled. Did someone scream? The aged one tip-toed to Kyllikki's door. She knocked and hastily opened the door without waiting for an invitation. The girl rushed into Mari's embrace. "Oh precious Mari! I'm going to drown."

"No, my child, you won't drown. The drowning one has a helper, Jesus Christ, your Saviour. In His name and blood. believe your sins forgiven!"

In the morning, Amelia Metsola and the old couple from Tuunala came, wishing the sorrowing home a blessed New Year.

"Now I have a truly New Year!" answered Kyllikki.

---

[1] December 26
[2] December 31; New Year's Eve

QUARRELS BREAK FRIENDSHIPS....

It was a snowy winter. For weeks gray clouds hung in the sky and shook down snowflakes. Cars were stuck everywhere in the snowdrifts. When the plows finally got the roads open, great heaps of snow rose over the ditches. In between there were windstorms and enormous drifts grew beside walls and fences. Then came a time when the temperature rose and rain even drizzled a bit.

In the village of Kurki the children gathered in the Koukkula yard. Enthusiastically they began making a snow-castle. Paul, Lawrence, Joseph, Henry, Tarmo, Miina, Justin and Anna-Kaisa rolled snowballs as big as themselves. George, Matt and Mataleena worked as building supervisors. Taavi and Tellervo plastered the cracks. Kreeta and Kerttu just looked on wide-eyed and shouted with delight.

The white walls now rose high over George's head. It was hard work to lift big snow chunks any higher. They laid the ceiling joists made from pieces of fencing into a neat row. For the roof they piled and smoothed the snow on deep. Finally Matt carefully climbed up the roof and shaped a beautiful light-tower using snowballs offered by the others.

"Mister Koukkula would surely give us one of his red paper lanterns," remarked Matt. They all crowded into Koukkulas'. There the master of the house brought out four lanterns, red, green, blue and purple.

"Which one of these do you like?"

"Red is prettiest!" exclaimed Mataleena.

"It's such a warm color!" Miina echoed her big sister.

"Then red it shall be," decided George.

"That's an old woman's color," growled Paul. "I choose green!"

"Green reminds us of summer," said Anna-Kaisa softly.

"It's got to be blue," insisted Lawrence.

"Blue is like the sky in spring," put in Tellervo, delighted, and Taavi naturally was of the same mind. But nobody cared for the purple.

The householder gave them three lanterns, red, green and blue. "Put all three on your roof!" he said, laughing. "Hey, Mother, bring these fine folk some candles."

But there was only one tower on their castle so only one lantern could fit. So a dispute arose in the yard over the color of the lantern. Finally they actually voted. Blue received six votes, green five and red four. Then George argued that Lawrence had frightened Kerttu into voting for blue, because otherwise she would have favored red.

"But we are going to put up BLUE!" shouted Matt who darted up the roof with the lantern. Paul, Joseph and Henry rushed after him. The roof crashed down and the lantern tower collapsed with it. One wall broke.

"It's your fault!" shouted Matt and he flew at Joseph. A fight broke out. The greens and the reds joined forces, eight against six. Blues took a trouncing.

41

The girls had a crying chorus. Matt's overcoat was torn; Paul lost his hat; Taavi's nose was bleeding. The castle's last walls fell and the blue lantern was in rags. Its candle was trampled into the snow somewhere.

The racket ceased for a moment, then rose again as Mr. Koukkula appeared in the yard. "I came to see how the beautiful building with its three lanterns was fairing under your joint efforts," he began. "But I can't see anything here--at least not anything beautiful."

The children became quiet, gazing crestfallen and embarrassed at the ruin. Here and there muffled sobs could be heard. "The words of the Bible, 'Behold how good and pleasant it is when brothers dwell in unity,' do not apply to you," said the man and he slowly walked inside.

Children who had just been wrangling sneaked out of the yard in three groups. Little Kerttu stood a long time in one spot. She hardly knew which direction to start; to her, all were just as good--and just as bad. Finally she ran straight home as fast as she could. The green and red lanterns were left in a badly trampled field. That night a big gust of wind rose and hurled them behind a great rubbish heap.

...BUT LOVE REBUILDS FRIENDSHIPS

Paul felt miserable. Lawrence was his best friend. They were both believers from believing homes! Did this quarrel over lanterns have to happen? Paul remembered pulling Lawrence's hair. Then George had come sneakily from the side and struck Lawrence in the face. Blood ran out of Lawrence's nose and mouth and Paul let go his hold quickly. Shame cut at his conscience frightfully. He had a mind to go thrash George, who earlier had sometimes acted despicably this way. "But hadn't we all taken sides in this humiliating situation? And hadn't the defenders of the blue been too daring?" On one hand he had a mind to run after Lawrence to make up and ask forgiveness. On the other hand, he knew his temper still boiled.

Paul reflected on these thoughts and walked to the field of the recent fight with his head hanging down. Mr. Koukkula showed up there also. "I suppose counting the cost of the lesson doesn't bring much happiness to the warlord," he said. "Sleep will come hard tonight, from what I know of you," he added gravely. Paul stood silent. "It happens to us grownups too, to say nothing of those your age," confided the man more genially. "Old Adam is wicked. He does many tricks during our lives. So we need often to bend his stiff neck that is within us, or even better, let the Heavenly Father do the bending." With that, the genial friend of the children trudged back to his house.

Paul knew all of this without being told but he became all the more remorseful. Instinctively his feet seemed to draw him to Lawrence's house. Tellervo, Taavi, Kretchen and Matt were still there. Lawrence was bathing his badly swollen face with cold water. When Paul appeared shame-faced at the door, Matt was still excitedly saying something about Paul and George.

All became silent. Mrs. Koukkula looked obviously pleased at the boy at the door. Paul, red and blushing, hurried over to Lawrence and choked out, "I'm sorry, forgive me!" Lawrence only kept on blowing his swollen nose noisily.

"You think you can get away with that?" threatened Matt from beside the window and he approached Paul. "Aren't you a hero? One of you pulls by the hair and the other strikes his face from the back!"

"Now, now, hold on!" said the mother. "We don't fight here, for this is the home of God's children. Besides, Paul, you did right when you listened to your conscience."

Lawrence turned quickly and came toward Paul and twined his wet hands around Paul neck, saying, "I do forgive you, Paul. Believe all forgiven in Jesus' name and blood. And forgive mine, too, in Jesus' name and blood."

But Matt slid out the door, grumbling as he went, "But who will fix my overcoat or pay for it?"

Paul went on to ask forgiveness from Tellervo, Taavi and Kretchen. Their mother also blessed him with tears in her eyes. "Go to Koukkulas' now while your feelings are still warm," she urged him gently.

Paul and Lawrence went together. It seemed almost that Mr. Koukkula waited for them. He sat in his shirtsleeves with his Bible beside him when the boys pushed through the door one behind the other. "God's peace," he greeted them.

"God's peace," they mumbled. "But can you forgive us after we carried on so badly in your yard and broke your lanterns?"

"Well, now, this is a precious mission that you brothers are on. How quickly the Heavenly Father was able to soften your stiff necks to bend in repentance. The sooner the better! Come here, precious brothers, so I can bless you properly with my arms around your necks."

And so they did embrace and bless each other with forgiveness. "Remember, it is Jesus' blood that truly does the cleansing. It mends a broken friendship and makes it more perfect than before," went on the father, moved with emotion. "Now go on home and sleep." Then he promised: "Come again, sheltered by love, to rebuild what was broken by the quarrel. I'm sure that we can still find lanterns and candles."

It was cold for three weeks before mild weather returned. There was activity once again in the Koukkula yard. Paul, Lawrence, Anna-Kaisa, Henry, Justin, Tarmo, Tellervo, Taavi, Gertrude and Kretchen had settled their old grudges and were rolling immense snowballs. Their faces were glowing and sweaty and their eyes sparkled. They spoke to one another in an even more friendly way than before. Nobody gave orders or argued.

Now Matt was nowhere to be seen, nor George, Joseph, Mataleena or Miina. Someone related George's remark that the whole business of building a snow castle was too childish. Someone else had heard that Matt still held a grudge, even though Paul and Henry had his overcoat repaired. Matt was the only son of the family with the finest house in the village and he was accustomed to giving orders.

But the rest of them got along well without a boss. The snowblocks joined together and the walls rose splendidly. Then Matt showed up by the corner of the fence and soon he started to roll a large snowball to the building site. He was subdued but at least his anger was obviously cooled. Lawrence and Paul gave him friendly nods. But not Anna-Kaisa.

"He has not yet apologized or asked forgiveness for things," she pointed out.

"Oh, well, let him first relent in his heart," Henry answered mildly. So the last one to join them could work hard peacefully, although he was not free and happy in spirit.

They were just about to put on the roof again when George, Joseph, Mataleena and Miina came noisily into the yard. They were loud and laughing, but their high-spirited voices were strained, to cover up apparent uneasiness. These late-comers went ahead to work along with the others, even though George especially still had lots of reason to ask to be forgiven. Lawrence and Matt averted their eyes, especially Matt.

"They just push themselves in without saying how sorry they are. At least George should ask for forgiveness," grumbled Justin.

"Let's wait and see if they are moved in a bit," counselled Paul.

The work gained speed and soon it was time to build the light tower. "This time we are going to have an ordinary snow-lantern!" Lawrence resolved. No one objected. Matt helped as directed and from snow he shaped a beautiful tower with a lantern.

Gertrude was sent to the Koukkulas' to get a candle. "Don't you want a lantern, too?" asked Mr. Koukkula with a twinkle in his eye. "We have a lantern right here."

"No, we don't! We won't argue this time," answered the little one briskly. She then took back the long thick candle, big enough to give light for many evenings. Matt lighted it.

"Christmas, Christmas!" sang Gertrude.

"A festival of peace, sure enough." Mr. Koukkula showed up with his snow boots on. The little childrens' eyes shone, but Matt dropped his head. George, Joseph, Mataleena and Miina drew aloof and really looked like onlookers, like uninvited guests. At this moment Lawrence approached George. George made a fist; he thought the time of revenge had come. But Lawrence grasped his wrist peaceably and said, "George, I've had very bad feelings toward you. Forgive me for that."

All were tense. Matt crawled on the roof to watch, as the lantern shone bright. George stared with wonder and was silent.

"He's pretending!" he thought. "I was childish even to come here."

"You have things which you ought to have forgiven you," his conscience persisted. Finally he yielded, hesitantly.

"You forgive me. I was most at fault!"

"I do, I forgive you in Jesus' name and blood," answered Lawrence soberly.

Matt slid down and joined them. "Forgive me also," he cried. "Forgiven, forgiven," came from so many mouths that the echo testified: "Forgiven."

Father Koukkula returned home with tears in his eyes. "What makes Papa cry?" asked his wife.

"I was out there in the yard while there were great services. I saw how love builds what quarrels break."

HARDENED SURFACES

One had to wait a long time for decent skiing that winter. Thawing weather lasted until well after Christmas. Then the Heavenly Father sent biting cold for weeks at a time and snow for days. Even the highest ridges had many inches of deep snow. The ground gleamed white and the woods appeared to be wrapped in cotton. But the snow was fine powder snow, like flour, and skis sank through it into stones and stubble. The waxed bottoms became scratched and pushing forward was tiring, particularly over the stony isthmus.

Then it abruptly turned milder and rained for two days. The trees cried. The woods were dark. The level of the snow sank, right before one's eyes. Folk feared that even the little bit of road would flee to Lapland.[1] Then the skies brightened and cleared and cold began to nip the tip of the nose.

One morning when Andrew dashed out into the yard, the crusted snow supported him. He strapped on his skis and slid down to the shore. Such speed! His eyes watered. The wind cut at his cheekbones. Even out on the lake ice, the skis slid effortlessly and the tip of the cape was quickly left farther and farther behind.

Soon the little fellow noticed that he was near his father's place of work. Men were busy by the lumber piles. Smoke from a nearby campfire rose in a slender column into the freezing sky. Andrew put on his best speed and dashed to meet them.

"God's peace, boy! Those skis must really slide!" greeted Bill Tasanen, Father's dependable workmate.

"What is there to skiing when the hard crust of snow holds you up?" rejoined the new arrival.

"The crust is hard, hard!" said his bearded father as he sipped his coffee. "Hard as a hardened conscience."

"The crust has to soften before it melts bare in places," agreed Bill.

Father went on, apparently leading to something serious and instructive. "If Andrew tried to smash away the hard crusted snow which carries him, he could stomp around and even then there would be hard, sharp fragments left. That is like a hard and unfeeling shell of a conscience. First God's severe law breaks it and the heart seems to be full of hard, sharp fragments. When God's grace truly softens the heart, when grace shines through the gospel, it melts even the thickest ice. Then spring comes to the soul!"

Father ended his little speech, shouldered his tool and started off down the logging road to get another load. Andrew listened and watched, leaning on his ski poles. He really could not understand all the thoughts of the men.

When Andrew was older, skiing in late winter with a campfire ax on his belt, he remembered his father's and Bill's discussions and understood them. His conscience too had hardened in enticing winds, but law's severe word drove his broken heart to the mercy seat where the warm reconciling word brought comfort for his agony and summer to his soul.

---

[1] After freeze-up, the logging roads could only be used while they remained frozen.

POINTING THE WAY

Father and Peter were driving to services in bitter cold. The horse trotted slowly over the frozen part of the lake. Peter tried to peek through a little opening in his scarf. "Why are there those small spruce on the other side of the road?" he wondered.

"So that we will know our way and stay on the road when we come back," explained Father. "It will already be dark before we come home."

When they came to a narrow channel, there were young spruce on **both** sides of the road. "Now, why are there spruce on both sides here?"

"Because the water has currents here and the ice is thick and strong only under the road. If we went to one side or the other, we could fall through the ice and drown!" answered Father, urging the horse to greater speed.

At the service Peter sat quietly in front of his father who was seated at the table in front. Father offered the prayer and then he paged through the Bible. He related: "Just now as we drove over the open stretch of the lake, Peter wondered about the guideposts along the road. I told him how they are needed so that we might stay on the road. In dangerous places, they are needed on both sides of the road.

"Our travel on the road to heaven is dangerous at every turn. If we are even a little to the side, we are in danger of drowning. That is why the Heavenly Father has carefully marked out the narrow road of life. He has given us the counsel and teaching of his gospel for guideposts. They are on the left side of our path to prevent us from slipping into sins of permissiveness and worldliness. There are also guideposts on the right of our path to warn us against hypocrisy and wrong-godliness. Now let us begin to study these guideposts."

Father then read for his text from the twelfth chapter of Romans, where the Apostle Paul counsels the Christians on how to live together in a new life which is acceptable to God. Paul particularly taught us to live in humility of heart, to love and serve one another, and to help one another with any gifts we have and whenever we have opportunity.

JOHN'S HEROIC DEED

John was given an air rifle as a Christmas gift. During the gray winter days, he diligently practiced target shooting. The little hollow-tailed pellets smacked into the painted center of the target. Once the boy even beat his father, who proclaimed him a man. "The major himself!" he called him.

Dozens of mountain ash grew near the fence and this winter they were just red with berries. How beautiful were the berries against the green leaves! When the first frost came, a flock of red bullfinches swooped into the ash trees. John pressed his nose against the windowpane to follow their activity. In the brilliant sunlight of bitter winter, their red breasts flashed grandly as they skillfully plucked the red berries with their beaks. For a while, there was delightful tumult and color in the dead of winter!

After the red bullfinch came the Bohemian waxwing. It seemed there were hundreds of them and their "Psst, psst, psst!" was everywhere in the courtyard. Surely they had a rollicking good time and no wonder, with such a dinner table! They lightly tilted their plumes of crested topknots as they ate their juicy meal. Then they suddenly took to flight, the flock circling about here and there until it swung as one mass to the top of a birch tree. There the birds sat without stirring, napping after their meal!

"Well, there are a lot of little roasts out there," said John's father.

"Roasts!" John was astonished.

"Yes, the meat of Bohemian waxwing is eaten and it is a real delicacy, too!"

"Then why don't you shoot it?"

"Just see how pretty and gentle they are! Father would rather watch them than eat them. Who would have the heart to kill them out there?" asked Mother. And so all three spent a minute watching the activities of the flock of waxwings.

But the wicked thought was now in John's mind. He imagined himself to be a handsome hunter with his knapsack, his guns and his horns, a perfect hero. Then he would grandly throw his bundle of birds in front of his mother and say manfully: "Pick these and roast them!"

Next morning, the lad stealthily stole out with his air rifle. He sneaked to the fence corner and behind the trunks of the pine trees near the mountain ash. But the Bohemian waxwings were not there. Perhaps they had hurried away because of the cold, to await Lapland's summer.

No! Here they flew into the lowest mountain ash. Happily, they ate a meal while visiting with one another. John crept closer, pine by pine. But another gray hunter sneaked along the fence. The pussycat took a couple of cautious steps and then froze again. She stalked the waxwings more for sport than for hope of a meal.

John had to act now! He no longer dared to move from his hiding place. There was more involved in this venture than target practice at home, but he could still succeed. The boy located a bird closer than those in his original field of view. His gun wobbled, then steadied. Ready. Snap! The flock of birds flew off in a cloud but one fell. John ran straight for it, but pussycat was quicker. She streaked under the fence with the fluttering bird in her mouth. John's jaw dropped as he watched. Then he walked inside, downcast.

At the noon meal, Father wondered, "What has become of our birds? I haven't seen them all day."

"Maybe they have already flown to Lapland," suggested Mother.

Hilja from the kitchen had a better suggestion: "Or that cat chased them. Just a while ago she had a feather stuck in the corner of her mouth."

"Yes, the cat always lies in wait for them," said John. He appeared detached and stared at his plate with fiery red cheeks. Mother closed the discussion with, "The poor cat does not understand the matter."

"But **you** understand!" said John's conscience within his heart. He left for the toboggan slide, but his conscience followed him. "Think of the pain the wounded bird had to suffer from the claws and teeth! And not only that, you were not honest at the dinner table!"

John stood on the hill and meditated. "The Heavenly Father has seen and heard your sins. Don't cover up or try to justify them!" spoke his conscience. Then it came again more powerfully: "Repent. Confess!" But the boy strove harder against it and fought it until evening.

Mother asked as they sat at the dinner table: "What are our young man's thoughts? He doesn't even remember to eat." John burst into tears.

"It is **my** fault!"

"What is your fault?"

"That the cat ate the waxwing."

"How could that be?"

"I shot the bird and the cat got it."

Mother and Father glanced at one another. "I think it was partly my fault, because I talked about the little roast," said Father without laughing.

"No, it wasn't. Father, you forgive me," sobbed John.

"Believe all forgiven, son, in Jesus' name and blood."

The Bohemian waxwings belong in the mountain ash; possibly they will arrive with the cold weather again next winter.

"MOTHER, REPENT!"

Nels Saari was dead. On his deathbed he received the grace of conversion. He called his wife and his only son, Nillo, ten, over to him. He cried and begged for forgiveness for his life apart from God. For a long time, Nels held his child's hand while saying, "Don't swear as your father has sworn. Don't offend your mother as your father has done. Don't take even your **first** drink. Then you won't go to the dogs and you won't be a drunkard as I have been. Don't scoff at the Christians as I did, poor soul, but go to their services and receive blessing from them."

Now they had the funeral service for the late master at the Saari house. David Tikkanen preached as Nillo sat beside his mother listening. "Perhaps this sad happening can be a blessing for his relatives and for us all. It would be good for us to become distressed over our sins while we still live. We may not be given a long and lingering illness but we all have sins...." spoke the preacher brother. Certainly Nillo had something to think about. He knew that already he had used swear words, had disobeyed his mother, had made fun of the children of God. His father had thought that Nillo was better than he really was, but God knew!

Nillo stood up. "Christians, forgive me! I have scoffed and said bad things about you." The living room stirred: "...forgiven, child, in Jesus' name and blood," was heard from all corners. An old lady named Sara came clear over to him, embracing him around his shoulders and blessing him. Then Nillo jumped into his mother's lap, saying, "Forgive my disobedience and sharp words."

"Surely I do, of course I do. Calm down now!" whispered his annoyed mother. But the boy didn't stop. With arms around his mother's neck, he continued, "Mother, you too repent so that we may go to be with Father in heaven." But Mother remained stiff. "Mother, repent! You will, won't you?"

The whole room followed this struggle with tense attention. There was hardly a dry eye in the living room, but Mother's face did not moisten. "Of what would I repent?" she asked.

"Didn't you and Father once laugh at the believers?"

"Oh, that was just a joke!" snapped his mother. She left for the bedroom and remained there for the rest of the evening. Guests at the service left, shaken and downcast. Finally only old Sara remained. She patted Nillo's head. "Freely believe, child. None of us can force anyone into heaven. We will leave Mother in God's care."

Nillo sat for a long time by the window, gazing into the night. Finally his mother emerged from the bedroom. "Go to bed, son, and stop your foolishness. You'll disgrace yourself and me!" Nillo went to bed, but he fell asleep crying.

This is how Nillo Saari's life in Christian faith really began. From the start, it was a trying and narrow path. But he has remained steadily on it to this day and he believes that some day he will indeed be with his father.

GETHSEMANE

Sam, the sixteen-year-old son of Jonas the pottery-maker, was much too quiet for a city boy. He was not at all happy in the company of the noisy young crowd in the streets and alleys of Jerusalem. He was an eager student in the school of Rabbi Sadok and he read the sacred writings fluently. His calm, quiet answers indicated that he understood what he had read.

During vacation times Sam slipped through the outside walls and wandered alone around the parks and among the groves. At other times he wandered from the Fountain Way near Rougel Spring and beyond, toward the Dead Sea. Sometimes he strayed to the Spring of Gihon and from there to Kidron Valley over the ridge of the Mount of Olives. More often, he walked from the Sheep Gate to quiet Gethsemane and further still to the cold mountain road toward Jericho. Often on these trips he stayed until he saw the red of the setting sun on Antonio's Castle towers and the last rays of the glowing fireball on the golden Temple dome.[1]

A person hurrying from the country at that time might see a determined schoolboy gazing on the slope of the Mount of Olives, his lips humming the old hymn:

> In Judah is God known:
> His name is great in Israel.
> In Salem also is his tabernacle,
> And his dwelling-place in Zion.[2]

The Passover festival was approaching and the season was spring-like. The streets were crowded. New visitors swarmed to the temple on all the roads as the town became more and more restless. In the early morning hours Sam threaded through the throng from the Sheep Gate and sneaked into the shadows of Gethsemane. The rainy-season dampness still lingered upon the earth. In Kidron, the water gurgled; in the fields, the barley stalks turned yellow and the wheat formed its heads. The mountains shone with the splendor of a blanket of flowers. Early in the day in the far-flung desert, a blowing, drying wind sprang up, bringing on its wings a choking, overwhelming abundance of odors.

Sam longed just now for perfect solitude and peace. The frame of mind in town was one of frantic bustle. Everywhere there seemed to be conflict and struggle. Jesus, Joseph's son, a Nazarene, was on everyone's lips. Some were for him, others were hotly against him. Rabbi Sadok was restless and absent-minded in his teaching. Finally he sternly and agitatedly warned his students: "Beware of that frenzied movement whose instigator comes from little Nazareth. He is an uneducated carpenter's son who suffers from a mania for greatness!"

Sam had seen the Nazarene three times and had heard him speak. It was impossible for him to believe that that man was evil. The proclaimer's face was kind. A light of blessing shone in his eyes. His voice sounded soft and warm. He conducted himself calmly and freely. This is why Sam's spirit rebelled against the bombastic harshness of the accusations. His teacher looked at him searchingly; possibly the famous rabbi had read his student's rebellious thoughts.

A time of anguish came to the young man. An oppressive feeling followed Sam to Gethsemane, stifling his breath, making him sweaty. A burning wind struggled like a fevered panting through the cypress and olive trees, as though to dry in one night the spring's luxurious growth. Shadows lengthened in the woods. The gold of the Temple glowed white as if on fire. Then darkness spread its wings abruptly over the area.

A strange lassitude overcame Sam. He knew that he should hurry home, but still he wandered about under the fig and almond trees. Suddenly he saw something. He heard a quiet conversation from the road. The red light of a torch swung toward Gethsemane. Sam felt his way into the shelter of a big olive tree trunk with its broad hiding places.

Sam heard a familiar warm voice:[3] "Sit ye here while I go and pray yonder." Then he heard the same voice, nearer: "My soul is exceeding sorrowful, even unto death: tarry ye here and watch with me!"

Then someone walked right past the young man's hiding place, fell on his knees and prayed, "Oh my Father, if it be possible, let this cup pass from me; nevertheless not as I will, but as thou wilt."

Sam held his breath. Bats rustled into flight from their roost, a wing brushing scarily against the boy's cheek. In the distance he could hear heavy snoring. The one praying rose and found his way to the sleepers. His words stabbed Sam's heart painfully! "What, could ye not watch with me one hour? Watch and pray, that ye enter not into temptation: the spirit indeed is willing, but the flesh is weak."

Again the steps came near to the young man's hiding place. Again the anguished man praying threw himself upon the ground and from the depths of his being he cried out, "Oh my Father, if this cup may not pass away from me, except I drink it, thy will be done."

Sam didn't dare to move. At times, chills made him shiver; at other times, sweat ran down his face and back. In the sultry night, the moments seemed endless. Close by, the man in prayer writhed in the grass. His groans told of a greater, burning pain as he prayed amid the even breathing of the sleepers. Once more he swayed over to the sleepers, lingered a moment, then returned without speaking to the place under the olive trees. "My Father," he cried, "thy will be done!"

Sam wished he could throw himself down on his face beside the one who prayed, but a boundless horror left his tender limbs without feeling. Then light shone amidst the darkness. A brightly shining being stepped down to earth before the now-silent man and laid his hand on his forehead. Sam then saw the pale face of the Nazarene and the deep glowing eyes. They seemed to look right at him---at Sam. Only the Father can look that way at his erring loved ones!

53

Sam recalled how old John had once caught him stealing figs from a bowl. Father brought the boy into the home's most holy place and spanked him. When the shaking child finally dared to look at his punisher, the boy saw tears on his father's face. Sam saw at that time the same luster which brightened the gaze of the man who had prayed in Gethsemane.

The angel floated away. The Nazarene arose and walked with firm steps toward where men's snoring still was heard. Sam heard quiet, sad words: "Sleep on now, and take your rest: behold, the hour is at hand, and the Son of man is betrayed into the hands of sinners."

Sam heard the sound of swords rattling and excited whispering. Tens of flickering red torches flashed between the trees. Dark shadows swayed near them. A slender agile man hurried to step forward. Sam heard a hasty kiss of greeting and then the response, "Judas, betrayest thou the Son of man with a kiss?"

Then a sword flashed. Someone cried out. The tumult increased. A cry for ropes and harsh swearing. Fleeing footsteps and panting were heard from the darkness in the woods. Someone ran very closely past Sam and panted, "My God! They arrested him!" Now the tumultuous crowd moved toward the town of Kidron.

Gethsemane quieted. Sam heard an owl's ghostly hoot somewhere far away and still farther a jackal's vicious bark. Sam collapsed into a hollow formed by the tree roots, leaned his head against the trunk and fell asleep. When the sun came up and dew glistened everywhere, a flock of sparrows chattered in the olive tree and Sam awakened.

He gazed at the ground, lost in thought. It was plain to be seen where a man had writhed in anguish last night. Fiery red anemonies were broken, but something else red glistened on the ground. Sam leaned over and lifted a stained leaf in his hand; it was bloody!

It has been told that when young Sam arrived at his father's house that morning, **nothing** could prevent him from joining the disciples of the Nazarene. He was baptized and given a new name: Stephen.

---

[1] You ought to be able to find each of these places on a map of Jerusalem in Jesus' time; notice how short the distances are!

[2] Psalm 76:12

[3] See Matthew 26: 36-57 and Luke 22: 39-54.

THE HARDEST THING

Sunshine of late winter baked the road. The crust of snow shrank so that the rye stubble showed through. A lark appeared, a tiny dot in the blue of the sky. A starling peeked into last summer's bird house. Joy was in the air. But Lauri walked with his head bent low as he came from the Good Friday church service. One point from the sermon stuck in his mind. The pastor spoke about Jesus' prayer of intercession: "Father, forgive them, for they know not what they do."

"Let this word remain and echo in your ears and hearts!" the preacher said emphatically. "It was a prayer for all of us. For all of us, the Lord cast the burden of our sins on his innocent Son, even the sin that we have not always been able to forgive or bless our enemies. Let the love of Jesus warm you this Good Friday, so that you can bless and do good to those who hate you."[1]

Matt had offended Lauri, obviously. Together, they had built Stonebrook Mill with its two waterwheels. Lauri's wheel turned like a windmill in the breeze, but Matt's was troublesome. Lauri bragged a bit about his own work and then, in jest, he called Matt's work a do-nothing rattle-mill. At that, Matt kicked Lauri's water-wheel to pieces. A scuffle started. Lauri pushed his playmate down on the wet ground but Matt was stronger. They struggled and Matt managed to get on top, hit Lauri and shout, "Lauri is a Black Jack! Lauri is a Black Jack!"

Lauri had been offended. But forgive? And bless? He wavered. He didn't feel like it. In fact, he felt just the opposite when he heard that Matt was sick. He had a high fever and they thought perhaps it was in his lungs. "**Now** he isn't a troublesome pest all the time," Lauri told himself. He might even have thought, "So there! He got his punishment from afar, that builder of water-wheels."

But recent days were a bit dull and long and lonely, playing alone. Besides, some tattle-tale had brought the matter to the parsonage! How else could the pastor guess Lauri and Matt's attitude toward one another? It's true that God's men can know in other ways, too. They are known to see right through one.

On Saturday, Lauri's mother reported that Matt had turned for the worse. The doctor said that the illness was actually pneumonia. "That is a **dangerous** illness," added Mother.

"Could Matt die of it?"

"Oh, yes!"

That evening was a sad one. Lauri hung around near his mother, who asked him: "Shouldn't we fix an Easter basket for Matt?"

"I don't know," murmured Lauri.

"You are good friends, aren't you?"

Lauri was barely audible. "Maybe." And there the matter was left.

"Pray tonight for Matt," Mother encouraged Lauri as she bade him good night. When Father and Mother came to retire, Lauri was still awake.

"Are you getting sick, that you don't sleep?"

"No, I don't think so."

"Then why can't you sleep?" The lights were turned out.

Lauri cried out: "Mother!"

"What, my son?"

"It is so **hard**!"

"What is so hard?" The only answer was sobbing. Now Father came to Lauri's bed to comfort him.

"To pray for your enemy."

"Who is such an enemy?"

"Matt."

"Matt! No, for goodness sakes, you are friends."

"We aren't any longer," sobbed Lauri, and then in anguish he related the whole story about their quarrel at the mill.

"You know, the fault was in you to begin with. In the end, you weren't left any better off than Matt," Mother said thoughtfully.

"I wonder whether Matt will forgive me," asked Lauri.

"Oh, I'm sure he will. And the Heavenly Father will forgive you also."

"Really?"

"Really, my child. All your sins are forgiven in Jesus' name and blood."

"Was Jesus praying on my behalf when the nails were hammered?"

"Yes, indeed."

"I will pray for Matt, too. Daddy, pray with me." Lauri folded his hands and said, "Dear God, bless Matt and make him well."

"Why was it so hard?" asked the boy after a bit.

"It is the hardest thing in all the world, for all of us," responded Father.

A minute later: "Mother?"

"What, Lauri?"

"In the morning, let's fix that basket. Is it hard for you, too, Mother, to pray for an enem...ah...for one you are angry with?"

"Yes, always."

Lauri went to Matt's on Easter morning. Matt's illness had taken a turn for the better during the night. He was sleeping when Lauri came, so they did not have the heart to waken him. But when he opened his eyes during the day, he saw the basket with its chocolate chicken and chocolate eggs. He also saw an Easter card: "Matt, forgive me. Lauri."

---

[1] See Matthew 5:44

SUFFERING JESUS

A picture of Jesus hung on the preacher's study wall. A crown of thorns was pressed onto the head of Christ so that drops of blood trickled over his pale face. A look of painful suffering was in the eyes of the gentle Saviour. Henry often stood under this picture. His thoughts turned sad and it almost made him cry. One day his father came upon Henry next to the picture.

"Daddy, why is good Jesus so sad-looking, and why does the blood trickle from his head?"

Father was very serious. He lifted his son onto his lap and told him:

"We have all been very bad. Your father has been bad. Henry has been a bad boy many times. God ought to punish us severely for our badness, and in the end he would have to throw us to the bad angels. But God has a kind and good heart. He does not wish anything bad for us. That is why He sent his own son Jesus to suffer in place of us.

"Jesus' face is sad because of our sins and the thorns are jabbed into the forehead of the good Savious on account of our badness. But Christ does not grow weary even though his pains are great, for He loves us. He gladly suffers and dies in place of us."

"Did Jesus die in my place also?"

"Yes, my boy."

"Oh, how good He truly is!" cried the child and he hid his tearful face against his father's chest.

EASTER SONG

The female lark was a small gray bird which flew and chirped a little like a sparrow. She hopped along the ground looking for her food and hid her nest of fine grass on the ground nearly two thousand years ago. She nested at a certain cemetery far away in the Mid-East and she hatched her eggs near a tomb in a rock cave in this peaceful place.

Occasionally a quiet melancholy man came near there; the keeper of the graveyard visited more often. The quiet man, Serious Joseph, had prepared his own last resting place there near a dark cliff. He often paused in thought and rested his chin on his staff placed upon the rock quite near the lark's nest. At first the bird was somewhat alarmed but soon decided that she was safe and was not upset at the discovery of her nesting place.

But then some upsetting things occurred. On one extremely gloomy evening the sun darkened and lightning flashed. The earth shook. Thunder echoed in the cliffs. The little lark crouched low on her nest and her heart almost stopped.

In the morning she heard the noise of footsteps. The lark abruptly flew off the nest and sat on the top of the gravestone to look. A funeral procession arrived at the graveyard. First came two pious-looking men, one of whom the lark recognized as the cemetery keeper.

Then the one who had died was carried in on a stretcher. Gaping wounds were in the body's feet and hands. The side was pierced. The forehead was covered with little wounds but the face was oddly beautiful. A wonderful calm and peace illuminated it. The lark turned her head away, her heart twisted with horror. "People are cruel. They have cut this good man to pieces until he died!" thought the lark.

The dead man was taken to Serious Joseph's rocky grave. A great rock was rolled up against the opening and once again it became quiet in the graveyard. One poor woman sat alone near the grave and cried. The lark stole to her nest, tired, but sleep failed to come.

That evening the peace was broken again. The lark had never heard such a noise in a sacred garden and she flew up in fright. She saw glittering helmeted soldiers marching toward the rock tomb. They milled about near the blocked opening of the tomb for a bit and then sat down on the rocks and grassy mounds, some leaning on their spears or shields. One was so close to the lark's nest that the poor bird didn't dare to sit on the eggs. Restless, she hopped about in the rocky holes and grassy areas. Whenever the soldiers stirred, their weapons rattled and the heart of the little bird quaked. It was a night of anguish.

But morning finally grew light. The highest cypress trees framed the rising sun. The rooster crowed in town. Dew glistened on the grass. Hundreds of little birds began their singing for the day but the lark could not sing even a single peep! She looked from the branch of a dry cypress at her threatened nest and at the drowsy soldiers and the closed grave. She could not forget that savagely wounded body which had been carried into the cemetery chamber yesterday. Such a lovely face!

But then the heavens flashed and the earth shook! A great and splendid being came down in front of the rock tomb there. Its clothes were like the snow on the mountain top when it shines bright in the sun. The soldiers fell to the ground like dead men. The heavenly messenger touched the stone blocking the opening of the grave and it rolled to the side. From the grave stepped forth the man just buried two days ago---alive! How beautiful he was!

The little lark seemed to burst with joy and she took flight. How her wings carried her in the light and bright air, higher and higher above the earth until Serious Joseph's grave became just a tiny spot. High in the clouds the little gray bird sang melodies which welled bright like the water burbling from a spring over a rock.

People in the towns and country-side looked marveling into the blue of the sky where a black spot gleamed. A musical flood poured from it, falling onto spring-time woods, mountains and lakes.

But no one who heard the music knew yet that the whole human race had been freed from sin and death's desolate winter, and that over them shone Resurrections's spring: EASTER!

SPRING

Oh, how the days have lengthened! When we awaken in the morning, the day is peeping out between the birch trees. The red-breasted finch has already wakened from his sleep. He has raised his little head from under his wing and now is lustily singing his morning hymn. He praises his creator for the lovely northern spring. We, too, fold our hands and say, "Dear Heavenly Father! Thank you for the warmth of the sun and the approaching summer. Give us strength to be kind and good-natured today."

Outdoors the snowdrifts have melted. Little streams ripple everywhere. Green grass is peeking out on the south slopes. On the edges of the fields, needle-like yellow flowers have burst into bloom. We hunt for them. Each flower found is a true treasure. We tenderly break it off and study it with great interest. "Dear Heavenly Father, how beautiful is your work! Let me find many kinds of these." And we do find them.

Soon we have in our hands a lovely bouquet of blossoms to hold. We run to bring them to Mama whose eyes beam with joy. Happily she arranges spring's first blooms into a coffee mug, pours water into the bottom and lifts the mug with its flowers up onto the windowsill.

Aha! Bubbles of water are showing along the shore of the cove. That is why Daddy is tarring the boat on the shore. He plans soon to lower into the water the fish net which is shaped like a bag held open by two or three hoops. The sunshine is already so hot on the boat that the tar melts into the seams. Its pungent scent fills the whole area.

Daddy has taken off his jacket; his white shirt sleeve is a real contrast to the black side of the boat. When we ask Daddy all kinds of things, he answers gently with a twinkle in the corner of his eye. Everything is so delightful! My own dear father here near me. And there in that blue sky is another Father who looks and looks on His children and sends a cloud of angels to protect us from all harm. What a blessed spring mid-day!

In the evening, Minnie carries in the bath-water. The mosquitoes come out to swarm next to the barn wall and we watch their dance long and earnestly. Now the church bells ring. This is Saturday night and tomorrow is Sunday. Daddy has paused in his work. He stands absorbed beside the boat which is now completely tarred and gazes over the inlet toward the church. We think he is praying to the Heavenly Father.

The steam gently bathes our arms and legs as we sit on the bath-house bench. It feels **good**! Daddy and Mama smile at one another. "This was the first real summer day today," says Daddy. Mama nods her head and her eyes laugh. Then Daddy is serious again: "The outside has spring's brightness. The body is cleansed from the soil of work and the conscience is made white with the blood of the Lamb. What more could sinful man hope for?"

It is as if we were sitting in church. Dusk gathers everything into its net. One is so tired coming to bed, but the evening prayer goes well all the way to the Amen. The eyes close.

SPRING TEACHES FROM THE HIGHWAY

Father and son were skiing on the road which was in pretty bad shape. The center of the road was dirty and at the shoulders of the road the skis barely slid for the branches and twigs from the fir trees. The sun on their backs was warm and Peter was red-faced and panting.

The boy paused. "Dad, why is the road today so full of rubbish? A week ago it was white and clean."

"The sun has shone on it."

"How so?" puzzled Peter.

"The sun is warm and good," Father explained. "All through the winter, the horses have dirtied the road in their travels, and straw and branches have fallen from the wagonloads. But new snow has always fallen and covered the trash. That is why, a week ago, the road looked clean but it was a false cleanliness. Now the kind warm spring sun has revealed the deceit. It has melted the snow and all the dirt under the snow is in plain sight, so our going is troublesome. Now let's move on again."

After a kilometer they had to stop again to puff. Father went on with his explanation. "Many a young boy is like the clean-looking surface of a winter road. He sins, steals, lies, teases his little sister, chases birds, uses filthy words, disobeys his father and mother, and **still** acts as though nothing bad has taken place. His conscience has fallen asleep. He can present himself very nicely so that the neighbor ladies think that he is a well-behaved boy. Let's move on."

Peter moved on, following his father and thinking. Once again before they reached home they had to rest. Now Father related: "I also was once a boy like that, troublesome and growing hard of conscience. But even then in my youth my steps led me to the services of God's children, where the Lord's word shone brightly. The word began to throw light on my conscience. Much dirt of sins became evident and I was miserable because of them. Life was like skiing on a dirty road and finally I couldn't go on any longer. I told God's children of my misery in sin. They preached unto me the gospel message of the Saviour of sinners and assured me that my sins were forgiven in His blood. The sun of God's redeeming love beamed warmly in my heart. It was truly a spring sun.

"Then I had the strength to beg forgiveness at home from Mother and Father. I went to my neighbor and confessed stealing turnips and asked forgiveness. I also had matters to settle with my teacher for causing disturbances and for once cheating on an exam by peeking in the book. That is what the light of grace was like in my soul and to this day I thank that spring-like God."

A tear rolled over Father's cheek and dropped on the dirty road.

THE GREAT CATCH

The school teacher's son John and Fishing Shack Charlie's son Gus were believing boys and good friends. They were enthusiastic fishermen too, especially in the spring when they were in a perpetual fishing bustle. John had three nets and setlines but Gus, who was of a poor family, had only a 100-hook line.

The ice was gone. It had damaged Peter Sharp's sawmill on its way crashing down the river. A couple of log piles had been knocked down with ponderous slowness. The river was still high and one could still see snow at the bends on the river-banks. The boys hurried with their fishing tackle to the fish camp which was also the sauna at Fireplace Rapids. The trawl crates slid easily on the towrope while each boy had a huge knapsack on his back. Steps echoed oddly on the frozen ground. Now and then their noses caught the strong odor of a recently tarred boat. The odor of pitch came from the woods, carried by the wind. A lark as little as a flea warbled at a dizzy height and its music rippled clearly over the landscape. **This** was something better than sitting bored on a school bench. It truly was!

The sun was already setting into the lap of the clearing when the youths quietly laid their burdens near the wall of the sauna. They could see the boat of their long gone grandpa still in its place. Grandpa from The Rushes had been there to tar it as had been agreed upon last fall. Quickly they pushed it down the embankment to the water. It didn't appear to leak a drop. They found the oars and paddle in the sauna. And so they got their nets into the isolated cove where they could watch the jostling spawning fish.

Then the hikers hurried into the warmth of the fireplace in the bathhouse. Gus gathered sticks of wood and brush and John split them. Soon smoke curled from the door and shutters of the bathhouse. The boys relaxed and sat by the wall to eat their lunch. Things were always divided equally, taking no note of the poorness of Gus' bread and butter. Bravely John bit into the sandwich while his neighbor munched on fancier leftovers from John's school-teacher mother.

It began to be dusk just about when the fireplace was finally hot enough to hiss instantly when spit upon and the smoke was rolling out. The youths cleared off the bench to the dry bare wood and lifted their knapsacks for pillows under their heads. They pushed shut the shutters and doors. It became dark as pitch. The noise from the river rose and somewhere a mouse gnawed on the floor. Gus shivered. "Let's sing the evening hymn," he proposed. "Let's sing our dead Grandpa's hymn of fishing."

Then he hummed a verse, tenderly and timidly. It went something like this:

A poor worm and pilgrim,
I travel many dangerous journeys.
On this way, I seek the Fatherland
And now await the evening hour.
No restful, sorrowless lodging have I here.
I hurry there with all my strength,
There where rest and peace enfold me.

    The boys folded their hands and repeated their evening prayer. Gus dropped off to sleep at once but John lay awake a long time. The blood in his veins seemed to race with the rapids. It seemed strange to lie here and think of the far-away village where the school was located. He thought of its paved streets and its idle people. He also recalled that departed old grandpa, a former factory superintendent in the big city, who moved to this country in his old age to live with his teacher son. Here is where his blood drew him--to these back woods. He stayed out here for weeks, especially in the spring. His son did not persuade him to stay but his grandson did. He carried the boy when he was a youngster, taught him hymns and prayers and showed him the wonders of the north country.

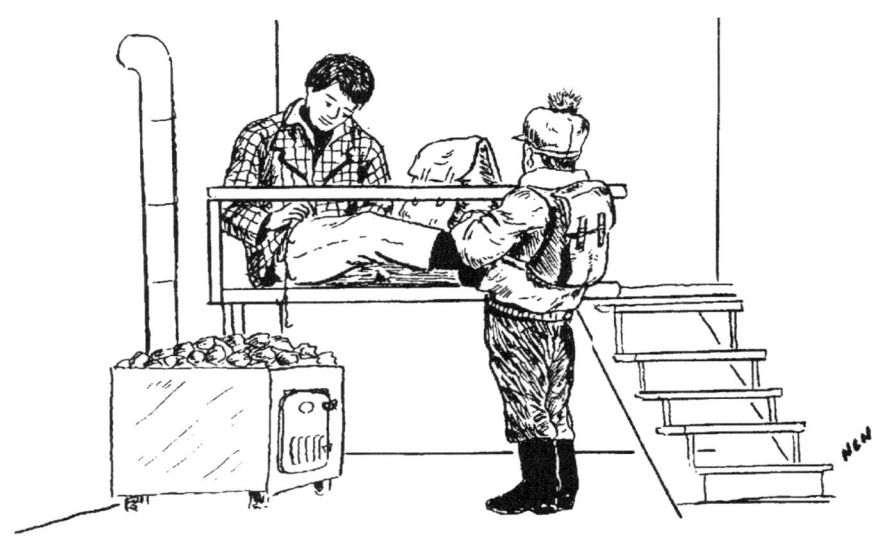

    At sunrise it was quite cold. Near the river bends the ground was frozen. Gooseflesh covered the boys when they ran from the warmth of the bathhouse to the boat. The wooden seats were icy to their bottoms. Their full nets threshed with the spawning fish as they struggled. Among them were a few little whitefish and pike.

Now it was time to bait. They lighted a campfire on the shore, put a coffee pot on the fire and began to thread the little baits onto their hooks by hand. They laid shrimp on their sides in the shallowest baskets and beside that the leaders and the baited hooks. In this way they baited the 200-hook lines. Now if only the good Lord would give the salmon the desire to eat.

Gus lowered his line almost to the waves of the rapids. John dropped his line into a more likely hole for salmon near the reefs. Usually they divided the catch equally. This time John thought things over and decided that each would keep what he caught on his own line.

At midday they looked at their lines and changed their bait, but they saw no salmon. John's line held a couple of worthless roe. By evening they were able to lower the third line and again John secretly decided in his mind that he now would keep what he caught on his own tackle.

This night John was not restless. The sun was almost up when Gus awakened him. Quickly they made their way down to the water. When John grasped Gus' line he felt a powerful jolt. A salmon's dark back was right by the side of the rock. Further off another hit the water with its tail. The boys flushed with excitement. There was shouting and rushing around before the beautiful huge creatures were in the boat. There were five on the top line, making a great big thumping tubfull. Even the smallest one weighed over two kilos.

From John's two lines they got a northern pike and just enough suckers to annoy him. Gus exultantly cried, "We **did** get a good start for fishing." But John almost looked sullen.

"What if we divide the catch evenly as before?" he thought.

"How did you decide yesterday in your heart?" asked his conscience.

When the lines were all lifted, Gus and John made another pile of cut-up bait. They put fresh bait onto the lines which they lowered into the same areas as before. And so they continued their successful fishing trip.

Afterward, the youths first had to stop at home and then on the next day divide up their catch. They could easily be divided into two equal piles of the same kind of fish. Gus stacked the fish. "Which pile do you choose?" he asked, overflowing with enthusiasm. John knew in his mind that he should choose the poorer pile but he did not. John's hands shook as they both began to stow their catch into their knapsacks.

Gus almost ran ahead towards home but John trudged after him, not being inclined to talk. His knapsack pressed. He perspired.

At home the people were delighted with the boys' first catch of the season. They kept lifting the salmon onto the scale and finally the women hurried off to clean the fish.

That night the boys retired early, but John could not sleep. "God saw your deceit!" thumped his conscience in his chest. In the middle of the night he crept out of bed and in reparation sought Gus's cleaned fish. He wrapped them in paper and left happier on his way to Fishing Cabin Charlie's little house. Grandma was still up. "Just why are you sneaking around at midnight?"

"I cheated Gus in dividing up the catch and I brought these fish. They belong to Gus."

When John was hurrying home that night he felt that **he** had made the great catch.

REWARD FOR SUNDAY WORK

John was allowed to work with the men to peel logs. Wasn't he already thirteen years old and robust for his age? The bark flew as the logs whirled in his fists. On the best days, he finished a stack two meters high. He properly brought every paycheck to his mother, for he was a fine, decent boy. It was true that he no longer had the courage to confess his faith as he did when he was a child. The poor fellow was afraid of ridicule from his work partners.

At his work place, there were many men who seemed to forget the third commandment. They took days off sometimes during the week, but on Sundays they kept strictly busy at log peeling. Even if some Christian rebuked them for it, they didn't care. They just laughed and joked. It was carefree bustle. John couldn't help being a bit jealous. A grown-up man ought to be that free and easy if he expected to get ahead in life.

Every Monday morning it bothered him to see the logs others had peeled on Sunday. "Why not you?" queried the enemy of the soul. And later in the week, it reminded him, "Why not you, the same as the others?" John decided to go along with the men to peel logs on the next Sunday.

Why did the decision keep him awake so on Saturday night? They had worked until exhausted and had taken a steam bath after. Mother had seemed to be a little suspicious as she talked about the wretched ones who no longer kept the Sabbath. "What of it? I bring her the money!" John turned to the wall and slept.

He awakened early in the morning. "The clock may not even say five yet. Now I can sneak off to work. Mother is still sleeping," decided John. He slipped into his work clothes quietly, but Mother woke up anyway.

"My boy, where are you going so early in your work clothes? This is Sunday!"

"So what, Mother? Others are peeling logs there too."

"Dear boy, do not go. It is sin!"

"I'm going, and that's that!" John pushed the door shut, as Mother sighed heavily.

John seemed to be troubled as he scraped the surface of the logs. The sunrise came. The pine pitch smelled good. He heard a lark trill in the sky. Yet somehow he felt badly. None of his partners happened to be nearby.

Old Miina Saari was on her way to church. She walked a path on the steep hillside quite near to the log piles. "Oh, poor child, are you here too?" she said. Then she sighed and went on.

The church bells clanged out their ringing. John recalled: "...that we do not disdain God's word and teaching, but gladly hear and learn it." Then he thought, "I really should leave when I get this measure completed."

But the trees were wicked and badly branched. He had to strike a full blow, starting his ax from clear behind his head. The ax slipped. Instantly, the sharp edge cut a gaping wound into his leg. He almost blacked out.

Workers came, tied a band above the wound on his leg and carried him home. "What's done is done," said Mother.

John had to spend two full weeks in bed, and he limped for many months. Finally the wound healed. Finally also the wounded conscience healed. John repented and believed his sins forgiven in Jesus' blood and name. He warned others of the rewards of working on Sunday.

THE BUTTING WOODEN COW

Aaro Rauhala was holding services at Taavetti Lokkisella's and that made everyone in that home happy. The children especially rejoiced, for Aaro shared in their life throughout the whole day. Aaro was a burly black-bearded man, but he was always smiling, his lively eyes beaming with warmth. He rocked the little ones on his knees and sang songs about Jesus to them. He told such fascinating stories about little boys in the Bible that his young audience was like one ear.

Besides the songs and stories, he had a most remarkable talent for whittling toys for quiet play. A piece of wood in his fingers was soon carved into a cow, a little pig, a squirrel, an old woman churning, a pussy cat or whatever he wished.

Right now Aaro was whittling a wooden cow for Lisa Lakinen to have as her favorite. When it was done, even the grownups came to admire and wonder at it. But Lisa was disappointed and asked, "Isn't it going to have horns? I don't want a cow without horns!"

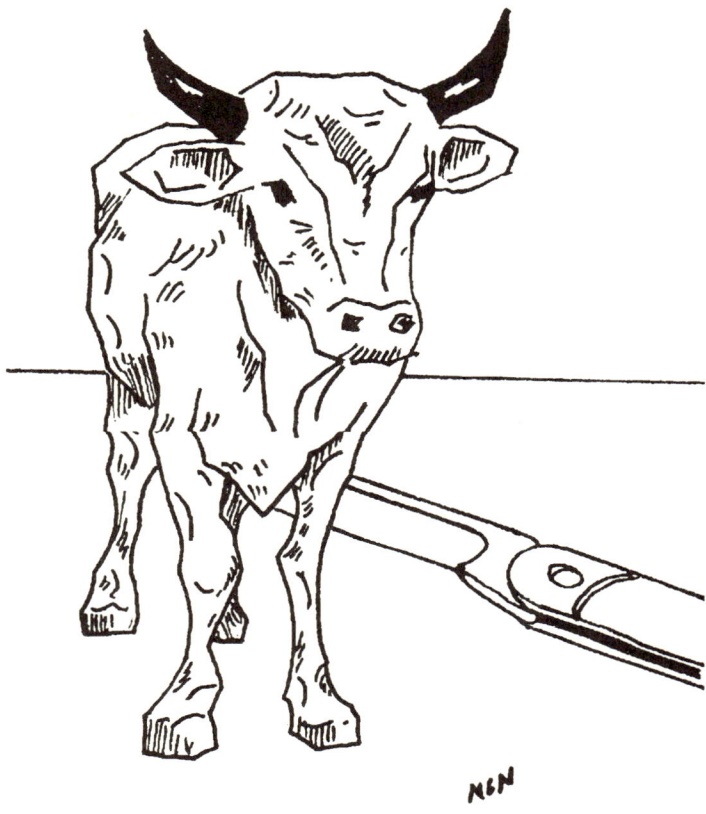

"Right, right, horns would be good, horns would be good," agreed the master mildly. And bit by bit from a blackened juniper branch he cut strong horns for the birch-wood cow. While he carved he continued, "Remember, Lisa, if you fall into sin and fall from faith, then this cow with its sharp horns will give your conscience a butt!"

Next day, just before the confirmation class went out for recess, they had a serious moment. The old pastor had reminded them how they soon would appear before God and the congregation to confess their faith and to promise faithfulness to the Lord. "Remember, the confession of faith will be read to you children while you are at the altar and then you will be asked if this faith is your faith. When you say yes, in the presence of the congregation and of God who sees all, it indicates that you confess yourselves to be believing young people."

"That is a time when many unfortunate children tell a lie. Not everyone in confirmation class really wants ever to become a child of God. Yet even these, when they are up at the altar during confirmation, will say they are believing. Now surely you would not dare to come to this holy place pretending."

Earlier the pastor had spoken in the chancel about another promise they were to make, a promise to avoid sin and follow Jesus. He mentioned then about confirmants he had known who made promises in class in the morning and then that same evening hurried to places of entertainment where Jesus would never be found.

When the matter of going to the Lord's table was discussed, the minister reminded them of Luther's words. "Acceptable is he who believes these words, 'Given and shed for you,' but he who does not believe these words or doubts them is altogether unworthy. For those words, 'For your sake,' require a truly believing heart."

He then asked what kind of heart every child at confirmation should have when coming to the communion table. All sat as if they were being tested; a couple of hands were raised, very timidly. When the pastor asked Lisa, she answered, "A believing heart."

At recess a group of girls stood by the belfry wall, laughing and shouting and screaming in their fun. Lisa sat between Laura and Anja on the stairway railing.

"I think that the pastor acts unbearably devout," said Laura as she wrinkled up her nose. "He's pretending," snapped Anja; she swung her boyish hair-cut up away from her forehead. Someone else by the wall cried out, "I suppose we should begin to shriek like Kaisa Aho does at services."

"This way: 'hih huh! hih huh!'" went another while she clapped her hands together and jumped around. "Or crawl through the narrow gate, like this," said another as she was crawling under the three railings. Laura and Anja looked at Lisa who forced her mouth into a smile. And then by the wall there was a whole crowd shouting and laughing and nearly all of them wanted to crawl through the narrow gate.

Suddenly the ones closest to the corner froze in place. The pastor walked from behind the belfry with the short slow steps of an old man. He stopped for a moment next to the noisy crowd and then continued on without a word and proceeded slowly into the sacristy.

"Now we will hear how honorable we are," Anja said sourly, breaking the silence. "He has a lot of nerve to spy around and lie in wait like a fox with chickens," Laura went on. But now no one laughed. "It's good that for once he heard the truth," decided Anja.

The bell rang, but as class resumed the teacher didn't mention what had happened. He did look tired and shaken and Lisa began to feel awful. The mockery of her companions had horribly cut her. The old pastor sat there as if waiting for a reason, for some explanation, and the afternoon sun shone silver on his head through the choir window. The words, "You will bring gray hairs in grief to the grave," came to Lisa then.

That evening Lisa settled with her books in her familiar study place near the hay-drying barn. Midsummer was at its most lush time: breezes wafted the fragrance of resin from the needles of the grove of pines; the mountain ash trees were blooming by the bath-house down by the beach; cowbells clanged from cows back at the home pasture where Lisa's mother was milking and singing as she milked, "A sweet resting place has been provided on Golgotha."

But Lisa's conscience spoke up. "Why didn't you speak up and resist the girls today? You joined in their derision and brought sorrow to your dear old pastor." Her conscience didn't let up: "And what sorrow did you bring to your Heavenly Father?"

"I haven't been any different from the others in school, and I really don't want to be!" argued the girl. "But how can I keep on being the only believer in a crowd like that?"

She got nowhere with her lessons. Her conscience bothered her, the mosquitoes were humming and biting fiercely, and she could hear her mother still singing, "He'll soon be able to bring us home from here."

Lisa's bed was across from the top of the stairs. She had moved her beautifully painted and lettered trunk over next to her bed, and on its lid were her school books, her recently-taken confirmation picture and Aaro's birchwood cow.

But this night she had trouble falling asleep. That cow, that child's toy, sat there on the trunk with its serious face and sharp black horns, looking at her. Old Aaro's words rang in her ears: "Remember, Lisa, if you fall into sin and give up your faith, then this cow with its sharp horns will butt your conscience."

Finally, toward morning, Lisa fell into a fitful sleep with mixed-up dreams that weighed heavily on her. The wooden cow became huge, but it still looked at her with the same patient suffering eyes. Suddenly it changed into the old pastor who raised an immense Bible over his head, threatening: "I will strike you with this!"

The next day, the last day of confirmation class, was painful and difficult. It drizzled outside and inside the church was humid and oppressive. Although the old pastor spoke warmly, he seemed even more worn than yesterday. Laura and Anja looked worried. Some in the class even cried, and Lisa felt like crying too.

Lisa stopped in at the store on the way home. The pastor came along just as she stepped out to continue on the road home. He nodded in a friendly way, and asked, "Do you still have Aaro Rauhala's cow?"

"Yes."

"Has it ever needed to butt you?"

"Yes."

"When was the last time?"

"Last night, while I slept."

"Yes, I thought it might."

"Are you able to forgive me?" asked Lisa. The pastor responded, "Believe your sins forgiven, my child, in Jesus' name and blood."

As they talked on, the old pastor became Lisa's own father confessor. When they came to the gate to the parsonage he said, "Bring greetings of peace to your home." And when he reached the front steps, he added, "And bring greetings to that calf of Aaro's which knew how to butt at the right time." Then he laughed.

Next day things were changed. The rain quit and the muggy weather cooled off. The sky cleared and turned blue as tens of summer swallows chased the clouds away. It was Mid-Summer and the day of First Communion.

THE CONFIRMATION GIFT

Gertrude Saari related this story to her daughter Helena:

>I want to tell you about the time just after my Confirmation school ended. The pastor, who has since gone to rest, was very grave and solemn during the last hours. We girls all cried and the boys were subdued and sober.
>
>Mother and I went to bathe together in the sauna that evening. Mother obviously had much that she wished to say but, being hesitant and anxious, she remained silent. I will always remember how we sat side by side on the bench as the sun curved behind Picture Point and the bonfire at Pike Rocks burst into flame. Then Mother grasped my hand and the corners of her mouth twitched, but she still didn't say a word.
>
>I was restless that evening of Midsummer when I crawled into bed for sleep. I prayed all of the prayers I had learned while I was little and repeated the Christian songs which I still remembered, but I didn't catch a wink of sleep until the early morning hours.
>
>The closing of the fence gate awakened me. Some had been close to me and had laid a sheet of paper on the lid of the trunk beside my bed. I snatched it up and recognized Mother's simple printing:
>
>>Dear child. Your father and I ought to give you a confirmation gift, but we are poor people. Still, we would like to give you those riches which even we possess by grace. When you were born, we were still unrepentent but the Lord took hold of us and we received forgiveness in Jesus' blood for our unbelief and other sins in God's kingdom. We became Christians, the most worthless of Christians. Even yesterday we should have spoken to you so that today you would have strength to confess your faith freely and kneel in faith at the Lord's table, but the evil spirit closed our mouths. Last night, your situation bothered us so that we could not sleep; your father rolled and tossed. Then I began to write this letter. It went poorly, but I think that possibly you will understand.
>>
>>We want to give you for a confirmation gift that peace of conscience which we now have. You probably have not denied your faith and you have been a well-behaved girl in every way. Perhaps you are timid about going to the Lord's house. Your father looked up in the Bible to find for you this king of confirmation gifts: "Fear not: for I have redeemed thee, I have called thee by name; thou art mine. When thou passest through the waters, I will be with thee; and through the rivers, they shall not overflow thee: when thou walkest through the fire, thou shalt not be burned; neither shall the flame kindle upon thee. For I am the Lord thy God, the Holy One of Israel, thy Saviour."[1]

If something disturbs your conscience, my child, come to us or go to the pastor this morning and believe your sins forgiven in Jesus' name and blood. We surely will pray in your behalf and ask the blessing of the Heavenly Father, that you will always remain as His child and someday arrive at home with us.

This is our only confirmation gift to you as we are poor people and such poor Christians. God's Peace. I don't know what more to add. Mother.

You cannot believe how I cried, reading this letter. I went to Mother and Father, who blessed me as we cried together. My father took me in his arms and spoke to me about the love of God. Before church I went to the pastor and he too blessed me with forgiveness of sins. At the altar I no longer had to cry; I just felt it was good to exist. I looked right in the pastor's eyes while I answered peacefully: "I want to believe."

I have read this yellowed and wrinkled confirmation gift many times since then, especially when under trials. Now I will give it to you, my dear daughter Helena, as tomorrow you will go to confess your faith and partake of the Sacrament of the Altar.

---

[1] Isaiah 43:1-3

DAVID'S FISH

Father's illness happened at a very bad time! Salmon spawning time was at the door and the parish catechetical[1] school was close at hand. There should be a tasty fish soup for the rural school dean and others at the festival, but now who would catch the water's harvest?

"We'll just have to make David the fisherman," proposed Father from his bed. "He's far too little for such man's work," objected Mother, "and besides, he would hardly know how!"

"Oh, isn't the boy already thirteen and sturdy? And isn't his mother well?" the father tried to joke. "Come here, David, and I will teach you how to catch fish."

The boy sat down on the edge of the bed and Father explained, drawing on a piece of board. "We have at least ten burbot traps for catching fish, but take only two of them. Be sure that there are no holes in the nets. Then get out a real white birch stalk from our supply of slender tree stems. Tie the fish trap to it like this. Chop a hole in the ice at this end of Roach Sound, near the middle. The water there is about three meters deep. You probably remember the place; it is the best around here. Push the birch with its fish traps through the hole, all the way to the bottom, like this. The fish will come!"

"Yes, Dad," said David. His cheeks glowed.

"There are three bow-nets on the fence at the dock, the kind that hang cone-shaped in the water. They have dirty strips of cloth dangling from them."

"Right, I've seen them."

"All right. Take off those dirty rags and Mother will give you new white strips. Tie them in place of the old ones. Then put the net into the hole in the ice, about halfway down. That ought to get the big mottled ones there! You see, the burbot is a very curious fish, especially when it comes to bright, white objects. They come right up to sniff. That's why we tie the traps to white birch and that's why we have a bright metal flasher piece in the funnel on the inside of the net throat and..."

David started to hurry off to look for his fur cap and mittens. "Don't go yet," smiled his father. "I will draw you a sketch of what you want to catch. Look at this, here is some of David's catch swimming toward him, a big, ugly, mottled delicious burbot! But remember, son, that only God gives you your catch!" Father concluded, without laughing.

David took the sled with which they drew water and slid with it down to the fence by the shore. He hunted up an ice-pick, a big dipper, an ax and the fish traps. At the storage building, he found a birch that was just right, cut the branches off and sharpened the end. He tied the lower fish net tightly to the birch, but left the others loose. He took off the dirty cloth strips and exchanged them for the bright clean ones.

When he was ready to go, he had quite a load to push through the thick snow. Sweat kept trickling down his forehead. He had to chop a hole through the ice when he finally reached the fishing site. It was hard work, but soon water came gushing into the hole and shortly then the hole was ready. He threw out the ice and slush with the dipper. When the hole was completely clean, he pushed the birch stick with the trap through the hole into the water. Luckily, it was the right depth! He could feel the lake bottom and the top of the birch was still about half a meter above the ice. Next he lifted the pole up and tied on the other trap so that it came just below the ice, just as Father had shown him. The sharp end felt well stuck into the bottom and soon the upper part of the pole would freeze fast to the side of the hole. Adjustment of the hanging bag-net also went without any complications.

Satisfied, David returned to the living room. "Did you remember to ask for the Heavenly Father's blessing on your fishing?" asked Father.

"No."

"My father never lowered his gear into the water without praying. I have never dared to do it either without whispering a prayer. I hope that in this house we always take the harvest from the land and the harvest from the water as something from God's hand!" Father's voice shook. His words struck the boy's soul as an order.

David intended to go the very next day to check on his fishing gear, but his father said, "You'd better let it go another day! The fish will keep fresher alive there in the water, and others will come when they see the first fish. The parish catechetical reading isn't until day after tomorrow. Just read your lesson today."

The lad ground away at his catechism and Bible history. They seemed to have gone well last spring and at the close of public school, he recalled, but right now his thoughts about this and that drifted to fishing.

On the day before the parish catechetical meeting, the dusk of the morning crept bleakly into the east windows of the living room. David tied a big woolen scarf around his neck, pulled his fur cap over his ears and dog-skin mittens on his hands and bustled outside.

A clear streak shone from far beyond Continent Ridge. Above it twinkled the last star. The birches in the yard were frosty and the woods beyond were completely white. Mother opened the barn door and a thick cloud of vapor poured out. David blew the air out of his lungs and a plume of vapor spread out at least a yard ahead. The cold was harder and harder to stand. The snow creaked under the stand at the pumphouse as the lad left to go to his fishing site.

The ice of two wintry nights broke easily in the fishing hole. The little fisherman hardly had the presence of mind to skim the chips of ice and slush away, because in the upper trap there was a considerable commotion. And there were several fish in the lower trap. The lad threw the black lumps into his box: "One...two...three...four..." In all, there were twenty-three! None was really big but none were little scrawny fellows either. Not until the trap was finally back in place did David notice the frostbitten tips of his fingers. The mittens went on quickly and he hurried home.

One big fish looked exactly like his father's drawing. The catch in the full knapsack was a real load. The whole crowd coming to the catechetical examination could lunch to their hearts' content! Mother cried out with delight when she saw the fish. David had to bring the knapsack near Father's bed. Then the sick man looked at his son with warmth in his eyes. "Praises be to the Heavenly Father!" said the man.

When the catechetical reading was over and the men from the church were lunching on fish soup, the preacher asked Mother: "Who caught these fish while our brother is ill?"

"David set the traps for catching the fish at the sound."

"This home will very likely have a young and capable master of the household! The lad knew his lessons well **and** how to catch spawning burbot, also. David will make a man!"

"The Lord grant it," sighed Mother, wiping a happy tear from the corner of her eyes.

---

[1] Teaching using oral question-and-answer methods.

ONLY TWO

This was the first time that the tenants on the Peterson farm grew wheat. God blessed them with a good harvest, too. Where they sowed ten kilos in the spring, they reaped over one hundred kilos at the harvest and the grain was beautiful! Father let the grain pour gracefully through his fingers and admired it with Mother, who also came to see. "Yes, times have changed," said Father. "Just think, now we can get white bread from our own field. All of southern Finland will change."

Then Father brought two big sacks of wheat to the local mill. He also took many smaller empty bags. When he returned that evening, he had five sacks to carry in from his cart. He lifted them onto the bench in the family room. Mother brought a lamp and the whole family hurried over to examine them more closely.

"Here is the best flour," said Father as he opened the first bag. "It looks as good as any imported flour," applauded Mother. "Right, and it will taste better in my mouth," declared Father.

"And these two will go in unleavened bread, with no yeast," explained Father as he opened the next two bags. "Yes, in muffins and pancakes and biscuits," allowed Mother.

"But these two are only for the pigs," Father said as rolled out the last two bags without opening them. "What do they have in them, then?" asked Peter. "Husks," was Father's answer.

After the evening meal and when evening prayers had been offered, Father looked at the flour and began to speak. "In the Bible, it also speaks of cultivating wheat. According to that, we people are God's grain crop. When harvest time comes, some are like chaff which the wind blows away. Others are the good grain and they are gathered and stored."

Mother interrupted: "But the Heavenly Father does not have five sacks!" Father agreed. "No, only two. People will stand in two flocks on God's threshing ground. The chaff he will burn with unquenchable fire. The others he will invite to everlasting blessedness.

"So, dear children, let us not deny our faith or pile up secret sins on our consciences. Then we may get to heaven as good grain." As Father concluded earnestly, tears rolled down from his eyes.

SUNDAY FISH

Sundays seemed long to Peter, especially in the summer. Mornings and noontimes went well, with going to church and walking outside with Father, but afternoons were different. Father lay down to rest on the living room couch and Mother sat by the window reading the Bible or humming hymns. It seemed that sleep crept out of its hiding place unusually early and filled the log cabin with stillness and lethargy.

Peter slipped outside. He watched the sparrows keeping house under the eaves for a minute and then he walked out to the dock at the shore. He could hear shouts from the next point, so he ambled over there. Art and Herbie Pinora, the neighbor boys, were fishing there and the fish were biting madly. Each boy had a splendid pile of fish, with the newly-caught ones still flopping into the air.

"It's going to rain!" exclaimed Herbie. "That's why they bite so. I hardly got the worm into the water and that bouncy fellow bit!"

"I'm sure Mother will be glad, since there's so little in the kitchen," Art said, glowing with satisfaction as he spit on his bait and cast it like a grownup toward the cattails. He glanced over at Peter at the same time.

"Hey, watch it!" cried Herbie just then. "Your bobber is going down!" Art struck, and the rod bent and shook. A vigorous northern pike rolled on the surface. "Don't yank, don't jerk! Play it, tire it out! Let me take it!" shouted Herbie. Art handed the rod to his companion, whose own hook and line were left to do as they pleased. Herbie slowly played the big pike toward the shore.

A splashing and commotion arose. Herbie yelled for his father to come and see. Mr. Pinora, a man of few words, growled, "What's to see! The deuce with your old fish!"

Peter returned along the shore to his own dock. A damp south-easterly wind caressed his legs and mosquitoes swarmed from the bushes. Wavelets rippled against the stones. The timid sandpiper cast furtive glances. A swallow flashed past, seeming to sweep the water with its wings. Peter heard the shrill call of a big brown curlew as it waded past on long legs. Clouds sometimes covered the sun, but mostly it was a sweaty sunny day even though it was almost six in the evening already.

"I could catch a fish to hang on the bath-house wall," thought Peter. But Father and Mother had strictly forbidden Sunday fishing. "On the Lord's day, one may do only that work which is unavoidable because of need or which Christian love demands," they had explained. "And," added Father, "we manage very well without breaking the rules regarding Sunday."

Peter felt annoyance. With others, it was different. Herbie and Art's grandfather only looked pleased with his boys' Sunday efforts. Could the Heavenly Father be so very strict in matters of this kind?

The fishing gear looked very lonely leaning against the bath-house wall. There were worms already in the cup under the porch and big fish were probably right there under the willow. "What if I caught such a big old fish? Then they wouldn't be complaining about breaking the laws."

Peter hurried toward the buildings. Only the bath-house roof could be seen from shore; they wouldn't see from the window of the house if he cast it just once. He would cast it just one time, right where that big fish jumped a minute ago.

The boy went ahead and put the night-crawler on the hook, his fingers shaking. The worm squirmed troublesomely, but did go on the hook so that the point of the hook couldn't be seen. He struck the spot with his first cast. The bobber rocked a moment on the wavelets, then sank! Peter struck. The fish was heavy and the mountain ash pole bent. The fish was half in the water and half in the air. Peter played his fish to the shore as his father had taught him. Then he gave a bit of a jerk and the fish thumped into the grass under the alder tree. Peter was on it, quick as a flash! It was a beautiful fish, bigger than any of the neighbor boys' fish.

But now Peter became scared. He did not dare to take his catch home. There were plenty of fish at home which Father had caught during the week. Surely this fishing was not because of compelling need or out of Christian love. Father would criticize him and Mother would become sad. He should have waited until morning to try his luck.

Peter decided to hide his fish until the next day. He would go out very early to the bath-house where fishing gear was stored, and add the fish to earlier catches.

He had a restless night. He had to go look at the clock many times. When it finally struck four, he grabbed his clothes and dressed and slipped out. The wind had shifted to the north. Clouds came over the tops of the pines and it was drizzly. Peter shivered and ran quickly to the bath-house, stooping to look under the porch. His hiding place was empty; a cat must have stolen his fish during the night!

The wind couldn't reach the water close in under the willow bushes. The bobber lay idly, not moving. The back of Peter's shirt was wet and his legs felt the raw dampness. He shivered again.

The clouds weighed down dark and heavy to the south. A northern storm roared far on the great ridge. Peter felt awful.

GIFTS OF HOLY COMMUNION

"I wouldn't give a mark, not even a penny, for such a preacher!" spoke Henry vehemently.

"I suppose because you fear being considered unworthy?" teased Katie.

"Oh, no! To tell the truth, if it weren't the long-time custom, I wouldn't even part with a penny!"

"Pastor **has** kept us on the torture rack," added Hilma.

"He is trying to force us to be believers! Phooey, that's shameful, that's hypocritical!" exclaimed Valerie.

"He is a man of God and hopes for the best for us," Sylvia suggested quietly. "Surely he does not expect gifts from us. Didn't he say, 'The best gift with which you can delight me is that you kneel as young Christians at the Lord's table'?"

"Oh, pooh! You are known as the preacher's pet. You probably will go over to the parsonage for confession soon," said Hilma sarcastically.

"I wish I could," said Sylvia as though to herself, and she started for the confirmants' cabin. Valerie and Hilma were already on their way to the parsonage with their gift package. They had been delegated to present the gift because they were thought to be the most outgoing and vocal of the group. Right now both walked in silence. Valerie's conscience accused her: "You are a hypocrite yourself! Now you are politely going to him after you have spoken so behind his back."

Hilma was recalling the last hour of confirmation school. The pastor had spoken calmly and seriously about tomorrow's sacred occasion. He had said that he knew that some students heard the Word but had hardened their hearts and now, only for custom's sake, intended to kneel at the altar. "Such wretched ones give the deceitful kiss of Judas to their Saviour when they confess belief and promise to follow Christ and to battle against sin. The lie soils their conscience which is already tarnished." Those words stuck distastefully in the girl's inner being. "Surely, he means me," thought Hilma. The pair slowed their pace.

In the pastor's double row of basswood trees, they met Sylvia who had a tear-stained face. She was slightly startled to see the girls, but then stepped calmly toward them. "You, too, forgive me for what happened yesterday. In my heart, I felt ill-will toward you," she asked.

"May it be forgiven," mumbled Hilma, annoyed.

"May it be on my part, too," echoed Valerie.

"Oh, I have such a good feeling now," whispered Sylvia, and she continued on her way. Hilma would gladly have gone with her!

The pastor sat in his lilac arbor reading his Bible. At the creak of the gate, he noticed Valerie and Hilma. "Come in, girls, come in!" The delegation stepped diffidently before their teacher.

"Here is a small gift from us all for our pastor," Valerie told him as she held out the package. He thanked them as he viewed the new little silver bowl.

"Thank you, thank you for your love. Let's put something very pretty in it at once." He broke off two lilac clusters and arranged them in the dish. "Have a seat and look at the lovely gifts from God in your gift of love," he urged pleasantly. "But I received an even greater gift just a minute ago. One of your classmates was here in this lilac summer chapel grown by the Heavenly Father, and he received mercy. He was already so burdened, poor child. It was my privilege to tell him personally about God's love and bless him with the with the gospel's forgiveness of his sins. He promised to believe and left feeling so fortunate. Tomorrow at least **one** of you will kneel with a believing heart at the Lord's table. There is rejoicing in heaven and I too rejoice."

"But doesn't one first have to confess sins?" cried out Hilma, a little frightened at her own boldness.

"Yes, our recent young friend did that, too. He sat right where you are and his unburdened heart was made lighter. I think that he left here to petition for forgiveness in his home, too, among his friends and companions. Faith bears such fruit. That is what we have learned in school, too.

"You remember how, in Luke 18:10-13, two men went up to the temple to pray. One, a tax collector, stood in a nook by the door at the back and confessed his sins to God in prayer, saying, 'God, have mercy on me, a sinner.' Another tax collector, Zacchaeus, promised to pay back fourfold to anyone he had cheated. I remember a portion from the small catechism dealing with confession. It speaks of the confession of those sins which gnaw at the conscience to the confessor father, that is, to some mature Christian who has received the Holy Spirit.

"In this same way, we confess our sins to God, to those people whom we have offended and to our confessor father. But the main thing is that we receive the forgiveness of our sins in Jesus' name and blood. Isn't that so, girls?"

"Yes," choked out Hilma. "But we must go now!" whispered Valerie in alarm. The girls waved farewell.

"Goodbye, goodbye. God bless you and help you, so that tomorrow you do not eat and drink of Christ's body and blood as a curse to you," he said gravely.

Subdued, Hilma walked slowly home. It was just over half a mile but her steps dragged as she plodded what seemed a long, long way. Those she met were puzzled at the confirmation school girl walking like a weary old lady and staring absent-mindedly at the ground.

The last swallows darted through the air and back again. Smoke from the saunas was mirrored in the water and rippled by the waves. The song thrush flew to the top of the spruce for his evening watch and began his lonely soliloquy in the glow of the sinking sun.

Hilma did not hear or see. This evening, she was listening only to her conscience. Oh, dear God, how uncompromising he was! "You have traveled to and from dances many times on this road. You've already agreed with Valerie about tomorrow's fun trip--first together to church in the morning, then to a party later in the evening where the folk applaud at crude humor. Is that what you think conforms to following Christ? Many times in the fall, you have taken turnips from your neighbor's field without asking. Stealing is thievery. You've had bad relations with Lisa Ratikka for two years. You have used abusive words to her and about her. Go make up with her whom you have quarreled with, before you go to the altar. At home, you went with your dancing friends early in the morning and ate apples from the apple tree. Later in the day, you lied to your parents. And you will go before the Lord to confess that you are a believer and follower of Christ? You hypocrite!"

Hilma sneaked directly into the storage shed. A white confirmation dress was there already, on the back of a chair. There was also a lovely gift, a silver wristwatch. What joy it could have aroused in the morning! Now even that accused her. What if Mother and Father actually knew everything!

Hilma Koivukangas stood in the pastor's yard, pale and nervous. Streaks of red blazed from the morning sun. A swarm of swallows was out frolicking again. A couple of busy bumblebees buzzed in the basswood. A rooster crowed in the back.

Hilma recalled Peter, who went out and wept bitterly when he heard the rooster crow. If only she were at least able to cry! Through the open dining room window rang the voices of children and adults, singing: "Every morning, grace is new. Why should we have cares!" Then the study window opened and the pastor appeared before it. He noticed the girl seated on the steps, dressed all in white. "Hilma! Did you have a question?"

"Yes," she responded, startled and rising to her feet.

"All right, go meet me at the lilac arbor."

Soon they sat there face to face, confessor father and first-time communicant, surrounded by clusters of white lilacs. Brokenly, Hilma related her distress and confessed her sins. The pastor laid his hand on the girl's head, assuring her: "Your sins are forgiven in Jesus' name and blood. What is forgiven here on earth, according to the promise of the Master, is also forgiven in heaven."

Then the confessor father continued freely. He unfolded the story of Jesus, who paid to reconcile **all** of us on Good Friday. Now, as a living Saviour, He is with his own each day. "He awaits you today at his grace table. Today at the altar, you can receive a strength and confirmation for the life of faith you have begun. You can see and receive in the holy sacrament an assurance that the body of God's sacrificial lamb was given especially in your behalf. His blood flowed especially for the forgiveness of **your** sins! Go in the peace of God, child."

"God's Peace." Hilma curtsied, a flood of tears in her eyes. Moments ago her eyes were timid and apprehensive, but now they became clear and peaceful.

How beautiful were the mountain ash blossoms on both sides of the road to church. The finches sang in the birch grove, almost bursting with joy. The bells commenced to peal and their ringing carried the news of celebration to the villages and the homes. There the old women rocked the cradles and yearningly hummed familiar morning hymns. The bells carried to farmhouses and to roads traveled by church-goers in their best dark attire. Here and there in their midst was a confirmation girl in white, shy, with a tear-marked face.

The prows of church-bound boats raised their wakes as they entered the sparkling narrow channel between the great open birch-covered islands. In one of them a proud grandpa watched with happy eyes as his grandson clutched his hymnal in a fist hardened by the ax handle. Today the boy would go forward to be confirmed.

CRY UNTO ME FOR HELP IN DISTRESS

Glen and Floyd went fishing. In the evening they lowered their nets and long set-lines before they went to rest in a make-shift hut used for storage and for cleaning fish. They slept soundly and peacefully that moonlit August night. The mosquitoes did not even bother their earlobes. The sun was already up when they wakened and they dashed to their boat. They shivered a bit in the cool morning breeze, but the anticipation of their catch invigorated them.

And there were fish! Right away Glen drew bream and pike and perch into the boat with his dip-net. Some were beautiful fish which made lots of commotion flopping around and some almost flopped off the hooks, so the boys were too occupied to notice when the wind increased more and more. Not until they left the shelter of the point and got out into open waters did they notice and become alarmed. There the white-capped waves dashed about like sea-horses gamboling on each other's heels before they were flung upon the shore in a thousand sprinkles.

Glen was barely able to make progress rowing back toward shelter, and the many waves breaking over the bow soaked Floyd's trousers. "We have a very tough trip to get home," panted Glen.

"How will we ever get the net up?" questioned Floyd. At last the set-line reeled in properly and was soon stored in the box in the bottom of the boat with the large heap of beautiful fish. Floyd bailed out water and then moved to the oars. The boat was tossed up and down by the waves and it seemed that the white foam-crested billows would bury men, boat, tackle and all.

Floyd was skillful at maneuvering the boat so that they came to no harm. Yet the boys' faces turned grave as they worriedly glanced at the sky, where gray tattered clouds sped from horizon to horizon, writhing as if in pain. In the wind, the trees on the islands bent into bows like yokes. It seemed that everything sprayed, rose, creaked and whistled. Gulls rising in the air glided over the crags for only a moment and then were hurled shrieking past the rocks. The first storm of the autumn was rising.

Finally the nets were brought in, making a wet tangled mass in the bottom of the boat. Then both of the youths took to the oars. At first they made some progress, yard by yard, but as the squall hit, the first real gust of wind and wave struck with such force and fury that it turned the boat broadside. A great white-cap spilled inside. "Unnhh!" grunted both oarsmen instinctively and their faces paled. At the same time, the nearly-foundering boat was slammed to the shore.

So there they were: two water-soaked youths, a boat half-full of water, fish, gear and left-over lunch, all in a perfect mess in the bottom. The boys swallowed hard to keep down tears and somehow managed to haul their boat up on the shore. Only miserable scrub pine and one patch of willows grew on an island like this. There was no protection from the wind, and spray from the waves wet the whole area.

Hour after hour passed while the boys cowered beside the pine. They gathered twigs from between the rocks but their matches had gotten wet. Only one flashed into flame and it sputtered out immediately. The soggy little bit of food which was left wasn't very appetizing, but it was something to chew on and somewhat eased their hunger. They didn't talk much. Instead, they mostly watched the far-away home shore in silence. Surely there was concern at home also, they thought.

Dusk began to fall, but it still did not become more calm. The rolling whitecaps still thundered onto the shore. "Let's pray," said Glen, and they sank to their knees, side by side near the pine.

"We've been bad boys," prayed Glen.

"We have been very bad," seconded Floyd.

"Good God, forgive us."

"Now we certainly will be good. Good God, give us calm now so that we can get home. Or let a big motorboat come near. Or perhaps, help us get a fire lighted for we are chilly."

"Let's recite the Lord's prayer and the blessing benediction," Glen suggested. They did. Floyd thought that things already seemed better.

"Do you hear it?" Glen suddenly shouted with joy.

"Hear what?"

"The thumping noise of a motor! Listen? Don't you hear now?"

"Yes! I see it now, just beyond the point! It looks like the Junti's motorboat!" The boys began to shout and wave. Finally the party in the boat noticed them and turned. Strong men soon had the youths' boat in tow. Once underway, it kept pointing the right direction although the waves pounded so hard that at times it seemed the boat must crack and split in two.

When the boys rested in bed that evening, their cheeks still red from cold, they said to their mother, "We have been bad boys."

"Well, how was that revealed to you?" Then the boys related all that had happened and could hardly keep from crying. Mother also had tears in her eyes as she blessed them with that best of all blessings, the forgiveness of all their sins.

STEPHEN'S FIRST COMMUNION

The Vasala cottage was all cleaned up for the Sabbath. After sauna, everyone sat around the table with glowing faces as midsummer filled the cottage. The cool of the evening wafted in through the open windows, swinging the curtains. Along with it came the sounds of summer: the clank of oars on a returning boat; the plaint of a frightened sandpiper; the splash of waves against the rocks along the shore.

Stephen had come home from confirmation school the night before. Tomorrow was the morning of Midsummer and he must return to church and then to the Lord's table. The minister had given him a Bible, a gift from the congregation. A verse from the Bible was written on its front page: "Fight the good fight of faith, lay hold on eternal life, whereunto thou art also called, and hast professed a good profession before many witnesses."[1]

Stephen's father looked at the holy book his son brought home. "The pastor has directed you to a good verse," he said. "You have been kept safe as a child of God up until now. I only hope, dear son, that you will always be able to walk with a clear conscience. May you always confess Christ with courage. These are very dangerous times in your life. You are just at the age when your father fell into the way of the prodigal son. Oh, I hope that you never need to tread in those paths. I have left a poor inheritance for you and it often burdens my mind."

Stephen hung his head. When questioned, he had claimed to be a child of God, but his conscience was restless lately. With his crowd of boys he had listened to swearing and to fun made of holy matters, even when his conscience urged him to warn his companions. He came to laugh and smile sardonically with the others at their jokes during the hour with the old choir leader. Even though he tried, he wasn't able to restrain himself.

Stephen approached his father and laid his shaking head on his father's warm chest. Haltingly, he confessed what was burning in his conscience. Father blessed him tenderly, saying, "Yes, my child, Jesus is your Saviour. He is the reconciliation for the sins of the whole world---and for the forgiveness of your sins also. You may believe all of your stumblings and failures forgiven unto peace and happiness." It was good to be there under his father's blessing hands. The room became quiet. His mother and oldest sister cried quietly.

Stephen was permitted to sit in the back of the boat. His mother and sister sat in the middle and Father was at the oars in front. Here and there the birch trees in their green attire bowed right down to the water. The glowing hot sun climbed toward its zenith, passing one white fleecy cloud sailing high in the blue. Swallows flitted past, like little shuttles over the weaver's loom.

Sister began to sing:

> We are on this earthly journey,
> Homeward bound for heaven fair.
> Though we may be hindered daily,
> We are safe in Jesus' care.

It began to feel to Stephen that the boat had floated straight to heaven where it is eternal summer. It felt so good when all of his sins were forgiven and all of his homefolk were dressed in Christ's white garment of righteousness! The bells of the church tolled the beginning of the service with their solemn booming.

The girls sat over on the other side, all in white. Taavi Viitala sat next to Stephen and Veikko Valkela in front of him. The organ softly played a summer hymn and then the pastor approached the altar with the communion cup in his hands. He first spoke about the confirmants who are battling against sin and repenting their transgressions. His prayer was that God, the dear Father, would keep them strong to the end in their precious faith, in these dangerous years ahead of them. Lustful desires are powerful in their young veins. The markets of the world have thousands of fine enticements to lay before them.

"May you be obedient to that Holy Spirit which lives in your hearts by faith. If your conscience becomes stained, don't cease from believing, don't separate from your Creator, but put sin away from you in repentance and faith in the gospel word. I suspect that all of you will be fearful as you think of all this. The question will arise in your bosom, 'How will a poor weakling like me overcome all difficulties? My faith is weak and my experience is shallow.'

"This is the very reason that the table of the Lord is prepared for your protection. It is a gathering place for the weak and for believers trembling because of their spiritual poorness. So approach this altar rail with secure minds, young brothers and sisters. Take and eat, for your journey is long. Take with the firm assurance that Jesus' holy body was given for you and that his blood flowed for the forgiveness of your sins."

Every word sank into Stephen's heart. All matters at that moment were perfectly lovely to him.

Then the pastor went on to speak gravely of those who had given up their baptismal grace. He encouraged them to repent and believe the gospel and then believing to partake of the sacrament of Christ's body and blood for the strengthening of their faith. One of the girls broke into loud sobs. Veikko Valkela rested his head on the back of the bench in front of him.

Summer's Sunday evening is lovely in the sun next to the wall of the gray house. But it is many times more lovely when God's peaceful calm rests in the bosom of those sitting there and when the Heavenly Father's blessing lingers over all creation. A fortunate boy sat on the beach near the front wall of the Vasala cottage. Sins were gone! Jesus' blood was shed just for the forgiveness of Stephen Vasala's sins.

On the opposite shore blazed a fire ready for Midsummer Eve. Sounds of music and laughter came from there. Stephen didn't have the least desire to be there with them.

"Peace I leave with you, my peace I give unto you: not as the world giveth, give I unto you," recalled Stephen.[2]

---

[1] I Timothy 6:12
[2] John 14:27

DISTRESS BELLS

Father and Mother went to the neighboring parish for Midsummer services. They left the house in the charge of Grandfather, a gentle believer. The old man had gone to church with the young folks earlier in the day. David and Daniel rowed while Grandfather watched from the stern. They all sang familiar church hymns as they glided along, through the narrow church channel and then along birch-lined shores. The girls' clear voices reminded of their late grandmother when she was young. As he listened, Grandfather's chin quivered a little and his eyes glistened. Sunday's spirit crept into his trials-torn heart.

By the time of the return trip, however, the young folk had lost their holy-day spirit. The boys at the oars dodged the boat around erratically. The girls whispered among themselves and glanced at the back of the boat with smirks playing round the corners of their mouths. Plans for the evening were already in place, first a dance and then an evening get-together.

For the first time in their lives, they felt an uncomfortable apprehension weighing on them, knowing that they planned to do wrong. They were filled with such thoughts as, "What shall I say to my boy-friend?" "How shall I answer my God? Lord, help me."

The young people became almost feverish as evening approached, their faces timid and defiant by turns. They often found a reason to go down to the shore and would return with knowing smiles. Grandfather sat on the porch and rested, glancing from the corners of his eyes occasionally at their activities, and prayed.

Then the activity ceased. The last one to go, slamming the door as she left, was Aune, the youngest, who had just completed confirmation school. Grandfather walked slowly into the living room after a bit; it was empty. So was the kitchen and the bedroom. The kids had jumped out the window closest to the fence; from there they ran along the ditch and through the field to the shore and then in the familiar boat with its tarred seams they hurried up the middle of the channel. Further on, at Lambcape, a bonfire swirled from which a draft of wind brought snatches of dance tunes.

"Oh, dear God! The children's souls are burning tonight! The burning wounds of sin heal with such difficulty---if they do heal! The scars which we receive in youth sometimes show up and smart even in old age."

Grandfather moved with great strides to the dinner bell rope and pulled, gasping for breath, pulled as one does when life is endangered or when fire has broken out!

BONG! BONG!   BONG! BONG! rang the bell, with distress in its tongue. Its peals carried far onto the ridges. The boat turned back, the boys rowing briskly, the prow furrowing a wave.

Grandfather met them at the shore, pale and shaking. Already from the distance, the girls had shouted, "Is it burning?"

"It is burning," answered Grandfather, with a sob in his voice. "The flame of sin has flashed up to burn in your hearts. I remember my own past trips into the world. I would not wish them on you!"

Aune burst into tears. The others slipped away without a word and lay sleepless in bed till morning, suffering under the Lord's angry eyes. When Father and Mother arrived home from services, they found four very repentant children and Grandfather crying for joy.

FIRST TIME / LAST TIME

"Tonight is the night that we start!" The Pajakankaan girls, Kertu at fourteen years and Alma, two years younger, lay awake and in suspense in their beds. "Why do Father and Mother whisper so long in their room next to ours?" It became almost too much to live with! If only the parents didn't suspect something or have the idea, "Tonight the girls are going out!"

Father and Mother's whispered conversation in the adjacent room faded into silence. Kertu put her ear to the key-hole. From behind the door she heard only the even breathing of sleepers. Now! Take shoes in hand and sneak to the door, quietly. **Quietly**! Oh, how the footsteps boom and the floor boards bend and squeak horribly. Surely Father will hear--he suffers from rheumatism and sleeps so lightly! What if someone hears! Oh, God!

Outside, they could hear music and the bawling of a drunk from the dance hall back of Spruce Hill. The cool night air penetrated their bones to the marrow. They shivered. The frightened girls looked at one another. "Let's go back," pleaded Alma. "Don't be foolish!" ordered Kertu brusquely, but her voice was uncertain.

When the Pajakankaan sisters arrived at the dance hall, the music stopped. A mischievous group of boys pushed out through the door. Adolescent upstarts proudly lit up cigarettes and seeing the girls, winked at one another.

"There aren't services here today," smirked one in an undertone.

"Or does the dance now draw Righteous Gus's daughters too?" asked another.

Kertu and Alma slipped inside, blushing. "Righteous Gus's girls." How those words stabbed painfully. Imagine that the neighbor boys would say anything like that. "The heck with them." Kertu tried to be defiant, but her voice had sobs.

Inside, the sisters joined the company of their neighbor girls, Sirku and Hilma. As they approached, the light-hearted chatter became more restrained. The others were uneasy in their presence and drew back from them, and the conversation was forced. Then, just as the situation became quite uncomfortable, the accordian player took it up again. Dancing couples swirled frenziedly on the floor. Girls whispered into boys' ears, the boys nodding. Bursts of stifled laughter were heard. No one seemed to notice the Pajakankaan girls, although they were regularly the object of surreptitious glances.

Kertu and Alma moved toward the darkest corner. Shyness and anger flared on Kertu's face; Alma stared ahead with a look of horror and confusion. "Oh, dear God, if only we could soon get out!" After a moment, Alma started running toward the door, disgustedly thrusting a couple of boys to the side out of her way, and pushed to the outside. She didn't stop until she reached the threshing barn at home, and Kertu was close behind her.

The girls didn't say a word, but sneaked quietly into their room. Meantime, the door of the parents' room opened. Their hearts nearly stopped in their chests, then pounded as the girls shuddered under their covers. "Oh, dear God!"

Father came into their room and paused by their beds, but didn't say a word. It would have been better if he scolded them! But no, he just stood there with tears on his cheeks. They heard Mother sob.

The hours of the night wore on slowly, but sleep refused to come. The covers were too hot, and the pillows had to be turned over every few minutes. They could hear sighs from the next room, where there was no sleep either.

"Let's go," whispered Alma. "Yes, let's," affirmed Kertu. The girls slipped quietly over to their parents' bedside and knelt there, sobbing, their shoulders shaking. Father soothed each girl's head in turn.

"You are forgiven, dear. Sins are forgiven in Jesus' name and blood."

"Poor children, dear children, sins are forgiven," whispered their mother, as the morning sun began to shine into the house.

FALLING INTO SIN

When their rich uncle related the story to Matt and Lisa as they sat by the picture Bible, they were greatly astonished at Adam and Eve's disobedience.

"I would not have been that foolish," Matt assured his uncle.

"Nor I," agreed Lisa.

Uncle decided to test the little ones. He brought them out to his beautiful country house where there was a lovely little park. A whole orchard grew there, with apples trees, cherry trees, pear trees, plum trees and a strawberry garden. There were shaded fields with many kinds of playthings. Goldfish swam under bubbling fountains.

The house was magnificent. In the children's room were stacks of new picture books, herds of wooden horses and a whole bevy of dolls. A table of delicacies was set aside in the dining room. In the middle of it was a golden dish.

"Here you can live freely and enjoy all of the good things of the house," Uncle told them. "Whenever you want something, call the servants to fulfill your wishes, but do not touch the golden dish in the center of the table. Do not lift its cover! If you do, all the loveliness will come to an end and you will be sent back to your poor home."

Matt and Lisa ran about in the park. Many days were spent in investigating it. Each day they found more tasty fruit there and discovered more amazing flowers. How the time flew by, examining the playthings and trying them out. Many bright mornings passed at the fish pond. Hundreds of delicacies vanished into the stomachs at mealtime. Sleep was good at night in soft deep downy covers. Life was lovely.

A whole month slipped by like a beautiful dream. On the first day of the second month the children walked in the park along a path bordered by trees. Lisa asked what they should do next.

"Let's go look for cherries," was Matt's suggestion.

"I don't care to," Lisa whined. "I've eaten enough of them."

"Okay, let's go fish for goldfish."

"You go if you wish!" pouted the girl. "I don't care to do the same thing over and over!"

At suppertime Lisa didn't care for anything on the table. "I've already tasted every dish and am not hungry for anything at all." Discontentedly she looked at the big golden dish in the middle of the dinner table.

Later the children twisted and turned in bed for a long time. They couldn't sleep. They stayed in bed late in the morning but even then they were tired. Yawning, they slowly dressed themselves and then began playing. The weather was humid and hot and surely there was a hint of thunder in the air. Lisa walked idly along the double row of trees and crossly tore leaves and flowers from the ornamental trees, throwing them on the road. Matt tried to fish for goldfish from down by the pond but they didn't care for his bait. He threw his rod on the ground and ran inside. There he looked at picture books but they seemed just too boring.

Neither of them was hungry for dinner. Lisa fingered the tablecloth and gazed at the alluring golden dish. "I wonder what Uncle could possibly have hidden in there," she mused.

"You wonder what?" Matt asked rather crossly.

"There must be the finest delicacies there with which Uncle wants to tantalize us when we have tired of everything else," Lisa continued. Matt didn't answer.

"I'll peek just a little. We still wouldn't have to taste," Lisa urged.

"But Uncle forbade us!" the boy opposed, looking at Lisa with wide eyes.

"How would Uncle find out if I just lift the cover a little bit?"

"Well, **I** won't take part in that!" and Matt arose from the table.

The following day was just as miserable again at mealtime. The same discussion arose. This time Lisa no longer held off. She rose on her knees and tried to lift the cover of the golden dish, but it was too heavy. "Matt, come look in the crack! I"ll lift with both hands," she begged. Matt came and Lisa raised the cover just a wee bit.

"Can you see?" she asked excitedly.

"Not yet. Lift a little higher."

"Do you now?"

"Not yet. It looks empty! Lift it a bit higher."

"Now?"

"Yes, yes, something black..." Just then a little mouse jumped out of the dish and ran across the table. Lisa screamed and dropped the cover back in place with a crash. "Get it, Matt, or Uncle will learn of this!" But the mouse jumped to the floor and slipped out through a crack under the door.

"It's gone!" Matt confirmed, shaken. "Now we'll have to go home to eat fish and bread every day!"

"Your fault! Why didn't you look more closely!"

"Your fault! **You** lifted the cover!"

A sharp quarrel broke out. Matt grabbed Lisa by her hair and Lisa pinched Matt's arm. The children did not notice when Uncle appeared at the door. He looked on at the tumult very sadly.

"Now you quarrel," he said finally. "You see? Matt is Adam and Lisa is Eve. You must now leave this house at once."

In school when they read about the fall into sin, Matt and Lisa were more serious than any of the other children and looked down at the cracks in the floor. They remembered with shame. Matt and Lisa never criticized Adam and Eve again.

THE ROSEBUSH

"Mama, may I break off a yellow rose from the bush?"

"Break it off, my child."

Little Mia dashed over to the rosebush. In a moment: "Mama! Mama! It hurts!" Mia ran frightened toward her mother. In one hand, she held a yellow rose blossom but blood trickled from the other.

"It's not dangerous," comforted Mother. "You just got a little prick on your finger. It will soon heal. But just think, child! A wreath for Jesus' brow was twisted from thorny branches just like this rosebush. It was shoved down **hard**, so that blood ran from his wounds and flowed down his gentle face."

"Why did he let them, Mama?" Mia's pain was forgotten and the girl gazed wide-eyed at her mother.

"Because he loved us! He patiently carried the crown of thorns so that some day **we** would have an everlasting crown of glory."

THE CHURCH TRIP

All week, folks had been talking about the church trip. From the little island community, there were some from every house and hut who planned to go. Virmala's big motorboat had been chartered to take them.

The exhaust from the departing boats was still in the air when the first of the church men who would operate the passenger boat appeared. Frank, whose father Peter had died, was in the crowd. He had earned his money for the trip by picking berries. After much pleading, his mother gave permission for him to go on the trip. "It is good if you go to hear the Word. After a month you will be going to confirmation school. So go now so that you understand more about how we are saved, for I have not been able to teach you well," she had said with tears in her eyes.

At the scheduled time the motor boat chugged into place at the pier and took on its load. It was clear that there were people of two different kingdoms there. Jaske Juustilla with his violin and case was going for an evening of fun. With him were Hulda and Eva Root in many-colored Finnish costumes. Two tenant-farm overseers, one from Suula and one from Roiva, were church men too, in their own way. Their eyes rolled sometimes and their speech was slurred. They had obviously drunk a bit of wine made from God's grapes. There were others who had likely been believers at one time. In the back sat Gus Kaarti, a preacher. His boys Walt and Aaro were childhood Christians. Hilja, who had been at Spring Communion, had just recently been converted. Her father's coarse humor and tippling embarrassed her. Father and Mother Rantola had been the first in the community to understand living faith. They sat side by side talking cheerfully with each other.

Frank stood next to Jaske and his violin, between the two groups. Entertainers for the passengers played in the cabin. The water murmured on both sides of the boat. As they passed from Tuuti Sound into open water, the surface shone silvery smooth and calm. The distant shore took on a faint blue haze. Nearby islands and capes showed fall's yellow touch, with spots of bright green rye grass among the yellowing birch. The morning air had a frosty bite.

Over the silvery waters, "Again to be released from grief and sins," echoed from the church tower. Beyond Firecape they could see the church tower and the boat then entered the long narrow church sound. The smell of coffee circled toward heaven from cottages and houses along the bluffs on the shore. The last shocks of grain had been cleared from the fields. Along the fences were mountain ash, bright with red berries.

The engine rumbled on but the sound of the church bell could be clearly heard above it. The jovial crowd quieted for a moment. The men from Suula and Roiva appeared reverent, with bowed heads. After all, they respected the church and ministers and other spiritual things, didn't they?

The believers began a new hymn and now they sang fervently:

> Help, Holy Spirit of God,
> Help us as we journey here,
> So that with the strength of the gospel
> We would travel on the way of faith.

Gustav directed the boat to the pier of Tuorila the storekeeper. The masters from Suula and Roiva hurried inside the *Drop of Joy* cafe for coffee, and so they were not to be seen at the Lord's house. Surely one could show honor to Him to whom honor is due from a greater distance . Jaske and his companions were in a hurry to "the house" for practice and other party preparations. Gus and his crew walked slowly toward the church.

Frank sat a while on the edge of the pier, watching fish play. Then he too left to head toward the church. But he paused a moment by Tuorila's stall. The bottles of pink lemonade were most enticing. And those lovely baked goods looked delicious. He sat up at a table. Immediately the waitress asked, "The gentleman would like lemonade? Right! And a couple pieces of the pastry, OK?"

Frank sat down, sipping from his glass and taking fair-sized bites into the edge of his tart. Half of his berry money went into that pleasure. "Mother could have used that for clothes and bread," said his conscience.

Restless, looking around him, the young church-goer moved back onto the road to the church. There was so much to wonder at on the way there. The off-duty storekeeper's boy was practicing high jumps bare-legged in his very official-looking black athletic shorts. He touched one hand to the ground, glancing with tilted head tilted first at the cross bar, then at his audience. After a few quick bouncy steps, he planted his foot, gave a shout and straightened his body in mid-air. The bar shook, but did not fall. Nonchalantly he leveled the apparatus and began to raise the bar with ceremonious care.

Keith Kalu had erected his stall on the edge of the market square. There he made his audience laugh with silly stunts and profanity and sold his cheap showy trinkets.

In these ways, the community around the church showed how it observed the Lord's holy day.

The entrance to the church had long been empty when Frank finally arrived. "The sermon must be nearly over," he thought and his feet seemed strangely drawn past the church. "I would fall asleep anyway on the benches since the strain of the trip kept me awake all night," he thought. And so Frank walked past the church, turned off at *Drop of Joy*, and ordered coffee.

"Well, well, a church neighbor," declared the gruff master from Suula.

"What will your mother say?" grunted his partner from Roiva.

"Who cares what old women say?" snapped the boy. The managers exploded into laughter and began a contest, offering to hire him, "...after you come back from services. Haw, haw!"

But Frank's bravado began to shrink as the noise in the coffee shop grew. He sneaked out toward the edge of the village. There he sat briefly on a stump. Soon the sun warmed him. He felt sleepy. There was still quite some time before the scheduled departure. He threw himself down full length near the red whortleberry bush. As he drowsed, disjointed memories flitted by. "___mother___home cottage___confirmation school that one could come to understand more about faith___that with the power of the gospel I would walk in the way of faith _____it shone red in the bottle____it went over, although the bar rocked_____a sponsor's gift for a namesake _____a hired-man's place_____go to church first_____." Word pictures flickered by. His conscience said something too. He felt badly but he was **so** tired.

It was dusk when he awoke. "The motor boat has left," flashed in his mind and his heart pounded in a panic. The youth dashed to the Tuorila pier. The men from Roiva and Suula had just arrived. Their swearing echoed in the air. The boat with the believers from Virmala had gone. "That punctual pig! He went to church with his fist on the bell rope!"

It was night before Frank could catch a return trip with the evening workmen. Nearly all of the men were drunk. They swore and sang bawdy songs. The girls giggled disgustingly beside them. Frank was cold and shivered as he crouched near the engine. In many ways his life had a bad flavor. "I wonder what Mother has been thinking?" The chugging of the engine through the darkness and the passenger cargo's raucous singing penetrated Frank as he made his heart's decision: "I don't belong to this crowd. My place is in that other group where the fire of the gospel burns daily giving God's peace in my heart.

Frank kept that decision. That very night he went to his mother's bed to seek forgiveness. After a month in confirmation school, a Christian young man from Taasila, a faithful hearer of the Word, was received into the service of God by a believing minister.

LESSONS FROM THE SWALLOW

The baby swallows were making their first try at flying. The parent swallows had to urge a long time before the little ones even dared to try. When one at last dared, its wings carried it beautifully. It quickly landed on the eave and looked about proudly, tilting its head. Then sisters and brothers did the same stunt as the mother commanded. Only the fifth one, frail and poorly ever since hatching out, was left peeking from the door of the nest. There were happy chirpings and sharp calls throughout the warm weather.

There was also excitement for the Davidson children who had gathered in the yard to have their afternoon nap with their father. "Father," asked Peter, "why do the swallows make their nests under the eaves?"

"They are shielded there from the rain and wind."

"What do baby swallows eat?" Marietta, the baby of the family, wanted to know.

"Don't you even know **that**?" blustered Peter. "Their father and mother snatch gnats from the air and carry them in their beaks to feed their children."

"Are gnats good?" questioned Marietta.

"They may taste good in the baby swallows' mouths, but **we** would not care for them," Father assured her.

"The swallows are tiny," observed Tommy. "Why aren't they here in winter?"

"They would freeze and besides there wouldn't be any food for them. Have you seen any gnats on a winter morning?" asked Father. Tommy had not seen any. Father went on: "Soon it will be time for them to leave. They will gather together in great flocks and then one morning they will be no more. They fly all the way to southern lands, all the way to Egypt."

"There where the children of Israel were?" asked Peter.

"Exactly," responded Father as he rose from the grass, took his scythe and started off to mow the barley.

That evening, Father took down Laestadius' *Postilla*. "Let's read from here about the swallow babies," he started.

> Little children, behold the heavens and the earth and everything that is in them, so that with four and twenty elders you can bend your knees before God's mercy seat[1] and thank the great Creator as swallows thank him for the first rain which awakened them on their nests. So should the Creator's little ones thank their Creator who has created all, and wait for the new heaven and the new earth where righteousness dwells.

"Mother, wasn't it said beautifully?"
"Yes." Mother had tears in her eyes.
"I'll read from another place now." He went on.

Praise him all ye titmice, snow buntings, swallows, praise him if you are able; for soon winter will come to the northland, and the swallows will have to move to that land where there is no frost or cold as there is here, nor a shortage of food as here where the little swallows sometimes cry in hunger and where great storms arise. Still, praise that great Creator who has given you life. Be patient in hope that you will be able to fly where the weather is warmer. Then you will know how to sing new hymns on Mount Zion and thank God eternally. But until then, be patient, be quiet on your nests and wait until the Ancient brings you food from the earth and the air.

Father closed the book. "So, our teacher father had eyes to read nature's great and beautiful Bible and ears to hear the words of the Heavenly Father in the great account.
"We weak Christians are like baby sparrows. That blessed nest in which we abide while we believe is Christ's congregation. We must live there in harmony, bearing up one another and supporting one another and being warm-hearted. A quarrelsome person soon falls away and dies alone without shelter or ability to fly. A cat could come and eat it. The eave that shelters us from the winds and rain is God's grace. The Heavenly Father feeds us with his word and sacrament.
"At times, there is cold and raw weather when we groan under heavy trials, hungry and chilly. At times, the daylight shines into the gray and worthless nest which is ours day and night. Winds of grace fill our bosoms and we twitter praises to the Creator, Saviour.
"Then, one day, the everlastingly beautiful summer morning comes when the Heavenly parent calls us from our clay abode. Then we'll get to heaven, to summer where the never-setting sun is the one in whose name and blood we now believe all our sins and weaknesses forgiven.
"May your father also believe?"
"In Jesus' name and blood, all sins are forgiven," rang from many lips.

The sun was just setting. Its rays still caressed the little swallows roosting on the eaves as they sleepily chirped a quiet: "Good night."

---

[1] See Revelation 4:10

A WORM-EATEN APPLE

"Daddy, look! Just look at that pretty apple! It's already fully ripe!" shouted Helvi.

"It does look like it," agreed Father, knocking the apple down with his stick.

"Why did it ripen before the others?"

"We shall soon see." Father picked up the red-cheeked apple from the ground and cut it in half with his pocket knife. "That's what I thought," he growled. "All worm-eaten!" Helvi looked. The inside was full of worm tunnels and an ugly black head peeped from one of the holes. "Phew!" she cried and threw the apple halves far behind the yard fence.

Father related the morning event to the whole family as they were reading the Bible and singing songs of God's children.

"See how even a Christian can become a worm-eaten apple. He tries to be better-looking than anyone else or more knowledgeable than others. Or he often tells of his profound experiences, sometimes exaggerating. When his God-given emotions start to dry up, he makes a great effort to maintain interest. He is often attractive on the surface. We might admire such a travel companion and think that he graces the congregation.

"We don't know whether the worm of pride and desire for respect has eaten to the depths of the soul of our most precious brother. In the end, that soul can be rotten, too. Christian pride prevents him from walking in the light. Secret sins are hidden in his conscience. Admiring one's self doesn't always give strength to overcome trials and temptations. Sin remains sin and the conscience is cleansed only by looking to Jesus in faith."

All listened without stirring. It seemed that the Heavenly Gardener came to examine his garden.

STRAWBERRY GIRL

The parents of Laila Heinonen lived in a little house beside the lake, on the edge of the village near Rytila church. They grew potatoes in a small field around the tiny gray cabin. Near the shore huddled an even tinier bath-house. The barn behind the house wasn't much bigger. Laila's father traveled on foot to nearby houses for day jobs. Mother sewed and cared for a flock of six children, of whom twelve-year-old Laila was the oldest.

As the family grew there also grew worry over the daily bread. "If only you were already able to earn sometimes!" sighed Mother to her firstborn. But the times were hard and it was difficult to get work. Laila had performed little tasks at the neighbors and she had earned a few marks for her work, but they did not make much difference in the little nest where need peeked in through every crevice in the walls. But the Heinonens didn't grumble. They had learned from the Word that the greatest fortune is to be godly and contented with one's lot in life. The Spirit of the Lord reigned in that little home and in their breasts dwelt that peace the world cannot give.

Laila was able to use the money she had earned to travel to near-by towns when big services were held. At every truck-gardening stand, she saw children selling strawberries. Oh, how tempting the little dainty morsels of cultured strawberries looked in little birch-bark baskets. But of course the money set aside for travel could not be used for such an indulgence! On the other hand, Laila saw that travelers opened their purses readily enough and the little peddlers seemed satisfied and happy. "I have earned thirty marks!" boasted one energetic girl.

"What if I tried that?" flashed into Laila's mind. "I'll ask my father for a part of the potato plot. Then I'll ask my school teacher for directions and where to get plants!"

At first Laila was timid about approaching her teacher. Laila was a good student and had received a good report card and certificate of graduation in the spring. That is why she was received with a friendly greeting. Her teacher promised to supply plants on the condition that the young gardener would pay for them from her first harvest. The price would be twenty marks for each plant.

"I'll try to choose especially good plants for you. I have two strains. I'll give you these Kasperns. They ripen early and from to my experience they bear a good crop. You can start with two hundred plants," explained the teacher.

"Oh, thank you! When can I come after them?" asked Laila.

"Come at the middle of August. That is a good time to plant and if all goes well you will have a good crop already next summer," replied the teacher. "But first the ground must be well worked up and you must find a suitable place. It must be a warm place, protected from the winds. That might possibly be near the wall of your cabin, where the sun can shine on them and the eastern whirl-winds will not get to them. Humus should be added to the soil about half a meter deep when the early potatoes are harvested. Turn the earth with a fork and carefully pick out all the weed roots. Then ask your father for two loads of cow manure and smooth it in with a rake. I will loan you one if you don't have one."

"Thanks!" replied Laila.

"I'll stop in to see your plot and show you how to plant them," promised the teacher.

"You are very kind!" said Laila.

Cheerfully Laila returned home, but Father was not so obliging. "Of course the delicacies of wealthy gentlemen weren't meant to be found amongst the laborers who live in cabins. Potatoes are more dependable."

Laila described the idea almost in tears. "You will see that it pays better than potatoes. I will get many marks for them at the news-stand near the Lattata Auxiliary. And I'll bring every penny home and I will care for my land myself."

"Well, all right, we shall see," said Father more mildly.

And so Laila had a deadline by which to get her plot ready for planting. It was five meters wide and ten meters long.

"I'm sure you will succeed!" earnestly encouraged the teacher when the time for planting in August arrived. Together with Laila, she brought the plants with their little clods of earth in the little planter boxes and set them upright and watered them just a little. With a piece of old clothesline they laid out seven parallel rows the long way of the plot, just over 70 centimeters apart. Then into each row they placed the growing plants about 30 centimeters apart. "Be sure that each plant is just a little deeper than it was before," taught the teacher. "If the clod has been broken from some plant the roots must be spread out evenly in the planting hole so that they won't be folded double. Leave a small depression around each plant for watering." Laila carried water from the lake with a pail and dipped a small cup-full for each plant.

Mother and Father thought that the planting was pretty and promising. "Just remember, child," said Father, "that God alone gives the increase."

"But we do what we can, also," added the school teacher.

Laila was busily occupied with her portion of the land in the evenings. She pulled noxious weeds and trimmed the furiously growing runners. She lightly raked the space between the plants and tended to their need for water. With money she had earned she bought a kilo of saltpeter[1] and sprinkled it around the plants. In October she spread rotted cow-manure between the flourishing plants.

Winter came and the snow covered even the highest growing green leaves. After the snow was gone in the spring, Laila carefully raked the soil between the plants, being careful not to injure the roots. She did not now have even a penny to buy fertilizer but she had gathered ashes during the winter and gave the garden about six kilos.

About the middle of June the first blossoms burst open. There were many! "Your strawberries beat mine," praised the school teacher when she walked past. "When the flowers wilt, water them a couple of times. Put about twenty grams of salt-peter in ten liters of water. Then watch how the cheeks of the strawberries will redden! You haven't watered them during the blossoming, have you?"

"No."

"Good. At that time it was not profitable but now, yes," coached the teacher.

When the cheeks began to redden, Laila covered the space between the plants with moss, so that the berries would not be mud-spattered but would lie clean on their beds.

On the sixth of July the first berries were ripe. Mother got to taste the very first one. Next morning Laila picked several of them and brought a cupful to Father at the "coffee break." He showed them to the farmer, too. "See how our girl grows things like this and intends to earn big money."

Every morning for three weeks Laila went to check on her strawberry patch. She made little birch-bark baskets and in them she arranged her ripe berries. She carried them in a hamper to a booth near the bus stop. She charged one mark for each little basket of berries and sales were brisk. Nearly always she was able to return home with an empty hamper, often with 15 marks jingling in the pocket of her apron.

Father was waiting his turn to have a bath when he got the first reckoning of the strawberry account. Laila noticed that his chin quivered like at services when Grandfather Joule preached.

The rising sun warmed the back of the young berry-picker. A southwesterly wind blew across the bay and lightly touched the pretty brown arms. Laila felt good. She hummed an old hymn, "Thank You Father for Thy Mercy." Laila could almost always bring home another ten marks each day. That was really something in hard times, almost half of Father's pay for a day!

Laila hurried to the bus stop and whirled into the booth from the middle of a dust cloud. Travelers rushed out from inside the station. The sweating gentlemen were in their shirt-sleeves. It seemed that some lady had fallen ill. "Girl! Girl! Bring some berries here!" They almost fought over the baskets and the money flew into the bottom of the basket. When one man got the last basket, he flung his money into the hamper as did the others and hurried to the bus. Laila noticed that the last money was **five** marks! The customer had made a mistake in his hurry.

"Call him back!" said her conscience.

"You don't have time," argued her reasoning.

"Call after him!" thumped her sense of feeling.

"Aren't you embarrassed to?" questioned the voice of reason.

Meanwhile the bus left the station. In the bottom of the basket there were now twenty marks. "But those four are not really yours," judged her conscience.

The day felt painfully and agonizingly long. In the evening the little house felt unusually hot. In bed Laila perspired even though she pushed back the sheet. The mosquitoes got in through a crack of the door. They whined in their high pitched tones and bit painfully. Worst of all, the money wrongly received picked at her conscience.

"You could easily have corrected the error, but you didn't want to," argued her conscience. No relief came and she spent an awful night. Next morning, Father could be heard sharpening his scythe on the porch of the shed. "Tell him about it," counseled her conscience.

"But that won't help anything," objected her reason.

"Tell it anyway ! Perhaps he will give good advice," persisted her conscience. The girl sat down on the rail of the porch.

"Father?"

"God's peace, child, are you going to the strawberry patch already?"

"Not yet. But I have a matter to discuss with you."

"What?"

Laila cried and related what had happened. At once it felt as though those extra marks had rolled from her conscience onto the planks of the porch. "Coveting overtook you," said Father seriously. "But isn't it good that you got remorse from it? Come here so I can bless you."

Father gave his daughter the blessing of forgiveness of her sin in Jesus' name and blood and then continued: "You must correct the error if you see that man again."

Several days later it happened that the same gentleman stood by the strawberry crate. Laila blushed almost as red as the strawberries in her birch-bark baskets. The customer threw his mark into the bottom of the crate and took his portion.

"No, no!" Laila burst out.

"What, aren't you going to sell to me? Am I so ugly, miss?" he laughed.

"No. No. But didn't you buy the other day too?"

"Yes, but do you sell just once to each one? That's a nice selling custom!"

"No. But then I got too much money. You gave five marks by mistake. Here is the change I owe you."

At that the gentleman stopped laughing. "You have truly remarkable business principles! Just keep the change and may God bless you."

Laila felt like running home, she felt so light-hearted. She related the incident to her father and mother in the living-room. "And so you see, Laila, that sin even attempts to come between the sales-person and the customer. But God is more powerful than sin." And so the discussion ended.

---

[1] Ground-up rock rich in nitrogen compounds.

MIDSUMMER SALMON

It was midsummer, and the "big services" were close at hand. Speakers were expected to arrive in Tasala in a couple of days. Folks understood that Pastor Olson would be there with Uncle Cain, that stout agreeable minister who always noticed the little ones around him and made himself at home with them.

At supper, Father recalled the first big Midsummer services in that community nearly thirty years ago.[1] The pastor who lived in town then was now dead and gone to Glory. There were only about twenty believers in the whole parish at that time, all of them poor, but the matter of their faith was precious to them and the desire to reach Heaven burned in their hearts.

At that time Tasala was a wretched operation of small tenant farms belonging to the Crown, as Father recalled, but the decision was made to house the speakers there anyway.[2] The means were limited, but God helped and all went well. "That's when the good Heavenly Father gave that big salmon catch, too," remember Mother.

Father went on. "The morning of the day before services I lowered my salmon net off the point which is called Gentle Breeze. It extends all the way from Morning Worship Cape to the mouth of Lamb's Bay. The wind blew softly from the south and it clouded over a bit. Brother Pasa was with us that morning and we pulled six salmon and a northern pike into the boat.

"I'll always remember when the minister came to the shore to meet us. Right away he looked at the catch and was pleased and impressed. Then he put on a mock-serious face and joked, "Shouldn't you say, 'Go away, Lord, for I am a sinful man'?"[3] Immediately tears were in my eyes from awakened memories and I embraced my confessor-father and begged for the blessing."

Aaro, the youngest in the house, who went to confession two weeks earlier, stood at the door listening to his father's tale. "Let's go, Dad, and we'll try!" he begged enthusiastically.

"Your mouth would water like Uncle Cain's on his way to the dining room when Mother carries the salmon to the table."

The idea became fact. Next morning until noon Aaro fished for minnows, catching about thirty with the bait net. Father arranged a back-line in the round wood covered box, putting fifty hooks on their short gut leaders. They put several small rocks into the bottom of the boat and about thirty big cork floats, each attached to a short leader. Mother packed lunch into the knapsack, a black coffee pot peeking its grimy spout out from the opening.

While Aaro rowed about eleven kilometers, Father baited the hooks with minnows and then arranged them neatly into the round wood box which had a cover. Again this day the wind blew softly from the south. Fair weather clouds rode high in the sky. The mountain ash were in bloom on the bluffs along the shore and the apple trees in Maki's yard also blossomed. It all looked like a great snowbank. Swallows shuttled back and forth between the snowbank and the rolling waves. A tugboat pushed a raft of timber. The back of Aaro's shirt got soaked with sweat but the youth worked hard and the trip went swiftly.

Beyond Pike Sound was the great open sea, with open water to the north as far as eye could see. There the waves were higher and the air felt fresher. They brought their lunch ashore with them to the little sauna/fish-hut on Leafy Island where Father baited the last hooks while Aaro boiled coffee.

Dropping the line was a fussy job. First a rock, then a float. Aaro pulled a couple of strokes with the oars. Father fastened a short hook and leader to the fishline. Another couple of oarstrokes. Father tied a float to the line. Two more strokes. Father explained, "The idea is to get the bait about a meter below the surface of the water. That's why we have the corks half a meter above the line and the hooks half a meter below the line. The hooks must be at least twenty meters from one another because otherwise a strong fish could jerk itself loose.

"Now when we bait the hooks, we start the hook into the minnow at the dorsal fin on the back and pull it through to the corner of the mouth. That way the little baitfish are in the water in a horizontal position and when the waves rock the corks the baitfish move as if alive and so they lure the King of Fish to the trap!"

The dusk of summer night crept from the shore to the open water. When the hooks were finally in the lake, Father threw the last float into the water, saying, "Now may God bless the fishing lines to provide the service fish."

Aaro couldn't get to sleep on the hard sauna bench. It made his hip just ache. As the sun arose, he was already lighting the fire in the fireplace to make coffee. He awakened his father from a sound sleep only after the coffee was steaming in the cup. "The salmon has stolen the sleep from the man, I see," smiled the father. "Did you remember to ask for a blessing on today?"

Aaro had forgotten the morning prayer. "Well, then, let's sing together! That's what the old dean did on our fishing trips together while he was alive. The old grandpa didn't have a singing voice, but night and morning he hummed the tune for at least a verse or two and read the blessing." Father began, "A blessed day arises, We already see its brightness!" and Aaro joined in timidly.

It seemed to Aaro that Father fiddled around with breakfast much too long. When he saw that his son was restlessly gazing out through the window, he explained, "It is the best time for us to eat. Let the salmon check out our bait." Finally they got out to the end of the fish line and Aaro backed around with oars. His father lifted experimentally on the line.

"Can you feel anything?" Father shook his head. Hook after hook came up and each one had only a luke-warm bait fish which Father picked off and threw far out into the water. A seagull hovering over the boat suddenly dropped itself to the water and rose with the minnow in its beak. Soon it had four or five shrieking companions. There was plenty for all of them. Aaro became so interested watching the sport of the big white birds that he didn't notice his father looking attentive, letting the line run through his fingers as something swiftly pulled it out.

"Got one?"

"Yes!"

"Is it big?"

"Pretty big." Father already had the club in one hand while with the other he drew in and fed the line into the round line box. The fish yanked again and the line sizzled over the edge of the boat. The line abruptly stopped and Father began to pull in again.

"Can you still feel it?"

"Not right now."

"It probably got away."

"It **did** get away," and his father lifted a badly mangled minnow into the boat. Aaro felt so bad that it actually made him hold his breath. "What a pain!" he almost cried. It seemed there was no use. More than one hundred hooks were already pulled into the boat and not one worthless fish was caught!

"I wonder what's going on now," his father interrupted through Aaro's gloom. "It has pulled down strangely...now it comes up...it is coming up...maybe it's a fish...maybe the Good Father **will** give us a salmon for our services...there...it is **biting**!"

The line began to sizzle. "Now, row toward the line! Row hard!" Aaro rowed so hard his shoulders creaked. "Just don't let it go!" he panted. The fish came in now without a fight. Now it was right beside the boat and Aaro saw its black back. The club struck the fish in the neck with a crack and it turned on its side, wounded. Then over the edge it came! It was big but it was not a salmon, only a pike. Aaro was let down.

"This is good, too, Aaro, real good," said Father, comforting him. "This will also serve as fish for the services. It weighs at least eight kilos! Probably there wan't anything else on the line. We started out too confident and the Heavenly Father humbled us. That's another blessing of the services."

"And I did remember the evening and morning prayers!" thought Aaro.

On the way home, Father rowed and the boy nodded in the back of the boat. The sun warmed the back of the tired youth. The trolling line slipped from his hand and ran from the reel and over the side of the boat into the water. Far back there was a sudden splash. Aaro awoke when the pole and reel fell into the lake.

"A salmon has it!" shouted his father and rowed toward the pole with all his might. "There it goes...there...grab it!" The line pulled the pole and reel erratically. Sometimes the whole rig disappeared, only to pop up farther away. Then by luck Aaro grabbed the runaway, but the line was slack. The boy began to haul the line into the boat just as it started to pull.

"There's a fish!" he whispered huskily.

"Bring it in carefully. I'll row toward the fish at the same time...take the club...now slack...not too tight...." the father continued to coach him. Finally another black back shone beside the boat. Aaro was almost numb from tension, but at his father's order he quickly hit the fish on the neck. It rolled over on its side. Father slid the net under it and the salmon thumped on the bottom of the boat. It wasn't the biggest, perhaps two kilos, but at least it was a salmon.

Aaro was not sleepy any more. And God had given a midsummer St. John's salmon.

---

[1] Near the birthday of St. John the Baptist.
[2] Depending upon the country, Crown land is either government land or land belonging to the royalty.
[3] See Luke 5:1-9.

A HAY-MAKING WEEK

Karl and Maria were allowed to go along with the others this summer to the distant meadowland for the haying. The meadow was so large that haying took a whole week even if the weather were fine the whole time.

At midsummer in this country the sky stayed light even at midnight. For the first two days of haying the mower ran all day and right through the night, with Father sitting ceremoniously in the driver's seat. The hired men mowed by hand the corners of the rows and along the mounds and drainage ditches, places that the mower could not reach. The children, however, slept at night in the biggest shed. Father had to make two trips to fetch food.

During the middle of one of the hottest and most sultry days, Father as promised took Karl and Maria berrying in the nearby woods. They came back with their mouths black and their birch-bark boxes full. On the way they jumped into the cove to swim. The day ran its course happily, the grasshoppers sang and laughter rang out from the men as they mowed. In the evening they sang hymns and songs in the shed and Father read the evening prayer. They slept even through the high-pitched whine of the mosquitoes. It was a week of weeks, a week of brightest summer, of joy of work, of sweat and pleasant fatigue.

Saturday morning they gathered to store the last hay into the last shed. Father, Big-Brother and the hired man Daniel brought huge wagon-loads to the door of the shed and forked great bunches inside. Margaret worked inside receiving the bunches and Maria and Karl chased each other around "helping" her!

It was really a busy hard sweaty piece of work. There was no breeze. The sun shone as though through a magnifying glass onto the low shed there on the edge of the woods. Beards and chaff from the hay prickled the skin. Even so, it was fun to grab armfulls of fragrant hay and carry them from the door to the back wall. It was even more fun to stomp the hay down firmly and then tumble down from the top of the hay pile! Between loads they sometimes ran out to drink a cup of fermented home-made summer drink.

During noon lunch break, Father said he believed that there was thunder in the air. He said that if they hurried they might get home and have a bath before the rain. "And surely a real bath after this dusty bath would be a treat. But we must hurry! There will be no time for berrying or swimming today!"

Toward evening the sky became covered with a gray haze through which the sun was a glowing red ball. The ones in the shed nearly suffocated. The men looked worried as they raced to empty the loads. Margaret didn't laugh anymore. Maria was weary. They all heard the rumble of thunder from somewhere far away.

Then it began to darken as though night were coming, even though real darkness did not come to the North in summer. A gust of wind rustled through the nearby grove. The far-away plaint of a sandpiper drifted up from the shore. Then they saw a flash of lightning through the door. "God is sending a terrible storm!" said Father. "Children, pray for yourselves."

The men hurried to get in the last load as if it were on fire. Panting, Margaret rolled the hay in bundles twice as big as before. Lightning flashed again and again. Thunder burst as if the roof of heaven had smashed into pieces and then it rumbled and shook the earth for a long time. The hay-cart squeaked up to the barn and the men dumped the last load just inside the door before they stopped to groan and pant. Daniel ran the horses in under an overhanging roof and Margaret got them water from the spring.

Father fixed a nice firm bed in the hay for the children and spoke comfortingly to them: "We won't get to go to Mother right now. We will have to spend a wild night here. But we can put up with a little trouble after such a beautiful week of haying, and anyway, the Heavenly Father protects his children."

As it got still darker, the lights of heaven flashed continually. Thunder boomed almost without pause. The time between lightning flash and thunderclap became shorter and shorter until they almost came at the same time. Maria pressed herself trembling against her father's side. Karl tried his best to keep from crying. Margaret got her lunch out but she and the men ate very slowly and were not really hungry.

"Will the lightning come in?" asked Maria.

"Does it kill people?" wondered Karl.

"Yes, it does sometimes come in and people have sometimes died from a bolt of lightning," answered Father.

"The last one was Jaffet Hongga," remembered Daniel. "I'll never forget it. We were haying like now, when an awful thunderstorm overtook us. Jaffet Hongga was not a Christian, I remember, and he would often swear. The rest of us were shaking in the storm but Jaffet just sat by the door of the shed and began to fill his pipe. He leered over at the master rather derisively and held up his pipe to the sky: 'Here, strike fire to my pipe!'

"'You shouldn't ridicule the Lord. It is dangerous sport...' The master's remark was cut off. The flash was blinding and the thunderclap blasted our ears. When we recovered from our fright, Jaffet lay charred and black in the doorway and his pipe smoldered far out in the meadow. I was an unbelieving man until then, I tell you, but that night my conscience was awakened. The master of the house preached the forgiveness of my sins to me and I became a child of God." Daniel voice was a little quavery.

"Right. The Lord will not allow himself to be mocked," added Father gravely. "We don't want to make fun of Him for He is our loving Father to whom we cry in every distress. Now let us pray that He will help us here and our loved ones at home." Just then the shed glowed dazzling bright and the thunder clapped so loud that it hurt their ears. Maria screamed and Karl burst into tears.

"You're all right," comforted their father. "God let the lightning strike the hill close by. Our time had not come. Now hear, the clouds are just pouring water. Just listen how it drums down! And the time between flashes and thunder is getting longer once again."

The little children quieted to listen and Margaret's appetite for lunch came back. Rumbles quickly became more distant. The rain lessened and after about an hour it stopped completely. The evening sun peered through from the edge of the sky. The newly harvested field steamed while the haying party struck up a hymn of thanksgiving. Karl and Maria lay down on their hay-beds with hands folded and fell into a sweet sleep.

They awakened early on Sunday morning and prepared to go home, but first the children ran up the closest hill with Father. A giant pine had been split down the middle and white splinters were thrown around everywhere. "The lightning did that last night," Father told them. "If it had happened to hit our shelter, there would no longer be any shed and maybe not any of us either. So you see, children, how our life and death are in God's hands."

"Truly," said Karl.

FOUR KINDS OF SOIL

An awakening occurred at one confirmation school. William Vitikka, Tamra Toropainen, Millie Metso and Charles Kuusinen attended the school along with others.

William's father owned the richest and grandest home in the parish. William behaved fairly well in class and knew his assignments quite well. The teacher never needed to reprimand him individually, but he remained uneasy about this presumptuous and apparently carefree student of his. William's thoughts wandered occasionally here and there. Now and then he told some dirty story he had heard. Sometimes he sneaked a glance over to where the girls sat and increasingly terrible mental images tore at his heart.

When a classmate seemed to be moved and was listening eagerly as he followed the teacher, William thought: "What are you thinking about? I know that false teacher, that misinformed and narrow-minded preacher. My father and mother are pious also and devoted to the Word and **they** don't have such a narrow-minded view of life!"

When the students all hurried out into the schoolyard after class, William always noticed something frivolous to laugh at, as when the simple-minded woman wandered out onto the road or a squirrel leaped in the nearby grove or when Vahas' young pig ran away. As the day of first communion was fast approaching, William decided, "I'll go along with the church custom like a man and go to communion. Then I'll get a gold watch from Father. There's no point in crying for nothing!"

Tamra was the flighty daughter of a believing home. Her voice rang out loudest at amusement places of the young people. Yet on the following Sunday she could weep at the services when young Paul Tapanella preached fervently. During confirmation classes and often at other times, Tamra would nearly bathe in her tears, yet that night she could frolic with the boys along the highway. Among the teacher's lessons, the stories and words of God's great love for sinners and Jesus' work of reconciliation moved her heart most. But her own sins didn't particularly pain her. Sometimes she was startled to remember suddenly a "little' disobedience, a "little" anger, "little" lies and thefts, "small and innocent" pleasures. When the moment for partaking of first communion was nearly at hand, these thoughts came to Tamra: "I've really not been a true believing Christian child of God for a long time. But everyone is going to communion."

Millie Metso was a quiet, beautiful orphan girl. A wealthy and upright uncle raised her after both her mother and father died in living faith. Millie did not even remember her father's departure, but the death of her mother was indelibly pressed on her five-year-old mind. The dying mother took her only child by the hand and said, "Stay a child of God until death, Millie!" Millie tried by all means to avoid sin and never dared to deny her faith, but her unbelieving uncle was reluctant to allow her to go to services. Eventually the poor girl became estranged from Christians. Little transgressions befell her and after them her conscience would be terribly upset. She would pray, "Dear Heavenly Father, have compassion on me and help me! Forgive me! Make of me a clean child." Once Millie bemoaned the plight of conscience to her uncle but he just stiffly snapped out, "Pray more to God!"

It seemed to Millie that the confirmation school words were spoken just for her. Oh, how all of her transgressions came accusingly to mind. If only this sin and that sin were left undone! How good the pastor's warm talks, concerning Jesus' complete and full redemption and finding security in faith, felt to her! And now school was coming to a close. "Before communion, I want to go to speak to my pastor to tell of my sins and the state of my soul. I want to kneel as a believing girl before the altar and be Jesus' own all my life. I hope to go to be with my mother and father."

Charles was the son of a Christian home, but he sank into the paths of the prodigal son. At ten, he stole five marks from the store. He concealed this deed with lies and did not humble his heart in repentance even though he was terribly miserable for weeks. At that point he began his downward path. He was seen in the company of drunks and at card tables. His whole being was restless and he avoided meeting people's eyes. He blushed easily. The reproaches of his mother and father gave him pain, even as he tried to cover his real feelings with a carefree manner and flippant answers.

Charles didn't care to go to services; it became too difficult to be there. From the start, he invented all kinds of pranks in confirmation school. The pastor spoke to him twice in class gently and in private more seriously and Charles did become attentive. It seemed the pastor was always speaking to **him** and mentioning **his** sins! How could the pastor know all this?

The youth began to withdraw from the other groups. He read his assignments and he knew them the next day. The boys joked, "Charles intends to excel in knowledge. He has become completely holy. But do you remember when he..." and they laughed about his former pranks.

The day of first communion fast approached. "Dear God, I do not dare, I haven't the courage," thought Charles. On the very last day of confirmation school, the pastor spoke clearly and seriously about the right and wrong ways of partaking of the Lord's Supper. Charles rose in his place with a pale face:

"I am such a great sinner that I don't dare!"

"Do you want to remain in your sins?" asked the pastor.

"No!"

"Then do you desire to become a child of God, to receive the forgiveness of your sins and live as a Christian man?"

"Yes, but I am so cold! My conscience doesn't even distress me any more!"

"Dear Charles," the pastor comforted. "Jesus has reconciled even you on the cross of Golgotha. Your sins are forgiven in his name and blood." The pastor crossed over to Charles and blessed him, saying, "You believe this, do you not?"

"I do believe," and Charles looked steadily into the pastor's eyes.

Millie had begun softly crying, deciding that this was the right moment: "Does God's grace belong to me also? I have been so bad, so bad," she moaned.

"Child, it does belong, God's grace belongs to all sinners. Be assured! Your sins are forgiven in Jesus' blood." Millie also now received the blessing and promised to believe that Jesus was her saviour.

Tamra felt like crying. She didn't know why, but the moment was so emotional and touching. Millie's tears had nearly ceased. When the pastor came near, Tamra threw her arms around his neck and begged, "Bless me too!" The pastor pushed her gently but firmly back down on her bench, laid his hand on her head and proclaimed the forgiveness of sins.

"Oh, I believe, I feel so wonderful now!" Tamra rejoiced.

William ducked his head and swore softly to himself. "Oh, I wish I could get away from this weeping mill and from you, idle preacher."

That evening Charles came to the parsonage and confessed his many sins to his confessor father. Once more he received from him the absolution. From there, he hurried home to ask forgiveness from his parents and his brothers. After this, he had time to go to many neighbors and confess his evil deeds and ask their forgiveness.

Millie also went to her pastor at the parsonage to speak of sins which had long burdened and troubled her. She begged for forgiveness from her uncle for transgressions against their home. She confessed her faith to the old man.

Tamra was just floating on a cloud. She felt so good, so good!

Ten years passed. **Charles Kuusinen** showed up at the parsonage again. The old pastor had invited all those who were confirmed in that class ten years earlier, but only Charles came. "Well, the good Father has protected you in faith?" the minister began. "Yes, although my efforts have been weak," acknowledged the young man. The evening wore on as they recalled Charles' confirmation class companions.

William Vitikka already presided over their home place as the bold young master. He drank sometimes, now and then made the girls laugh, and swore and spoke sarcastically about the Christians. He came with his father and mother to the summer communion only once, and fretted the whole time about the minister's hopeless narrow-mindedness.

Tamra Toropainen partook of grace for almost a year. She often rejoiced at services during those days and thanked the Lord with upraised hands. Then the joy faded! The girl became discouraged and thought that she had lost her faith. The Christians tried to counsel her that even when she felt cold and dry and troubled, she should cling to God's imperishable promises of grace and love. They reminded her also of how precious are the promises of grace when the enemy of the soul frightens with accusations of former faults and failings, or when a believer falls into sins of weakness which wound the conscience.

But poor Tamra was known as a good Christian, so how could she humble herself in that way? No, she tried her utmost to regain those former good feelings, to be touched as before. But instead she gradually had to pretend. Between services, hopelessness weighed heavier. Then the enemy of the soul set a trap.

Tamra got a job in a respectable place of business. The young people there were especially kind and attentive. In their idle talk, they asked, "You are a pleasant girl and upright, but how can you stand being in the company of those detestable hypocritical Christians?" Tamra herself had some of these thoughts recently. Services began to be a heavy duty or obligation to her, and finally she stayed away altogether.

Some believing sisters went to call on her and talk with her, but after they came, Tamra's manager annoyed her with caustic remarks. Finally, when one Christian auntie came to see her, Tamra snapped, "I am no longer believing and you don't need to come here to pry!" Not long after, Tamra took out her grievances by going to her first evening dance. Two years later, a pastor in a nearby parish was asked to baptize Tamra's out-of-wedlock child.

Millie Metso remained faithful to her belief in the heavenly call for eight years. Then it happened that a wealthy neighbor boy began to approach her. He was shy and gentle. Millie had secretly admired him and yet feared him for a long time. The young man began to attend services to impress Millie, but her instinct was that he understood nothing about Christianity. Still, he didn't speak evil of believers, but rather assured her that he respected them. Millie began to imagine that she might win him over to Christianity later in their married life. Furthermore, her uncle continuously represented this proposed marriage as a great temporal benefit. "An orphan girl should accept such an offer, thanking God for it as a gift from heaven!" When the girl seemed to be yielding, the uncle who had been so cold these years now became very cordial.

So Millie Metso became the wife in the Tuorila house. To be sure, her conscience was timid and restless. But her husband was decent and good natured, the home was lovely with plenty of pleasing activity, and Millie gradually became content. She enjoyed having plenty of everything her very own. She admired the view in beautiful mirrors or through living room windows at bountiful fields and full feed boxes. There was less and less time to sit with the Bible received as a confirmation gift and even less time to sit in services. When the pastor happened to meet her, Millie hurried past almost without a greeting.

"So you see, Charles," spoke the pastor, "Jesus told of four kinds of soil where the seed was sown. Here they are. William's heart was a hard-trodden road. Distracting thoughts were those blackbirds which plucked from his heart the words of God which he heard.

"Tamra's heart had just a thin layer of soil over a bed of rocks---too little, too little. The seed soon sprouted, but the plants did not grow sufficient roots. The first sunny day burned up the plants. There was much true work of the Lord in Tamra. She was truly sincere, but shallow, not deep, a very flighty changeable nature. That's why Christlike feelings moved in her breast but not her conscience. In an awakening there always is a sense of emotion, but it must not be the most important matter. The main thing is that the conscience must suffer from past sins.

"Tamra's transgressions did not press her down greatly. She only had some indefinite longing and feeling of weakness. God's grace produced mainly feelings, not desire or will. Her freedom from her accusing conscience was vague and indefinite. She was only a fair-weather Christian. The first adversity and testing disheartened her. In living faith there is also emotion. It is incredibly good at times to be refreshed by God's grace so that one must praise the Lord aloud. At other times heaven is clouded over and the heart is cold, hard and troubled. But these are side issues that do not affect our salvation. The main thing is that in faith we hold fast to His promises of grace, being obedient to keep faith and a good conscience.

"Millie Metso's soil was deep and tilled but the cares of life and desire for riches slowly drew her into permissiveness. They thrived in the shadow of her beautiful intentions. They finally smothered the heavenly plantings.

"But you, Charles. I hope that your heart is in that good soil which carries grain into heaven's granary."

"I hope so, too. Pray, dear confessor father, that I, a tired and weak Christian, may endure to the end," said Charles thoughtfully.

HOW OLLE GOT SERVICES

Olle lived in a village which was far in the wilderness. Olle was a believing boy from a Christian home and although he was only eight years old, he was big for his age. Once, in the winter, services were held in Olle's home with Daniel Kukka speaking. Daniel taught Olle many Christian songs and showed him pictures from the big Bible. He spoke about the Heavenly Father, of Jesus and of God's people. **Then** he took pieces of wood from the shed and carved a horse and sleigh.

Olle never had such happy days! In the evenings, even though he didn't understand everything, he was able to sit and listen without nodding while Uncle Daniel preached to the grownups. Daniel and Olle agreed to put the horse and sleigh under the bed for the night "to eat oats in the stable." The boy became so attached to the guest that when Daniel left he burst into tears.

Over and over that spring, Olle asked when Uncle Daniel would arrive again to hold services. "When we can get enough supplies together that we are able to plan for services," Father replied.

"How much do we need?"

"At least a couple of hundred marks."

"That's big money, isn't it?" bemoaned the youth.

Auntie Kerho came to the backwoods to hold the spring 4-H meeting. Olle pushed to go, although the big boys scoffed. "A stub of a boy can't work with men." Auntie spoke to the club about gardening in club plots and at one point mentioned how during the past fall some children near the church had earned hundreds of marks. "Money for services!" flashed into Olle's mind. He made his way into the Agriculture Club room to speak about joining, but Auntie did not promise to take him. She said that members had to be at least eleven years old. Olle almost cried.

Sadly he made his way homeward without looking back. There he sat huddled in the doorway. When Mother learned the reason for his disappointment, she promised to rent for him a little piece of land where he could plant onions **without** belonging to the 4-H club. Olle cheered up!

Then oh how slowly the land thawed! During the day the brooks rippled and bare spots appeared on the hillsides, but at night it froze hard and the poor sun had to begin its work again from the beginning. At his mother's suggestion, Olle put ashes on his plot. Also, because it was a warm southern slope, the black ground appeared when there were still drifts of snow most places. Before the last frost went out of the road, Father hauled three wagon-loads of well-rotted manure to "Olle's Field."

When all the snow was finally melted, the skylark warbled in the sky and the finch twittered in the woods. A water-thrush chirped and strutted, picked up a worm and fluttered away.

Olle was off to his field like a grown-up. He spread the manure evenly over the whole plot before his father arrived to start plowing. Then they cultivated about five kilos of slaked quicklime into the field. "So that root-worms won't come there," according to Father.

Then using a steel rake, Olle smoothed, leveled off and raked the whole plowed area and mixed the white lime into the soil. He broke up the lumps and plucked out the roots of undesirable weeds and the stones and short pieces of roots. His shirt was soaked with sweat and an amazing number of potatoes disappeared into his stomach every night!

One afternoon Olle measured the plot and marked off the spaces for the rows, about 30 centimeters apart. He stretched a cord taut for each row and drew a groove along each row with the handle end of his rake. Then he watered the little ditch and pressed the onion plants into the soil four centimeters deep and fifteen centimeters apart. In all, he planted 2,200 onion plants! Olle's day began early and often lasted till evening, even though his mother helped some at the last.

Sunday church bells already were sounding from far away when Olle shuffled into the house, muddy and tired, where he could kick off his boots and hurry after his father to the bath-house. They bathed and then on their way back to the house they went together to glance at "Olle's Field."

"May the Heavenly Father bless your planting," said Olle's father in all seriousness.

"You know that it is really a planting for services," Olle informed him.

Olle's crop was blessed when August came. Every planting site was like a bird's nest with its eggs. Some bunches had fifteen onions! Olle kept weeding all summer and once or twice in the evening he had to water heavily when the weather had been dry and sunny for a spell. After watering, the soil had to be loosened. If seed stalks appeared, they had to be cut off. Sometimes midnight came before Olle could slip into bed. At harvest time, even the club leader marveled at Olle's harvest.

"When you harvest the onions, bring them directly from the garden to the drying barn to dry. After a week, twist the tops together by hand and hang your onions on the beams in the drying barn. Warm the drying barn with a little juniper-twig fire, but see that it doesn't get too hot," directed Auntie Kerho.

Olle did as he was told. When the onions had been dried in the harvest baskets made out of shingles, they were put into sacks and weighed, and behold! There were 130 kilos! He paid his father thirty kilos for his work with the horse and he gave thirty kilos to his mother for all her help planting and weeding. The rest, seventy kilos, he sold to the cooperative store for four marks per bag or 280 marks in all. What a thrill!

The boy rolled the new paper money in his hands and put it under his pillow for the night. Next morning he wrote to Uncle Kukka:

> I have been so lonesome for you. The sleigh for the horse is broken. Come to our house soon. I still know those songs of God's children. I am enclosing 100 marks to pay for your trip. I got it for onions I raised. Remember to come. God's peace. Olle.

The uncle did come. He kept services all week at Olle's house. The children swarmed around him during the day and the adults gathered around him in the evenings. In the daytime, his skillful hands carved wooden horses, cows, dogs and sheep. In the evenings, God opened the door of his word and gave birth to children unto himself under the gospel word.

"This is sweet onion rain!" said the old preacher with tears of love in his eyes.

WHEN GOD BLESSED THE SEED

When the sun peeked into the Paanas' living room, it saw two ragged and pale youths. Phil and Gene had experienced real hunger during the winter. Father had worked various weekly jobs but Mother had been ill, and Father's meager wages were eaten up for medicines and finally for the hospital.

Now Mother was finally home but she was weak and tired quickly. She sat wearily in her rocking chair and was hardly able to smile at her boys' play.

They had had a hard winter in the Paana cottage but God's sun shone warmly again. Bare spots in the field got bigger every day. The brooks chuckled happily. The finch flitted nimbly in the birch trees around the house and puffed out its red breast and trilled its brightest song.

One morning as he was leaving for work, Father said, "The vegetable garden should be started, but poor Mother isn't able and I don't have time." The boys heard. Father's words rang in Phil's ears all day. That evening he asked hesitantly, "Dad, do you think we would be strong enough to work up that vegetable field?"

"Probably," decided Father. "Tomorrow I will get out the tools for you and give you some directions."

Next morning, Father gave the youths each a spade and showed them how to turn over the soil. It was sweaty business. As they turned the soil, the spades sometimes reached white frost. The work was hard and Gene threatened to quit, but when he saw his sweet mother watching through the window he again shoved his spade down clear to the frost. An odd feeling moved in his breast. A starling fluttered onto a bit of sod, pecked at something there and flew away, but the boys hardly had time to eat.

When Father arrived home from work that evening, the garden soil was all turned. Mother's supper stew barely went around, yet there was happiness in Father and Mother's eyes. Even though the sun was sinking to another place, the living room seemed to be flooded with the brightness of summer. "You know, these toddlers will become **men**!" mused their father. And a warm emotion was surging in the boys' breasts, too.

On the second morning Father instructed that plenty of manure from behind the barn should be spread over yesterday's newly turned soil. The boys found a small hauling box and undertook to do the work. It was heavy, dirty work and their hands were already sore from their work the day before. Mother moved onto the porch to sit in the sun with her knitting, giving the boys extra incentive.

On the third day the manure was turned over and mixed into the soil. Father came home a bit early from his work and took a spade to work at finishing the edges of the plot.

The fourth day was sowing day. The boys raked the soil evenly and cleaned out bits of stick and roots of weeds. Toward evening the wind quieted.

Father had promised to arrive in time for planting, so the boys waited impatiently for him. When he finally came, he praised the boys' work and told them his plan.

"Let's leave half of the field for potatoes. We will plant them later. For now, we will plant starting from this edge. First a row of lettuce, this little flat white seed." Then he took a stout cord from his pocket, gave one end to Phil and told him to take it to the far edge of the garden. Along the line, Father scratched a straight little furrow about one centimeter deep, using a little stick. Into the little furrow the boys dribbled seeds. Father covered the seeds with the back of the rake, carefully pulling fine dirt over the seeds and then patting them down. The the cord was held for another row about 35 centimeters from the first. They sowed carrot seeds in this one. They planted many rows of carrots and then beets, each row 35 centimeters from the other. There was lots of squatting and their backs became tired, but the work had to be done before the church bells rang on Sunday.[1]

Father looked at the spring sowing and his face turned ever so serious. The boys thought they saw something glimmering brightly in his eyes. "Dear God, bless the seeds in the field," he asked. Phil and Gene's dirty hands were folded. Mother came out on the porch: "Come, men, and have some stew." Her voice seemed to be unsteady also.

It was a different Saturday evening. The food tasted good. The bath tasted good. Sleep tasted good. Sunday morning came bright, light and peaceful. The Paana boys knew for the first time the joy of work.

But they weren't through. There was something to do all summer. There was weeding, very slow and tedious work, but Phil and Gene's determination held up. There was grubbing and hoeing of the soil. Then there was thinning that must be done, leaving 7 centimeters between carrots and 10 centimeters between beets.

God in his goodness gave sunshine and rain. First, little green spikes and oh so tiny leaflets peeked from the ground, but with the passing days the leaves of the beets became as broad as a man's hand and the roots as fat as a man's fist and the roots of the carrots like giants' fingers.

One Saturday in the fall they got ready to harvest. They had been eating potatoes since the middle of July and carrots and beets all through the month of August. Now it appeared that they would have a **really** bountiful harvest. According to Father's weighing, there were 350 kilos of potatoes and they had eaten 60 kilos during the summer; that meant a total of 410 kilos! And then there were 500 kilos of carrots and beets.

"Now," said Father, "quickly figure how much you earned. Those potatoes would cost at least 40 pennies per kilo at the store and the carrots and red beets 60 pennies per kilo."

"We'll have to have pencil and paper," protested Phil.

Father chuckled. "And a little elementary arithmetic, too. Boys, you have earned over 464 marks for us!" "Oh, wow!" burst from the boys together as from one mouth. Indeed, God had blessed the seed.

---

[1] See Exodus 20:8-10 and note the parallel in the story.

THE THOLE-PIN

As Mother Anna looked sadly out at the open sea, a freezing north wind beat on her face. Gray clouds in the wintry cold sky extended down behind the southerly edge of the woods. High foam-crested waves boomed onto the ice-covered rocks on the shore. The month of October was coming to a close and whitefish were plentiful. Despite the fact that Mother had tried to dissuade him, Brother went with his neighbor, Thomas, to fish for spawning whitefish. They **could** have gone--in fact Fishing Inspector Niira had begged them to go--to milk spawn at the nearest fish hatchery.[1]

The boy's confirmation school would begin on the first day of November. Brother did poorly with his lessons in the spring at the parish catechism examination. The pastor encouraged him to study hard before school began in the fall but the books were left untouched, such was the pull of the water for the young man. Mother hoped to talk with her first-born about those serious matters to which he would have to give answer in front of the Lord and the congregation in the coming fall. That is why she was sadly gazing now at the heaving boat bobbing in the surging sea, struggling to get to the Gullsound fish camp.

Brother rowed into the wind with difficulty. Thomas also pulled with his steering oar from time to time. Slowly the boat worked its way toward the rocky island camp. Often the crests of the billows splashed over the edge. The gunwales shone icy. The water in the bottom froze. The pace of the rower remained steady; obviously the boy was in a situation that suited him. When icy water drenched his seat now and then, he just laughed. The main thing was that the little barrel holding the net would stay protected so that the nets, dried in the smoking sauna, would not get wet and frozen.

At last the boat banged hard into the camp-shore dock. They loaded their lunch on board and were once again on the water. Thomas moved to the oars. It was Brother's turn to stand at the proper place to haul the icy nets into the boat. They could see that the spawning run was at its peak. From six 30-meter nets, they lifted seventy-two nice whitefish. What would they see in the morning when they looked at twenty-one nets taking that prime catch!

It began to get calmer toward evening. The nets ran out smoothly from Brother's freezing fingers into the water beneath the overhanging rock formations.

"There may be ice to chop in the morning before we can use the boat," guessed Thomas.

"Probably," agreed Anna's oldest.

---

[1] Ed.: Spawn (fish eggs from the females) and the fertilizing milt (from the males) are gently squeezed or "milked" from captured adult fish for use in raising hatchery fish. If the adults are hatchery stock, they may then be returned to the water. In this story, the "milking" involved fish which were then intended for the kitchen.

Satisfied, the youths made their way to the fishing hut. Brother set a lighted candle on the table. Thomas fetched some dry pitch-wood and some birch-bark from a familiar hiding place. Soon a steady fire crackled in the fireplace and its flames caressed the black cheeks of the coffee pot. The boys munched their lunches while the hut warmed up. Brother hung his trousers in front of the fire to dry. It felt good to stretch out their tired limbs on the benches and then quietly wait for sleep.

The wood, now mostly coals, crackled here and there and finally tumbled still deeper into the coals. The light of the flames gradually flickered more weakly on the ceiling and the log walls. The warmth became more even, with a more soothing effect, pleasant and relaxing. The room grew dimmer and dimmer. The waves still broke hard on the rocks, covering the end of the dock with ice-works.

"I'll bet your old mother was left grumbling," yawned Thomas.

"Never mind!" was the curt reply which he heard. Brother had just thought of the same thing and his conscience tended to hurt a little. It had been eased to some extent with the thoughts: "Wouldn't it have been wrong to quit fishing at the best time? Can't I read twice as much when I get to school? The others don't pay any attention to the pastor's suggestions either."

Now Thomas had pulled the covers off the thought and Brother's conscience ached again. "Brother didn't **have** to come! Had not Father promised to go with Thomas? Mother very likely had something besides his lessons on her mind. Had she not hinted all summer long about the importance of the confirmation period and her fears that her son would sink into having a hardened conscience?" Sleep was a long time coming.

The open, spread-out camp took care of arousing the campers. Shivering and chilly, the boys quickly gulped their morning coffee and ate their bread and butter and salted whitefish and then hurried to their fishing.

It was hard work to break the ice off some of the nets but the inconvenience did not damper their enthusiasm. The nets came in perfectly, filled with the silvery whitefish. The catch was more than 210 fish! The big wooden fish box began to fill up and the seagulls made happy cries and chatter. As the wind freshened, the morning grew lighter and lighter. They heard the chugging of a motor from the direction of Great Point. Inspector Niira was coming for his morning "milking."

The boys already had the net stored in the shed. Next the boat was pulled beside the dock. Thomas drew it toward the rock on the shore. Brother stepped on the thwart, straightened out his legs and jumped to the high dock. The boards of the dock were icy. Stiff from cold, Brother slipped and was thrown between the dock and the boat and onto the boat. His head banged hard against the side of the boat where the thole-pins were stuck in their holes to make fingers which held the oars. He was knocked unconscious. Thomas was petrified with terror; it looked to him as though the sharp hard thole-pin had pierced Brother's temple!

The fallen one eventually stirred. He got up with difficulty and, white-faced, started to crawl toward the shack. With relief, Thomas saw that the thole-pin had not penetrated Brother's head after all.

"Thank God!" escaped from the boy instinctively and earnestly. When Niira arrived at the rocky island, he met two very sober people beside their great catch. Inspector Niira extracted a whole wash-basin full of roe from the few brood-fish he squeezed. He poured water into the yellow mixture and stirred his "porridge" with great ceremony. He poured off the water and added fresh water to stir it again. This he repeated until the rinsing water was no longer cloudy. He poured this cleansed roe into a milk can and set it out as "tobacco."

"I suppose you'll come again tomorrow night with your nets?" he asked.
"Oh, no we won't," answered Brother, feeling the lump on his head.
"You're not taking offense at my joke, surely?"
"There is confirmation school."
"But that doesn't begin till the day after tomorrow."
"Well, there are other reasons we won't come again."
"Well, if not, so be it," laughed the state inspector for fish preservation. "And thank you for the excellent porridge. For sure now, whitefish will multiply even more because of it." Niira turned his outboard motor toward open water, waved his fur hat, started his motor and was off, chugging toward Boyhood John's fishing waters. Soon the boys' boat also was off, flying with the wind toward home.

"That was God protecting us," said Thomas.

"It was, truly."

"Do you know what I remembered after I was knocked out?" asked Brother at the oars.

"How should I know?"

"It jumped into my head about when Jesus told Peter to follow and that he would make them to be fishers of men."

The Brother who related this story has travelled through the land as a dedicated preacher since long before I write it for you now.

THE RELUCTANT OUTBOARD MOTOR

We were driving around Stony Lake's lovely straits and open seas with our old outboard motor which was a gift from dear friends. It had served us faithfully for many years, but now it was sometimes troublesome--like a case of rheumatism in old folks.

So it was now. At first we just couldn't get it going. We turned this thing and that. I yanked the starter rope and, "Putt, putt, putt - - putt, putt - - putt." Then it stopped. We tried again and again and again. Sweat dripped from my forehead under my familiar dirty gray fishing hat. My fingers got black and blue and old cracks opened in the knuckles.

Finally it started and we whizzed forward as brilliant reflections shone around us in the waters. On the shores the birch were thrusting out their first buds. The weathered grass in the meadows took on a new green look. Men were harrowing the fields to cover the seeds and swallows swept over the surface of the water. The motor purred smoothly. Delighted, I straightened out my back and let the soft breeze dry my face.

Suddenly, the motor began to run even worse than before. It jerked and balked; it huffed and puffed. It slowed and then raced violently. Then it sputtered mischievously and stopped. I pulled hard on the starter rope--a little lurch forward, a pop, and it stopped. We were stalled for some time. A bit ahead of us on our course a rowboat came closer, then drew away again. My forehead was wet with sweat again and the skin of my thumb knuckle came off. The "Old Adam" brought me close to swearing.

Victor drummed on the oars and wondered a bit, "Is this the end of the motor that earns us a living?" The motor was now completely silent; it wouldn't even give a cough. The wind was calm enough for mirror reflections on the lake and then arose just enough to nudge us toward Pioneer Head.

I examined the needle valve and could find no defect there. I unscrewed the spark plug. Aha! It was wet and very dirty. I cleaned and dried it with care. When everything was tightly in place, I pulled on the starter rope. The motor started at once and ran steadily. We continued the trip toward the fishing hut in the cool of the evening.

While I waited to fall asleep, gazing at the fire going out in the fireplace, I thought about myself. "Am I like that machine, stiff-necked, obstinate, ready to be junked?" That is how we Christians, big and little, old and young, often really are.

How difficult it is to start off on that journey to Heaven's harbor. God surely can bother one's conscience in one way or another. But He is patient. He continues his work until New Life in Christ begins, and a soul embarks by grace on the way to that blissful eternity.

But we are still obstinate on the journey, even though we are under the care of the guardian. We are poor at staying in line even in the hands of the

Master. Our consciences become soiled. If we cover up the stains and defend them, the river of grace is cut off from our souls. Our faith is strengthened when we find strength to confess like children for the forgiveness of our sins in Jesus' blood and to live in the light and walk in repentance before people. Then the candles are kindled again and we can fight against the storms of the world. We are in the care of him whose hands are beautified by nail holes. The prow of our boat is turned toward an eternally sheltered harbor.

THE CUCUMBER FIELD

The village of Hallilammi was growing fast. A railroad was being built and the place was alive everywhere with strangers. Even the smallest hut was crammed full of short-time renters. Grocery prices rose. Most people rejoiced over the new "good times," but some of the small-scale farmers became skeptical and cautious.

The folk who lived on the Pentfield place were depressed. The old steady, secure way of life seemed to be disappearing. Ungodliness such as they had never known increased and spread rapidly. Drunks brawled from Saturday evening till Monday morning. The clamor of dance-halls was heard late into the night.

The master of the Pentfield house sighed heavily as he went to lock his doors. The Pentfields kept a vigil in the back room on nights like this. Mother and Father carried their children in prayer before the Lord and talked with each other in whispers about the dangers which threatened their children's souls. They were especially concerned for Kullervo, who was to be confirmed in the spring. His spiritual welfare was upon their hearts. If only they could think of some interesting, challenging work to occupy his time, there wouldn't be such an attraction to "go visiting."

Father pondered. "What if we give him a piece of land to cultivate as his own? It would be close to home and things from the garden would surely sell well."

"We could let him keep what he earns," suggested Mother.

"Good. That's what we will do."

Kullervo was enthusiastic about the idea. When he finished working for Father for the day, he would press on with work in his own field, often late into the night. He had already planted radishes, red beets and carrots when their neighbor Anja stopped one evening to watch over the fence as he worked. Anja was the the wife of one of the construction engineers.

"So, you are keeping busy becoming a gardener here?" she greeted him cordially. Kullervo assented bashfully.

"I suppose we can buy garden produce from you next summer, then?"

"Oh, yes, surely you can get them here," he responded.

"Now that would be a good place to grow cucumbers! It has a warm protected southern slope and on the north side, the building and a thick spruce grove to protect from the wind. And our grandpa **loves** cucumbers!" she added.

"I've never even seen cucumbers. How would I know how to grow them?"

"Oh, I'll come over some evening and help you. There is no hurry to plant them yet. I'll order the seeds. Just leave a strip of land about 2 1/2 meters wide on this side of the house, right under the window." And the enthusiastic lady waved a lively goodbye and was soon far down the forest path.

Anja kept her word. One May evening, she showed up with a little bag of seeds in her hand and then the diligent work began! Anja used the cover of the seed package for paper to sketch the criss-crossing of the cucumber ridges. At the same time, she explained that the rows were to be terraced in tiers, like steps.

"That square in the middle should be compacted manure. Do you understand? Good! Now then we will use a rope to mark the ridges, two meters apart. In between, we will mark a pathway 30 centimeters wide. Now, bring old rotted horse manure to the center of each bed---about 30-40 centimeters deep and across for each bed. That's the way. You carry great loads!" said the enthusiastic instructor. "Now, spade soil in from each side so that there will be 25 centimeters of dirt with the manure."

Kullervo shoveled until his shoulders steamed with sweat. Anja meanwhile enjoyed a cup of coffee which Mother offered.

"All right, now the ridges are ready," Anja approved. "Now we'll mix this nitrogen-phosphorus fertilizer evenly into that loose surface, about 15-20 centimeters deep. There is some in that little sack which the workmen brought into the yard just a minute ago."

Anja got involved herself in mixing the strong fertilizer into the loose, moist soil. "Now, make a furrow on these terraces with a hoe, and water them like this. Then I want to plant this way myself, always two seeds in each spot, about 7 to 10 centimeters apart. Damn! **Three** went in at a time!" cried out the planter.

Kullervo flushed. "You shouldn't swear," he said seriously. "Father says fields do not grow with curses." The lady also sobered.

"Pardon me. Excuse me. It is an ugly habit. You are believing folk?"
"We are."
"Let's go on by sprinkling loose dirt over the seeds just a half centimeter deep, in rows. We'll discuss the matter in a friendly way later."

Just then, Anja heard from behind her, "May the Lord bless the seeds in the earth and grant refreshing rain." Father had appeared. He explained, "That's how they have prayed at these tenant farmer's fields from the time of my late grandfather, and our good Father has marvelously heard our sighs."

Anja suddenly turned red and had trouble continuing with her work. A shadow like a flying black shuttle on the weaver's loom flitted past the sower of the seeds. "The first swallow!" Father roared joyfully.

"Ah, perhaps spring has come!" exclaimed Anja, straightening her back.

Soon the seed leaves popped out in the terraces. Wherever two appeared side by side, Kullervo picked off the weaker one. Once a week, the boy watered his plants with a mixture of 20 grams of nitro-phosphorus to ten liters of water. He had to be very careful with this so that the concentrated fertilizer did not touch the leaves. When the weather was dry, he watered the plants every evening. Kullervo tested with his hand that the water temperature was the same as the air.

One morning, during the week before midsummer, the wind shifted to the north and the raw air really raised goosebumps all over. Then the biting wind quieted toward evening. The bright cold cover of heaven turned out to rise even higher.

Little swallows sought shelter by the wall to gather the day's last sunshine to their white breasts. They twittered to each other with heads tilted as they complained of the cold.

"It could come on Midsummer night," siad Father solemnly.

"We'll have to cover the cucumber plants with sacks," decided the boy. "We know that cucumbers are especially tender."

But after midnight the Heavenly Father brought a thick cloud in from the western sky. After raising his threatening head, Jack Frost finally sank back into the mud, taking his little urchins with him.

The first yellow cucumber blossoms appeared on the first of July. About that time, Kullervo pruned the tips off his plants. Blossom after blossom fell off, and in their places appeared tiny hairy, green cucumbers. The engineer's wife had instructed that now the sprinkling of the nitro-phosphorus water must cease. The young gardener placed spruce twigs under the runners and the beginning fruit. And how the cucumbers grew! They sucked the sun and the warmth of the air into their roots, bringing nourishment from the moist fertile soil. They looked like longish green lumps, with rough creased skin.

"Now we can have a taste!" exclaimed Anja when she came to look one August morning. She cut one of the largest cucumbers with her knife. "See, it is almost crisp already."

"I wonder if it perhaps tastes like an apple," wondered Kullervo. Mother and Anja whispered in the kitchen for a minute. Then buttered rye bread with slices of cucumber appeared on the living room table. Kullervo eagerly took a bite, and did the delicious bread and freshly-churned butter ever disappear! But the sliced cucumber, an example of a gentleman's delicacy, was almost too good to eat. Anja looked on, her eyes twinkling. She ate heartily, praising the cucumber's excellent taste.

"Well, it **might** taste good," Mother admitted.

"That's how it is," confirmed Father. "Many healthy foods taste strange when you first eat them, but they become necessities as time goes by. Our Christianity is like that, too. It is a healthy treat for an anxious or uneasy person. Yet it must seem a bit odd or even bitter to you, Anja, when we mention first one thing and then another which is most precious to our hearts."

"Yes, yes," conceded the guest, who looked for a long time through the window with tears showing in her eyes.

The cucumber yield increased daily. Anja and her husband and other workmen's wives came, competing with one another to buy cucumbers. Other garden produce went along with them. When Kullervo finally figured his earnings in late fall, he had 478.50 marks all clear! That was something! "May I really keep this all for myself?" the boy inquired, his cheeks aglow.

"Yes, you may," affirmed his father. "For Mother and me, the most precious things are that we have had you at home and the good God has kept your heart in faith and your conscience clean."

In August, the engineer and his wife moved to a new place. Anja left knowing that she had been a little help to those around her. She also knew that she had been touched by that kingdom which shows itself through righteousness, peace and joy in the Holy Ghost.

THE RETURN

A small hill covered with fir trees rose near the house gate. Recent rains and periods of sunshine had melted snow from its southern slopes. Dark stems of the heather threaded themselves around the gnarled pine roots. The loganberry leaves were still green and here and there showed a flash of bright red berry highlighted by the sun. Again today the sun shone pleasantly warm and the fir trees gave off the pleasant pitch smell. The ice was melted from the road and everywhere rivulets ran into ditches from big puddles. Seven-year-old Henry stood in the calm of the pines watching the road.

The sandy soil in front of him was all cleared of grass and roots. Along the road was the whole Mannerheim Line[1] of defense, a division each at Taipale and Summa. Trenches just wide enough for a running soldier wound between the boulders, with machine-gun bunkers in the bends. Behind the boggy area were two grenade-launchers. A whole battery of cannon was protected by another swamp higher up the hill. A zigzag barrier of barbed wire stretched in front of the emplacement, with oblong stones standing upright along either side to protect from a tank attack. Two dugouts carefully reinforced with alder branches were behind the front line, with spruce cone soldiers standing watch at their stations. Everything was in order. Let the evil enemy come!

This was where Henry and Charles worked and played all winter. During his period of convalescence, Uncle Paul worked with them as their busy supervisor. Uncle Paul had fought at Taipale; Father was with the infantry in the front lines at Summa.

The winter had been amazing to Henry in every way. Last fall, the police came in the middle of the night to knock on the door. Henry had awakened to see Mother, teary-eyed, packing clothes into Father's Home Guard knapsack. She packed a New Testament on the very top. Then Father had pressed his cheek against Henry's, saying: "God's Peace, son. Grow up to be a capable man."

Mother had jumped up and put her arms around Father's neck and blessed him. Father then quickly swung the knapsack onto his back and hung the rifle on his shoulder with the gun-sling. He briefly touched their cheeks with his hand and the door creaked shut.

Henry had looked solemnly at Mother and asked, "Did Daddy start off for communion service?"

"What do you mean?"

"Well, you blessed each other just now."

"Yes, maybe so. Go back to sleep now."

"Or did Daddy go to army reserve training exercises?"

"Perhaps he did. Only a little more than training." Just **try** to understand what adults say! Mother and Father had been so mysterious all winter!

Henry did know that Father had been detained "there" somewhere. Henry's Uncle Paul had gone "there" also, and Stephen Mattson and Big Victor and many other uncles. Cards for Henry and letters for Mother came now and then, sent from places like Dugout Hill and Rock Stump Camp and others. Henry scribbled his greetings and wishes, "May the Heavenly Father bless my father," tucked into letter which Mother sent. Henry noticed that many of Mother's tears had fallen between the lines of the letters.

One January evening, Uncle Paul appeared in their living room, his right hand bound with a large white bandage. The evil enemy had shot it with his rifle. Uncle was very subdued. He did not swear even once!

Sunday night Uncle went to Torvola to church with Mother. It was said that he became a believer. Certainly he was more tender. That was the time when he spent all his time with Henry and Charles up at the pine hill. It was then that the whole gallant Mannerheim Line with all its dugouts and fortifications was begun. Frost nipped the tips of the boys' noses and made it difficult to widen the trenches for all of the dugouts. The shouts of play could be heard in the living room and far down the road. Many a parent passing by heard the noise and turned around to wonder.

"That's Pine Hill Front. Imagine what the racket is like where there is actually the real battle!" someone said.

"Right, you can't imagine," responded Uncle Paul and he suddenly quit laughing.

Finally Uncle Paul had to say good-bye. His hand was healed and the white bandage was gone. "God's Peace, boys," he said, lifting each youngster from the ground and gazing warmly into their eyes. "When you grow up big, build even stouter barriers of iron and concrete at the borders so that mothers may do their household chores in peace." Then he leaned against the pine tree and looked into the distance at the Koliman expanse, with tears running down his cheeks.

Only two weeks later, Uncle Paul returned. Isaac, the old hired man, went and fetched him from the station in a white casket. Mother, the other aunts, Charles and Henry sat right on the first bench in church. Mother cried and Charles sniffled. They brought a wreath of sprigs of fir, with clusters of scarlet mountain ash berries tied on with light blue ribbons. Mother and Henry laid some yellow flowers brought from town onto the grave.

"God's Peace, Brother!" Mother said sadly. Just then Henry recalled how his uncle once leaned against a tree on Jack Pine Hill. Gazing at Jack Pine Hill, Henry burst out crying.

Back in the sleigh, Henry gave a fierce look into his mother's eyes. Sounding like a grown-up man, he promised: "When Charles and I are big, we will built at the borders such barriers that...." "God grant that it may be so," Mother responded, squeezing her son's hand.

Next morning a hero's grave was dug under the only birch on Jack Pine Hill. Charles' favorite beautiful tin soldier was laid there in a match-box coffin. Spruce tree twigs and mountain ash berry clusters were placed on top of the mound of earth. Some time later a cairn of polished rock appeared, a hero's memorial.

"I wonder what poor soul's death that is for," Tina Tupala remarked as she walked past. "I think that surely Henry's father will be brought home soon."

But he was not brought home. Instead the enemy's birds came! It was a terrible day! Henry and Charles were just conducting the changing of the guard on Jack Pine Hill. Suddenly the local blacksmith began pounding furiously on the iron triangle hanging from a branch of the big pine in his yard. They could hear church bells clang afar off.

Isaac drove past at breakneck speed with his load of hay, shouting an alarm, "An air attack is coming!" as he glanced back at the sky. Great huge gray birds came thundering overhead. Terrible fright seized Henry.[2]

"On your knees, Charles!" he ordered and the boys sank to their knees, flattening one trench and two machine-gun bunkers.

"Help us, Heavenly Father! Help me, Henry, and Mother and the whole country of Finland!" he yelled. "You too cry out!" he ordered his speechless comrade.

"God can hear, even if we **don't** shout," returned Charles. Mother found the youths just then and led them off to the shelter of the potato cellar.

In the morning they heard that yesterday Captain Sorvo had shot down four enemy aircraft flying over Koliman. "God **did** hear when I cried aloud," Henry told Charles that evening as they repaired the broken equipment and completed the changing of the guard.

The family knew that Father had been slightly wounded once and had been detained at the patrol, even though the war ended some time ago. Henry sighed and continued to watch the road. It was time for the bus, but the bus was always late. Now it finally came round the bend in the road, dashing so that it spattered mud. Would it go past as it had so many times? No, it slowed and stopped. A soldier jumped to the road from the back door of the bus.

"Dad!" Henry jumped up to run but stumbled over the supply dump of a machine-gun battery. Panting and trembling, he scrambled up and raced down the hill. The soldier put down the items he carried in his hands and met the child, hugging the youth in his arms. Henry felt the bearded face wet against his.

The bus stood still as riders gazed through the windows. Mrs. Daavetilla, whose husband had been brought home in a casket last winter, sobbed aloud.

Mother was watching through the living room window when she saw father and son start down the lane. She rose to run gaily to meet them but her knees gave way and she only sat pale in the face watching the door. Father set down Henry at the door and walked slowly across the floor as though approaching an invalid. When he reached his wife, he knelt before her and laid his head in her lap.

"Thank God!"

"Thank God!" she echoed.

But Henry looked on in alarm. "Father! Take your rifle from your back before you poke Mother in the eye!"

"Right, son," laughed his father and his mother smiled too through tears pouring down her cheeks. The rifle thumped into the familiar gun-rack.

"If only it were never needed again," sighed Mother.

"May the Lord grant your wish," Father said, looking through the living room window over fields to the shore beyond, past the sauna to where the water shimmers on the reef.

"But if these fields and these docks are again threatened without cause, I'll take my rifle again at my government's command. If I am not able any longer to carry it, Henry, you take it from the rack onto your shoulder and start down there where your father just came from! Right, son?" And Father swung round, lifted Henry in his arms and looked into his eyes with warmth.

"And we will build a stout border line with steel and concrete," threatened the youth.

"Oh, you heroes!" laughed Mother.

---

[1] Field Marshal Baron Carl Gustaf Mannerheim, Finland's highest-ranked military commander and later Finland's president.

[2] See Appendix on Finnish History.

LITTLE GERTRUDE'S WREATH

Peter and Paul were at the oars, wearing their soldiers' uniforms. Father manned the stern of the boat and Mother sat in the middle. On one side of Mother was fashionable Big Sister, just arrived from the city, with a beautiful flowered wreath in her lap. Little Gertrude huddled on the other side, leaning a little against her mother. Gertrude had a buttercup bouquet in her hand, tied with blue and yellow paper ribbons. Written on the yellow ribbon in clumsy small-child's writing was this message: **TO MY HERO BROTHER   GERTRUDE**

Big Sister wore a proper mourning veil. She was rather vain about it and fussed with it often. At that time there was honor in having a hero-brother. She grieved in solemn dignity. She cried briefly and neatly when guests deplored the family's misfortune. She scolded the family over the preparations to attend the funeral. Her mother only had a black scarf for her head and a clean handkerchief around her hymnbook as she usually did for the trip to church.

"Mother, **must** you still wind your book into a bundle like a child?" Big Sister tossed her head as they departed. "And you, Gertrude, throw those flower buds into the trash!" Mother turned away without answering and Gertrude burst into tears.

"Allow us to keep our customs," Father said gently, though he was annoyed. "Try not to be annoyed."

Paul growled a little and lifted his little sister into his lap. "Don't cry, Gertrude," he consoled. "If George saw these, I'm certain that he would rejoice more over your pretty flowers than over fancy wreaths. Would you have brought these spring buttercups if I were the one who had fallen?"

"I would! I surely would have." Gertrude stopped crying and was cheerful again.

"Yes but what will people think?" Big Sister muttered.

"We are people, too. We may even be closer than the others," Paul concluded the discussion.

That is why they sat in silence the rest of the trip. The boys pulled steadily and vigorously. Father helped at times with his steering oar. But Big Sister sat with her back stiff and straight and with an offended and disdainful expression on her face. "Everything here in the country has to be so old fashioned! They just don't know what's up-to-date. Phooey!"

Mother had done her crying earlier in the winter. Today she only gazed absent-mindedly at the ridge; her face was pale but there were no tears. Gertrude looked past Cliff Island, still rocky here, at its docks, its wharves and at its seines, those large fishing nets with floats along the top edge and weights along the bottom. The birch trees were bright today in their brand new pale green attire. A sandpiper flew from rock to rock and piped dolefully. One could occasionally see fish swimming to and fro under the flat calm surface of the water.

Gertrude remembered spring fishing trips when the boys had taken her with them. George bundled her up warmly in the prow of the boat. They cooked coffee together over the campfire by the dock while Peter and Paul were out at their traps. George whittled a whistle for her from a weeping willow branch and then he hummed: "From a willow I made a weeping flute, a weeping flute."

She recognized a place where they fished for carp and perch with hook and line. Happy shouts carried over the pools and narrow channels of the water. They competed with each other to show the most admiration for the catch of the other two, who glowed with happiness over their catch in the nets and the weir. (The weir was a fence woven of sticks and brush in a channel to make a trap for fish.)

Gertrude saw the point of a cape where they made a campfire at one time. They hid on that island once when a surprise rainstorm overtook them. They took cover under their upside-down boat while they lit a campfire which never burned well. Here she saw a place where George caught a big pike on a trolling spoon. A storm once threw their boat into that bay over there; at Paul's command, they all fell on their faces to pray for God's help.

Now George was no longer. He and his brothers volunteered to go in the reserves. "I **have** to go!" he had exclaimed resolutely.

"If you must, then go in faith," his father acquiesced.

Afterward they had held going-away services. The boys begged to hear forgiveness preached by Mother and Father. Then they hugged Gertrude around her neck, saying, "You also forgive us, sis, for when we have teased you."

"You have always been so good to me. But believe sins forgiven in Jesus' name and blood," answered Gertrude. Then they sang together: "We are on this earthly journey, homeward bound for Heaven fair." They sank to their knees beside chairs and benches. Father prayed on behalf of the boys, the family, the people of the whole nation of Finland and their beloved fatherland.

Gertrude came back to the present, crying. Mother caressed her hand and still looked out to the open sea. "Why do you cry?" asked Paul, rowing nearest to her.

"I remember George and our fishing trips!"

"Me too."

Father's chin trembled as he steered the boat into a slight curve with his oar. They pushed on toward the narrow channel to the church as the church bells began to ring. Peter began singing, "We are on this earthly journey..." Paul joined in and Father hummed with them. Gertrude overcame her crying and sang with them in a lovely child's voice. Big Sister remained silent and annoyed. Mother's face trembled again with emotion; she could not sing.

A sister in the congregation came to meet the Konlonniemen family at the door of the church. She squeezed each one's hand with a kind twinkle in her eye and directed them to the front seats. Big Sister walked first in line, very dignified. Mother came last, leading Gertrude by the hand.

Gertrude did not grasp the pastor's words and barely heard the hymns. She just stared ahead. On the altar were white lilies. Sixty-four candles burned on the railing, lighted in memory of the congregation's heroes. The one on the end, nearest the door to the sacristy, was for George. Word that he had fallen in battle arrived last. His candle burned with a flickering flame and almost went out when the door was opened.

Suddenly Gertrude jerked to attention. She heard the minister saying from his pulpit: "Look at the candles on the rail. They are lighted there as symbols of the sacrificial flame which burned in the hearts of the dead heroes of our congregation. Fifty-four have already been covered by the earth in our cemetery here at home. This divine service today is our last heavy task. It is our duty of love to bless by this heroes' funeral the distant resting place of ten such heroes who were left on the battlefield. They are Master Sergeant George Konlonniemen, Sergeants Matt Luokkonen and Sulo Tuuraniemi, Privates..." He named them all.

Big Sister leaned over to Peter: "Did you notice? George was named first! Was he really a master sergeant?"

But Peter was silent. He was remembering how his younger brother had led the troop in a major counter-attack at Taipale. His face was resolute and his voice bright and clear: "Peter, bring your rapid-fire gun into position over here. There is the enemy's machine-gun emplacement. Fire when ready!" Paul crowded with them into a protected corner. "Paul, don't have your boys killed needlessly! Assault the enemy from behind those rocks! Ho, boys, up and at them, up, forward! Hey-oh!"

Peter remembered the last time, after midnight, when George sneaked into his dugout. He put his arms around Peter's neck, saying, "I'm going out on patrol again. I have a strange feeling it may be the last time. Bless me again. Bring greetings of God's peace to Mother and Father, Tyynie, Gertrude and Paul!" The boy did not return from that trip. He slept on the battlefield with the blessed. His comrades right to the end were too exhausted to bring back his body.

Bright warm spring skies were over the waters surrounding the area of the parish church, the overgrown old cemetery and the hero's grave. Flags hung from their flagpoles in pretty folds. The senior clergyman of that parish, a grim-faced greying man himself wounded in battle, stepped to the head of the grave under its flags. Hundreds of voices powerfully sang out the old battle-hymn: "I am wretched, a worm, a traveler on earth." Little Gertrude felt like collapsing where she was, so touched by the overwhelming ceremony. She hardly heard the beginning of the funeral sermon but suddenly the words reached her.

"Look and behold how the summer-like sun radiates a blessing over the beautiful part of the country where he was born. Look at the familiar open blue seas with their islands and peninsulas. Look at your young tender crops just come up and at your flowering meadows. God's blessing, the gift of God's grace in creation, covers the whole earth, the same earth where these blessed heroes now sleep in their far-off resting places. The land there is blessed earth of God's holy fields.

"Remember that God's sacrificial Lamb took away the sins of the world on the cross of Golgotha. By the grace of redemption, the whole world is consecrated earth where believing brothers sleep. But they will arise glorified, transfigured by that Lord who won the world's bitterest struggle and cried: 'It is finished!' There in that land of peace, all the exhausted warriors will sing a new song of the honor and glory and blessing of the Lamb.

"With these thoughts we bless you who have given all, you at these home burial grounds and you in your far-off resting place. Into the land God created and blessed with grace and redemption, into God's great field:

"Departed hero George; dust thou art and to dust thou shalt return. Jesus Christ our Saviour shall raise you on the last day.

"Departed hero Matt; dust thou art and..."

The face of the minister became radiant. These were his boys, his confirmation school children, his comrades in arms! All those around grieved as though they were one family joined together in a common distress.

After the battalion and village wreaths were laid, Big Sister Tyynie hurried to stand just to the side of the grave. She cried with real emotion as she spread the silk ribbons in a graceful fold. Then she read, subdued and solemn: "For our hero! You suffered much, endured much and at last arrived at peace. Father, Mother, Sisters and Brothers." Gertrude leaned hard against her mother. The buttercups were already wilted a bit; the whole bunch of flowers now looked rumpled and trivial. Perhaps Tyynie was right after all!

Many wreaths were brought, each more magnificent than the one before. Many had broad silk ribbons and were bigger than Big Sister's wreath. Finally it appeared that all wreaths were laid. Then Paul took Gertrude's hand and said cheerfully, "Now we go!" The girl looked shyly at her brother, but his face shone so kindly and his hand squeezed so securely that the little wreath-placer forgot her fears. She set her buttercups beside Big Sister's wreath and said very clearly and entirely from memory: "For my beloved hero brother. Gertrude."

Mother cried against Father's shoulder. Father clumsily wiped his eyes. Tears fell from the minister's eyes. Quiet sobbing was heard all through the multitude of the procession. Little Gertrude gazed around in amazement.

IN DARKNESS

Lauri received permission to go to his aunt's to play with his cousins. As they said goodbye, Mother begged him, "Now come home before five. It is late fall and it gets dark early, and besides it is cloudy and there is no moon. By six we might as well be in a sack."

"I know, I know," exclaimed the boy and with a delighted shout he happily waved goodbye.

His cousins suggested game after game and time passed quickly and unnoticed. "Hide and Seek" was at its height when Lauri noticed that dusk was creeping into the yard. "I really should go home," he thought, "but I'll play this one more game." He darted off to hide, but he was the first one caught. It would be embarrassing to quit then, since he was "it." So he called out his warning and set off to seek the "men" hiding in the woods. The darkness grew deeper and he became concerned. He gasped from tree to tree, but in the darkness it was hard to find those who were hiding, and cousin after cousin slipped by to the shelter of "home." Lauri was "it" again. Almost sobbing, he searched after the hidden ones. This time he was more lucky and was able to catch the first cousin.

At once he shouted, "All in free!" to the others, bade a hurried goodbye to his aunt and uncle and the cousins and broke into a run toward home. It was getting really dark and the way was difficult. It somewhat scared him right away and tears started in his eyes as the road left the open area. In the woods it was even darker and he had to feel his way forward carefully.

Suddenly he heard a car horn and headlights flashed around the bend. He hastily ducked to the left and fell into a water-filled ditch. The auto whizzed by. When Lauri crawled back onto the road, soaking wet, he really did feel like he was in a sack. Fighting back tears, he groped onward. Then he saw a glimmer of light from the Williamson's shack and with that as a guide he knew when to turn off the road onto the path that led home.

But now the difficulties really started. Here there were not even ditches to direct his path. Again and again he fell over rocks and stumps. Finally it seemed to him that the path came to an end and completely vanished from under his feet. He stood trembling and prayed with his head bowed: "Dear Heavenly Father, forgive my disobedience and help me yet this once to find my way home." Then he saw a light twinkling and oddly swaying between the trees. "Hey!" he hollered.

"Hello, hello," echoed the answer. It was his mother's voice. Mother had watched for him for some time and then started to meet him.

"Why did you stay so long?"

"I was playing with my cousins."

"Didn't you remember what I told you?"

"Yes, I remembered, but I didn't obey them. Forgive me, Mother!"

Mother set down the lantern, put her arms around Lauri, and blessed him. "Child, your sins are forgiven in Jesus' name and blood."

Then Mother marveled, "How did you get this far?"

"It was hard." Then Lauri related his experiences.

"Ah, yes, that is what this world is like," said his mother. "This kind of a dark night of sin covers the whole world, and yet we must press on toward the heavenly home through this kind of darkness. We cannot go forward without a light, but not all lights help us. The lights of the auto only blinded you. There are many such lights about us in the world. They dazzle us for a moment and then leave us beside the road more helpless than before. That's how it is with worldly amusement, with human praise and commendation, with riches and human wisdom.

"But it is safe to travel with this lantern. The path shows up for several yards ahead, but its light doesn't blind our eyes, not even for a moment. The Word of God is like a similar light on our road of life. Its light does not dazzle us with fine words of splendor and clever thinking, but it gives appropriate counsel and comfort in the difficult moments of life. In its light, our conscience sees all of the lurking dangers, all the temptations to sin. Then we know how to avoid them and thus find the narrow way between the stumps and stones which brings us home."

When they reached the home gate, a warm light from the fire at the living room hearth gleamed into the night air. Lauri grasped his mother's hand and squeezed it, intensely happy with his good fortune. "You are so good to me!"

Father noticed in wonder that evening at the hunger with which Lauri listened to the Old Testament psalm about the Good Shepherd. Lauri sang from the bottom of his heart: "Your word ever shines for us so that we may walk in its light, and finally from the valley of shadows we can arrive to be with Him in heaven."

JUDGMENT

On the evening of Judgment Sunday, Michael had a dream.[1]

In the dream it was midsummer and the sun swung low in a completely cloudless sky. Swallows shuttled between the heavens and the scorching hot ground. The purple pond was smooth as glass as the day became slightly dusk.

Believers were holding a meeting in Mikkola's yard. All the people from around the village of Tuukala were gathered, even the shoemaker who denied God! Some sat sprawled on the grass, some leaned against the fence around the yard and the steps to the granary were filled with people. Young boys sat on the ladder. Michael was among them, squatting on the bottom rung. Santtu from the cape spoke in a quavery old man's voice, every word penetrating clearly.

"If Christ should come now, this crowd would split in two. You ungrieving friend there would sink groaning into the ground, and from your lips would arise an endless cry of torment. You pretending friend, you who are carrying secret sins under the cloak of piety, you too would roll there as a worm! But you with pure feelings, you tired believer, you would be carried to where the sun shines brighter than at the crest of this hill."

"Same old hymn," murmured the shoemaker.

"The old man could vary his tune a bit," agreed Esa from Survi, who was sitting beside him.

"Once more we are being picked out and judged," complained the pious wives seated on the steps of the porch.

Just at that moment the earth shook. A strange light grew and became dazzling white over houses, fields, woods and water. There were no longer any shadows. Everyone suddenly raised up erect. The boys fell from the ladder. All others were frozen in their places. The ground shook again slowly as a strong gust of wind went over the yard. As it did a cry arose, piercing to the bone and marrow: "All people to judgment! All people to judgment! The Lord is coming! The Lord is coming!"

Michael looked up and saw angels. They descended onto the top of Kuolio Hill like an enormous flock of swans and set up a shining chair. A bright living being, too bright for a frightened boy to look at, seated itself on the shining chair. Michael's eyes grew big as he watched.

The angels floated across the hillside area and down toward the place of the services, some of them into the midst of the people. One now carried the old speaker toward that shining chair, that throne, and set him at the right side and then returned to his place. Santtu from the cape, seated there near the summit of the hill, changed to become as radiant as the one seated on the throne.

Over there, another angel dragged along struggling Justin of the Vale of Tears, who confessed faith but was a wine-drinker in secret. The poor wretch sank at the left side of the throne, his face turning to black as he grated his teeth. Soon he had for company the shoemaker and the pious women from the porch steps.

The angels brought more from those gathered for services, one after another, until the courtyard became empty. The number of the transfigured there at the right side of the hill grew larger, but that other crowd whose cries rent the air swelled even greater.

Michael trembled. Very early, the angels had brought his mother and father to join those at the right. But Michael's older brother, who had gone away to high school and college and who laughed at the Christians, was carried to the other side where the unfortunate groaned and gnashed their teeth. Oh, how awful he looked!

The group of boys around the ladder was shrinking. Many had walked in the light on the sunny side of the hill; many others on the dangerous side of the hill fell from the hands of the grim angel into darkness. Finally, Mikkola's whole courtyard was empty except for three boys who huddled there shaking. Three angels hurried down the hillside toward them. Michael caught his breath.

"Into which crowd! Into which crowd?" His heart pounded. He tried to cry out to his father and his mother, but his voice only rattled in his throat. Oh, Good Jesus! Those who came for the individual boys now arrived. Two faces shone warmly; the third looked grim. And the third came toward Michael.

"And he is going to take **me**! Take me into darkness! Oh no, **no**!"

Michael awakened. His big brother was poking him in the ribs and scolding, "What are you bawling about? Why aren't you letting people sleep?"

"I had a bad dream!"

"What about?" Michael told him, in a shaky voice. Big Brother listened to the dream. Neither of them slept any more that night. Michael never heard his brother ridicule Christians after that. He seemed contemplative, pondering in thought and sometimes sitting with the Bible. Now and then he was seen at services. In the spring when he graduated from college, he promised Mother that he would commence studies to be a minister.

Only Michael knew that his big brother's conscience was awakened on Judgment Sunday night by that amazing dream of Judgment.

---

[1] Last Sunday before Advent (or fifth Sunday before Christmas).

THE BROKEN SLED

The November days were grey. Either the clouds almost touched the ground or they lay like a damp wet mass flowing over the woods. Roads were muddy. Great flocks of crows hovered over the dirty meadows and fields. Sometimes it froze at night and other times the weather turned very mild. The children were anxious for winter and snow.

As winter came on, the ground froze on clear moonlit nights. Birches became white with frost and the cove near home reflected like a mirror. Then came some milder days when clouds crept over the sky and snowflakes filled the air. They fell on the roofs and branches and roads and fields like soft downy feathers. Before long the Heavenly Father had covered his autumn-like earth with the linen of freshly fallen snow.

For Brian and Emily these days were like holidays. At first they had to try out all of the skin-thin frozen coverings of meadows and mud-puddles. Then they got Father's permission to try on their skates and venture onto the ice in the cove near home. At first they frequently tumbled but before long the skate blades began to bite more firmly into the cold bright surface. Finally they brought their sleds out to the hill in front and began coasting down dizzily. Each child had his own sled from Santa almost two years ago. Emily happened to get the one which glided better, so that it got the name Nimble. Brian's sled became known as Sulky and Brian gradually became annoyed with it.

Sometimes Emily and Brian traded sleds entirely peacefully. At other times they slid together on Nimble. Then they had long giddy exhilarating slides. But once Brian secretly took his sister's sled and that is when the regrettable incident occurred.

The evening was already growing dark and Emily had gone inside, tired out by the day's activities. Brian snatched her Nimble and ran hard over to Jorma's narrow channel where only the big boys dared to slide onto Kerto's ice. When he got there the hill was empty. From far away down the ridge came a boom as the ice cracked from the cold. A grouse fluttered in a nearby fir tree.

Brian was actually almost terrified, but he screwed up his courage, threw himself onto Nimble on his stomach and the sled started sliding down the frozen hill at great speed! All went well at first, but quickly the speed became unmanageable as his eyes watered and blurred. Alarm seized him. He let go and threw himself off the sled and onto the ground. When he quit tumbling and could get himself up, Nimble had vanished! It had been thrown off the road and over the ditch into the trunk of a birch tree. Brian shook it loose and took a look. His sister's sled was smashed!

The boy knew he had committed an outrage. He left the sled in a snowdrift and started slowly trudging home. From somewhere in this darkness there was still a magpie which appeared on a fence rail to laugh at him.

At home, Emily tried to draw her brother into joking, but every now and then he forgot himself in his own thoughts. That night in bed Brian had an idea: tomorrow he would bring the broken sled to Henry Kero to be repaired. He finally fell asleep while making his plans.

Very early in the morning Brian was at Kero's blacksmith shop with Nimble. Henry certainly understood the situation. As soon as the sled was in good condition, Brian paid for the repair work from his Christmas money. It was disappointing but nothing else seemed to help.

During the day Emily was surprised at some of the scratches Nimble had gotten, and it didn't seem to glide as it did before. Now it seemed that **Sulky** gave longer, more dazzling slides. However, there was no fuss over the matter. Just the same, **Brian's** mind was disturbed. Every time they went to the hill or were pulling their sleds together, he felt downright badly.

Sunday came, and the sled rested in the shed while the children hurried off to Sunday school. There the teacher happened to speak about hypocrites. He explained that a hypocrite is one who covers up his own evil deeds and presents himself as better than he truly is. Then he told a story about a crooked merchant.

"He patched and painted a rotten old boat to make it look sharp and beautiful and then he sold it at a good price to someone in the next parish. On his first excursion, the buyer got caught in trouble with his sporty boat in a fierce storm and he was about to drown. A hypocritical person is like that fancy beautiful rotten boat. When the storm of death approaches, that poor soul is in such serious danger of drowning!"

Brian listened with a pained conscience. "Now the teacher surely means me and Nimble! How could he know? Henry Kero promised to keep it a careful secret!" To everyone's astonishment, Brian burst into tears in the middle of the class.

"What's wrong, Brian?" asked the teacher.

"I---I---I am a hypocrite!"

"How is that, Brian?" And then Brian told all about it.

The teacher's eyes also filled with tears. He blessed the sobbing pupil and assured him of forgiveness of all his sins in Jesus' blood. Then he led Brian over to Emily.

"Emily, do you forgive your brother?"

The girl rose immediately and threw her arms around his neck and said, "Believe your sins forgiven in Jesus' name and blood."

LEARNING CONTENTMENT

"Mother could fix better lunches for us," Arvi grumbled.

"I sure wish I could figure out how to get a catch here with less hard work," growled Sam.

The boys were huddled under their overturned boat at far-off Cat Island. Their campfire barely smoldered while an autumn storm raged. Waves rolled with fury onto the boulders on the shore. It rained and sleeted. Darkness now covered the big open sea as the lads munched their lunch in low spirits. They cut slices from a big loaf and spread them with butter from the lunch box. Between eating slices of bread, they bit into salted bream and took long drinks of buttermilk from the can.

"Those lines did go into the water somehow, but with the ice it will be like real stone-cutting to lift them out again in the morning," remarked Arvi.

"Yes, we're likely to knock some skin off our hands," agreed Sam. Sam was a sturdy thirteen-year-old. His job on these fishing trips was to row. Arvi was a year older, but lanky and much thinner. The line ran smoothly into the lake through his skillful fingers. He knew how to play the wildest pike until it tired and how to use the landing net. When he baited, the worms curled up on the hook as fast as one could imagine doing it.

Toward morning the wind eased a bit but the sleet grew more violent and the weather became colder and colder. The fishermen awakened shivering beside their dead fire. It took a long time to start a fire for making coffee. At last, however, the blackened pot began to bubble as the flames licked it and the boys warmed up, sipping its contents noisily.

At first the line rose well and they fed it into the crates. Again and again big bream came along on the line and now and then a small nuisance fish. Soon the brothers were soaked all through. Arvi was freezing; his face turned blue and his fingers ached with cold. One big walleye got away because their fingers became stiff and clumsy.

Ragged clouds hung down over areas studded with multi-colored islands. A cold reddish glow lay just above the horizon. The boys worked hard and finally got all five hundred hooks coiled in the box. Sam put twenty-three walleyes, each over one kilo, a couple of two-kilo pike and a number of smaller fish into the fish box. The catch cheered them but they hated to think of the trip home---over ten kilometers rowing against the wind in such weather!

"Let's go to Tuola Cape. There is a small tenant shack there where we could warm ourselves and dry our clothes," suggested Arvi. So they did. Neither of the boys had ever actually been in that hut before, but the gray hovel stood close to shore near a spring. The fishermen stooped inside through the low door and then looked at each other in solemn surprise. The hut was small, barely three meters long. Near the door was an open fireplace built of gray stones. The other corner was filled with a wide bed made of unpainted boards. It was full of dirty shreds of clothes and in the middle slept four stuffy-nosed children. Only two of the four windows had unbroken panes; the other two were stuffed with shingles and rags. Before the window was a box used for a table and a couple of stubby hassocks. The grey, cold house had only a dirt floor. Then the oldest child awakened.

"Where are your mother and father?" Arvi asked her.

"Father is in the hospital. I suppose Mother is either milking or gathering brush for a fire," the girl answered as she shrank in fear back into the litter.

Just then they heard sounds in the entry. The lady of the house came in with her apron full of wood and brush. "So, the brothers from the police are here, are they?" she greeted them. "How did you happen to come to such a miserable place?"

"We came to warm ourselves after we got wet fishing in this weather," explained Arvi, a bit puzzled.

Soon a fire blazed in the fireplace. The boys put their kettle on to boil and went about trying to get dry. All the children wakened and timidly slipped closer to the fireplace to warm themselves. Each wore only a dirty shirt. "Mama, give me bread," begged the youngest. The mother went out and brought in a half loaf of hard bread and a pail with a little milk in the bottom. Each of the children took a piece of bread and soaked it in the milk with their dirty fingers, eating it and drinking in turn out of the edge of the pail.

Meanwhile, the boys opened their knapsacks and began their meal as the children gathered about to look on. Sam cut each of them a slice from his loaf and spread on some butter. The faces of the little ones shone as they bit eagerly into the treat.

"We are very poor here," explained the mother. "If only Father were well!"

"God makes well," piped the smallest one, crawling into Sam's lap.

"If these children were able to catch fish, then sometimes we could have fish soup! But they can't do it yet," said the lady. Arvi slipped out to the boat and brought in two large walleyes.

"Fix these," he encouraged her.

In no time, the soup was boiling in a little pot. Sam added the butter which was left in his lunch box. He also left the rest of his loaf of bread and the salt fish at the hut with the family. "The Heavenly Father sent you here!" said the mother gratefully as they said good-bye.

"We'll come again!" promised Sam. The boys rowed against the wind in silence. They were more solemn than usual at home, no exuberant enthusiasm or bragging. Arvi recalled long afterward that he left his childhood in that tenant farm hut. The harshness of life there touched his heart and opened his eyes for the first time. In the evening the fishermen lay awake in their beds even though their bodies were fatigued.

Sam spoke first. "Mother! I will never again grumble about poor food or poor clothing."

"Nor I!" joined in Arvi.

"How is that?" wondered Mother as she dressed for bed. So the boys related to her about their stop at the Tuola Cape hut; Sam burst into tears.

When the boys went fishing for the last time that fall, they went again to Tuola Cape. They brought a basket full of food and a bag of clothes that Mother collected. And each boy gave the mistress twenty marks from his savings.

THE HAT

Charles was the oldest child of the village carpenter and was a ten-year-old full of promise. While they were playing in the school yard, Charles was not intending mischief when he grabbed Andrew Sorola's worn old hat and threw it into the air. Andrew himself only laughed. But just at that moment a fierce gust of wind whizzed over the cove and sailed the hat like a saucer amidst a whirlwind of leaves. When the hat finally fell, it dropped into the open mouth of a well. Charles took off like lightning and ran to the well, but could only stare numbly into its depths.

Soon a whole crowd of boys was there. The remarks rained down on Charles from the teasing gang:

"I saw it. It was Charles' fault!"
"Charles' fault, Charles fault!"
"Andrew, run tell the teacher!"
"Teacher will lock you up in a room alone!"
"You'll have to pay for it!"
"What will your father say? You'll get trounced at home!"

Andrew didn't say a word. He was nearly in tears and his lips quivered as he turned to run home. Now, Charles was a good student and not a troublemaker. He was not only the oldest child but also the only son in a wealthy home. Beside all this, he was a believing Christian lad. This was a good time for an act of kindness which might relieve some of the envy of the other boys. Charles knew he should run after Andrew but something held his feet where they were.

At that moment the bell called them all in for the last hour of school. The teacher did not notice Andrew's absence but he did wonder a couple of times at Charles' inattentiveness. The boy seemed restless and preoccupied. He stepped on the wrong foot in gymnastics and turned toward the wall when the rest turned toward the room. He didn't heed the teacher's instructions because he didn't hear them. His face was red and his life was miserable.

On the way home Charles walked alone. Many thoughts crowded his mind. "If only I could get the hat fished up. Maybe Matt, our hired man, will help me later tonight...What if Andrew's father, the shoemaker, is at our house?...He **is** a pretty kind-hearted man...When Father is angry he punishes hard!...I have enough in my savings box to buy Andrew a new hat. I'll dig the money I need out of there!" The way home seemed long. Right at the edge of the woods, Charles had to sneak past the Sorola cottage.

All was quiet at home. "Mr. Sorola is a very fine man. He is my parents' brother in faith. Maybe he won't come." But that didn't seem very likely. For some reason, Charles almost wished that Andrew's father would bring his boy and come storming and accusing. Nothing happened. The night grew dark. Soon one would not be able to see more than a step ahead, even with a lantern. The hired man Matt did not show up, so Charles could get no help from him to try to fish out the hat.

Charles was shaking his savings box to get money out when his mother came by. She took a long look and he gave up the effort. Charles' dread grew: "Andrew won't be in school tomorrow. The teacher will ask why. I'll be whipped and locked up!"

The words danced around before his eyes as he studied his lessons. During supper, one bite remained in his cheek so long that Mother asked, "How is it that our young son is so lost in his thoughts?" That made the bite get stuck in his throat and the youth choked with tears in his eyes.

Charles had to turn his pillow over at least ten times after he went to bed and it still was too hot. Over and over his evening prayer got tangled with that hat in the well and the prayer was never finished.

"Charles, why are you tossing and turning?" asked his mother. "Ask for the Father's blessing and forgiveness and sleep in peace." Then Charles began to cry: "But...that...hat..."

"Are you sick?" Mother asked by his bed.

"No, but...that...hat..."

"What hat?"

"That hat of Andrew's!" Finally the boy was able to tell the whole story. His mother comforted him.

"Tomorrow we will go to Sorola's and apologize and ask for pardon. From there we can go to the store to buy Andrew a new hat. That old one was pretty tattered and with winter coming it is about time for fur hats.

"It was just horseplay, wasn't it, but there was damage in the end. You have learned that too **much** frivolity can be harmful. Now believe, Charles, that this and all other sins are forgiven in Jesus' name and blood."

THE CONVERSION OF PETER JUUTI

The harvest had been threshed. Potatoes were in the pit. The plow-shaped V-formation of migrating cranes had turned its shrieking front end to the south.[1] The ground was frozen and during the day the wind blew off the last leaves from the birch trees in the schoolyard. Fall arrived at the slough area also, with sudden vigor. School opened. When the children thought about it, they saw that fall had its good side too. For the boys, it was a time to tromp in their smart new boots on the icy and puddle-filled road to school. The girls had their own fun, tricks and whispers while their cheeks glowed and their noses reddened.

The smaller coves were almost frozen, but there were still waves in the open water and ice was soft in the middle of the sounds. All the boys of the area went skating at the fish-clubbing area where the burbot concentrated near the shore as a last act. In that area, the fish could be dazed by striking the ice with a club. Then the ice was quickly broken away and the fish could be thrown out bare-handed. By evening, the fastest young fellows had a good-sized pile of fish and burbot soup was considered a delicacy.

The shoemaker's son Peter Juuti was always big for his age and by the time he was in the upper grades he looked quite mature. He also thought it showed that he was grown up when he smoked both at home and away from home, and he frequently shouted swear-words and dirty songs. He learned these bad ways at home, for shoemaker Juuti had a reputation for cursing and denying God. George was the son of a tenant farmer. Since he was a neighbor and in the same grade at school, he often walked to school with Peter. Now George was from a believing home, quiet, peaceful, good-natured. He often admonished Peter, "Why don't you quit the swearing and the off-color songs and the smoking?" But his companion would just grin.

"What's the matter, does it irritate the spirit of a child of God?"

"No, but it does upset me sometimes," deplored George, often near tears.

That fall a spiritual awakening moved in the slough area. Services were held for three weeks. The school teacher was converted in the living room of one of the farm houses. He promised to repent and asked for forgiveness from the children for his unrepentent life and his false teachings about faith. Then the class hours in Religious Study changed. The Bible stories began to live. The teacher even began to understand the catechism somewhat, and it became like a new book. First one and then another of the students came to the teacher in the evening to ask for forgiveness for disobedience or laziness or deceitfulness in school.

Only Peter Juuti remained hard and scornful. He devised many aggravations for his teacher and his classmates. Once he brought to Religious Study class a dove which he had shot with his bow and arrow. In the midst of their study of the third article of faith, the part about the Holy Ghost, he threw the bird in front of the teacher, saying, "There you have the Holy Ghost." The teacher went on as though nothing had happened. No one even smiled. Peter was nettled.

Then, when the last hour of the day came and prayers had been said, the teacher called Peter to his room, where just the two of them met together for a time. Flushed and sniffling, Peter finally emerged where George was waiting for him. "Why do you stand there, you child of God? To gape at a heathen like me?" Peter spoke harshly.

"But you are **not** a heathen!"

"Yes, I am too! I have not seen God nor got a penny top. Nothing!"

"Well, I will still pray. Nothing is impossible for God. My father once denied God also, but now he is a Christian and Mother says he is a completely new man."

The boys walked the rest of the way without a word. As he turned into his own path, Peter spoke up quickly: "Shall we go club-fishing right after supper?"

"We can," agreed George.

The fish were surprisingly hungry. Peter rowed like a storm from place to place. The club boomed and then he waved a cluster of burbot in his other hand. George was lucky enough to catch a pike weighing over one kilo and a couple of cod. The full moon was already risen in the heavens when George reached the mouth of the Kuha Straits and suggested that they go home.

"I think I'll go to the edge of the strait to try it," panted Peter. He was a little jealous and irritated by George's pike.

"Don't. You'll be disappointed there," warned George. But Peter went at full speed. Under him, the ice cracked and split and snapped and bent. His club rose and fell. Then there was a great splash and the boy sank out of sight. He rose and worked to the edge of the ice, coughing and choking. The ice broke, with jagged edges, and Peter sank under water again. It went just as badly the second and third times.

The fourth time the ice held, but Peter was so tired and numb with cold that he didn't have strength to climb onto it. He could barely hang on. George had disappeared and he could see no one. The cracks in the ice kept widening. Peter was terrified. "I'm going to drown!" He cried for help. Then he heard George's voice from the shore.

"God will help us, for sure. I am coming from shore with a boat." But the going was slow. The ice would hold the weight of the boat and the boy for a bit and then it would give way. George was soaked through. Chills shook his youthful joints but he strained hard and finally drew the boat next to the drowning Peter. He almost blacked out as he pulled and twisted Peter over the edge into the stern seat. The boat tipped badly and it was even harder to get back to shore. George was nearly exhausted. In the back, Peter never moved even his hand. He may have been unconscious.

"Dear God, have mercy! If Peter dies while he is still godless, what then?" whispered George. Peter already was living in another world. He knew nothing about how they got to shore nor about how George finally carried Peter on his back, crawling on hands and knees to the nearest house. Peter was floating in cold slush when suddenly a big bright white swan flew close to him. It grabbed Peter and lifted him to its back. It felt lovely to rest in the warm feathers as the bird rose to where the sun shone as in summer. From far away at the home of the swan, Peter could plainly see the gray cottage of Juuti the shoemaker.

In the yard stood a stalwart boy who aimed his slingshot toward the sky. Whiz! A stone flew clear up to the clouds and dealt the swan a blow to the head. The bird changed in a moment into a crawling snake and a nasty voice from somewhere said, "There you have the Holy Ghost." At the same time, a crouching creature began to plunge headlong at him. Peter gasped for breath. Soon he saw nothing. Round about him he heard the nasty voices swearing and speaking ugly words. Then he heard George's voice saying, "Pray!"

"Lord help me and have mercy on me!" cried out Peter.

Later he opened his eyes a bit and made some groans, reviving a little. He saw bustling about a small, alert, good-hearted man, the believing master of the house in Valkola. "Thanks be to God!" sighed George, who was resting from his ordeal. Color began to return to his face which had been terribly pale.

The boys were taken to a bedroom in back to rest, as it was already midnight. There Peter burst out, saying in tears, "George, will you forgive me everything? For now I surely believe that God hears prayers."

"In Jesus' name and precious blood, dear Peter, believe all sins forgiven. You also forgive me for the times I found you troublesome and even disliked you."

The Hanhineva shoemaker came in the morning to fetch his boy home. With oaths, he burst out at Peter, "Haven't I warned you that you would kill yourself following after good-for-nothings?"

"Father, do not curse. You should really thank God and thank George here. Without them, last night I would have sunk into eternal damnation!" Peter looked serenely into his father's eyes, but the father avoided his glance and became silent.

On the third day after all this, Peter went to talk with his teacher. Afterward, they came to class together. Peter was pale, and his eyes were red and swollen with weeping. After prayer was recited, Peter stepped in front of all his classmates stammered out, "All of you children of God, forgive me, for I have made fun of you and teased you and made trouble in many ways."

"Your sins are forgiven in Jesus' name and blood," was heard from timid voices in the group.

"Now Peter, too, is a child of God," spoke the teacher. "His past is forgotten in heaven and we also have forgotten it all."

Peter suffered a lot because of his faith, first at his home and later when he grew up and took a log-cutting job. But he never denied his faith in the good God and the Saviour of sinners. George became a speaker in the area and sometimes called Peter to his side to read the text at the start of a service. They often recalled that hard fishing trip, when the heart of a trouble-making boy was shaken by a blow from God.

---

[1] *Kurkiaura* translates literally to "crane plow", the flight formation.

JESUS, LITTLE AND POOR

Young Jacob's very first earnings were five brand new silver coins. During the cold fall he had walked along behind the plow in the potato field and picked up the hidden potatoes left behind. Father had promised one mark for every full potato basket.

The tramping was heavy because of the muddiness of the plowed field. Thick clay soles had stuck to his shoes. But by the time Peter and the hired man got the potato field plowed, Jacob had five baskets of potatoes. Then Father had given him those bright silver coins. Of course, he had to keep them very carefully in the pocket of his pants so he could peek and admire them every little while. But he intended that finally they would go into the savings box, just like the gifts he had been given earlier.

Jacob went to church with Mother on Judgment Sunday. The preacher spoke an unusual message about feeding poor Jesus, clothing naked Jesus and visiting sick Jesus. He then talked about how Jesus goes about concealed in his littlest brothers and sisters here on earth. "Is it helping Jesus," Jacob asked his mother on the way home, "if I give money to some poor child of God?"

"Of whom are you thinking?"

"Gus of Rapids Isle."

"Why do you think particularly of him?"

"He sat by me in Sunday school and a toe peeked out from each shoe. You told me you think that Gus doesn't always have enough bread, either." Jacob made up his mind that on the next Sunday would give the money he had earned to Gus.

During the week, Jacob played with Lauri Keiska. They examined the five coins many times. "What are you going to buy with your money?" Lauri wondered.

"I'll put it into my savings account," slipped from Jacob.

"You are a real pain," remarked Lauri.

Jacob did not understand these words at all. But when mean old man Tuohi was being called names like "a real pain, pain in the neck," he understood it to be bad. He didn't want to be in the same class as Tuohi. "I guess I won't put it in my savings account. I will give it to Gus of Rapids Isle."

"You **are** a foolish one. I sure wouldn't want to. The village government helps the needy," answered Lauri smugly, having heard the words from his father. Jacob was stunned as he walked beside this nonchalant playmate.

"What would **you** do then?"

"I would buy caramels and licorice and whatever from the sweet shop," he countered and with excited enthusiasm they began to recall the delicacies in the store. Jacob's mouth watered as they entered the store like grownups. They walked down the aisles and sat in a booth where they dined on goodies. But Jacob had a horrid feeling. Somehow he felt like he did on those days when Mother's jam bowl secretly emptied itself. The jam tasted delicious at first but later it didn't seem so tasty.

The following Sunday in Sunday school, Gus' toes showed themselves even worse than before. It was frosty already and his toes glowed red as coals. That drew one's eyes to them!

Sunday night Jacob had a bad dream. In his dream the end of the world came. The heavens shone brighter than ever. An angel led Jacob along the side of a high mountain. Other young boys were led by angels toward the top. In this way, a gathering of youths became a great crowd surrounding a gray rock at the top of the mountain. On the rock sat Gus of Rapids Isle with torn shoes. He cried. All the angels cried with him.

The heavens continued to brighten. They flashed a thousand times brighter than a crackling fury of northern lights.[1] Jacob choked in his throat.

An angel pointed at Gus' feet and cried all the more loudly. Then little Gus pointed out his need. Suddenly he became a grown man. His whole being began to shine. "Jesus," whispered a tearful angel. The Lord cried too. He looked at Jacob and said, "All that you did not do for one of these the least of these my brothers, you did not do for me." The whole angel throng burst into a groan. Jacob could not breathe.

"Jacob, Jacob, what **is** the matter with you?" asked his mother. "You yell in your sleep and awaken everyone!"

---

[1] Aurora borealis

LITTLE ARTHUR'S ENDURING DECISON

It was another of those strange dreadful nights. Arthur could hear that Mother was not sleeping. Over and over she sighed in her bed, arose, slipped over to the window and gazed out. A fresh wind was blowing and wisps of clouds sped over a moonlit sky. When the clouds covered the moon, the room darkened and a shadow passed over Mother's pale face. When the clouds passed again, a silver spot appeared on the floor under the window and Mother in her white nightgown looked like a bright white angel. A steamboat whistled somewhere, menacing and evil. The surf boomed on the shore down by the bath-house. Father was not yet home.

Arthur recited his evening prayer three times but sleep still did not come. He heard a shouted song from the road, growing nearer. The gate creaked and then banged against the fence. Someone swore harshly. The crude singing got louder and moved to the courtyard. Soon there were several men at the door. Arthur shrank under his covers. Mother slipped over to the door.

"You don't dare, old woman's man," Arthur heard from outside. Then the whole house shook as a huge rock crashed against the door. The key from the door flew under Arthur's bed with a clink. The hook gave way and the raw night air flooded the house. Three drunken men pushed in through the door.

"Coffee for visitors!" roared Father. No answer was heard. "Get up, old woman! Coffee for company! Don't you hear me?" ordered Father.

Arthur heard departing steps from the birch-lined walkway between the house and the gate. His heart pounded violently against his ribs. "What are you lounging around for? Coffee for the guests!" shouted Father. Arthur peeked in at the one fallen in sin. Father was kicking Mother as she lay on the floor. Arthur rushed in, shrieking, "Father!" After that, the room was flooded with bright moonlight. Mother's pale face! A big man's dark face!

When Arthur regained consciousness, it seemed that the silver splash under the window was changed to the sun's golden reflected image. The deaconess sat beside his bed. He could hear his father snoring somewhere.

"Mother! Is Mother---?" wailed the boy.

"Mother is fine. She went out to milk the cow. She only fainted last night, and was soon revived."

"But Father kicked her!" The deaconess nodded her head and a tear rolled down her cheek.

"I'm going to go kick Father!" he gritted through his teeth and his face quivered with anger.

"We must never return evil for evil," answered the deaconess, attempting to calm him. "Your father did not know what he was doing. Usually he is a good man."

"Then why does he have to drink?"

"He has acquired a thirst for alcohol."

"But why?"

"When he was young, your father took just a little drink in a group of men. Then he did it again and then a third time and even tens of times until his body began to demand it, more and more often, more and more drink. I can't explain it better. But try to sleep now."

"Can even God help my father any more?"

"Oh, yes!"

"Well, I will pray then that Father will be able to stop drinking completely." The boy's fingers folded into a cross. His lips moved slightly and his eyelids closed. He fell asleep again.

When he awakened, the sun had already rolled around to shine through another window. The dust danced oddly in its shaft of light. A fire crackled on the hearth and the fragrance of coffee filled the room. Mother sat by the table. Father was next to her, his head in his hands, crying.

"Mother," whispered Arthur. Mother hurried to her child. "Mother, I will never take even a little drink!"

"God help you to keep your promise," said Mother.

"God help you," echoed Father.

God did help, and Arthur grew up a believer and a sober man who never took a drink.

A CHRISTMAS ROAST

Although Junnu had waxed his skis, snow still stuck to the bottoms. Water dripped from the tree branches. Every now and then a great mass of snow slid with a thud from pine tree branches somewhere. Quail flew nimbly enough from tree to tree and a titmouse sang plaintively.

Junnu was on his trapline rounds along a barren arctic hill in the Piessa area. He was exhausted and sweat ran down his face and a curl of black hair was glued to his forehead. Junnu was the oldest of three brothers. He was still quite a short little fellow, only about 110 centimeters tall.[1] He was only eight years old but his jobs were grownup ones. His dear mother had been left a widow a year ago. His sister Maija was older and a bit taller but she was needed to help Mother in the gray cabin near the Root of Danger on the rim of Pierkku Rapids. And anyway, she would not have made a woodsman for she was a skinny girl. No, these were especially heavy journeys! How the skis dragged, probably from the ice and snow stuck on their bottoms.

Mother borrowed flour from the storekeeper in the early winter. Junnu had to hunt the willow grouse in order to make payments for the flour. Mother helped set the snares in the fall but then the whole task of trapping was left in the care of the youth. And he caught grouse! Mother said she prayed to the Heavenly Father who sent quail for the children of Israel in the desert. She taught Junnu how to pray also, and now a large flock of grouse covered the edge of the barren hill of Piessa. How exceedingly good the Heavenly Father is! Even now He looked down from the heavens and sent his angels to protect all who travelled near the edge of the gully. Thus Junnu was protected from falling into a chasm.

Today was Christmas Eve. Yesterday there were as many birds as Junnu could carry, but Mother took all of the catch to the storekeeper. Today the snares were empty, even though he really hoped for a Christmas roast for himself. Junnu checked twenty more snares and then he reached the trapping grounds of others. He stopped and scraped the ice from under his skis and again clawed his way ahead. He got his skis to slide a bit going downhill and then suddenly tumbled down into a patch of young spruce. He heard the furious beating of wings. "There must be at least one," he panted as he struggled from one snare to another, but they were empty. He listened intently.

Again he clearly heard it, wings now beating feebly in the snow. "Probably it's a bird in Pier Uula's snare. I'll leave it there! Let it be, even though it might be one of the large European wood grouse. It should still stay there." Junnu stood there and leaned on his ski poles. "Maybe I should still go over and look. Such grouse are sometimes caught in this kind of cover. I can still leave it there in the snare."

The boy crept on ahead. Beside a stump was a black chunk, a large European wood grouse, sure enough. It had struggled as long as it could, but now it lay without moving, with eyes turned up, still warm. Then the evil one entered

Junnu! He loosened the snare and took the dead bird with shaking hands and covered his tracks in the snow.

Then with pounding heart he hurried toward where he could hear the roar of the Pierkku Rapids. It was dusk. The clouds dropped even closer to earth. The wind was rising and snow shook down from the pine tree branches. God no longer looked down kindly from the skies, but the Luossavaara Ridge appeared, a dark slab of rock like a Laplander's old statue. The thunder of the rapids increased, the wind howled even more wickedly. A big driving blizzard was coming. "That's good. My tracks are being covered," said the lad as he tried to steel his feelings.

"A thief's tracks!" accused his conscience.

Junnu thought he heard the sound of skis behind him. Perhaps Pier was coming to get back his grouse! Strike him with the ski poles! Pier was already a big boy and quick tempered. But there was nothing there--his ears were deceiving him. Liar's ears!

Junnu threw his pack onto the porch and clattered into the house. "What kind of Christmas roast did God give you?" asked his mother.

"Not any, really." But Mother went out to the porch to look. She clapped her hands together and cried out. "God be praised! Junnu, did you remember to thank the Heavenly Father?" she asked as she turned back into the room. Junnu did not answer.

That evening, porridge and roast grouse steamed on the table. Mother even had brought candles from the store. The other children expressed their delight, but Junnu sat in silence. "We are eating stolen bird," his conscience ground at him.

Mother read about the stable, the manger and the baby Jesus. Then she knelt down and thanked the widow's Protector and the orphans' Heavenly Father who helped so wonderfully and even directed such a large catch into Junnu's snare. "And how does the thief pray?" asked Junnu's conscience as the boy knelt there beside his mother.

That night all slept except Junnu. The Pierkku Rapids roared. A Laplander who was rich and proud and who lived on reindeer had drowned in those rapids. It was said that on blowing stormy nights one could hear him cry out and gnash his teeth. The wind howled and whistled in the attic vent and snow rattled against the attic window. Junnu became fearful.

"Thief! Thief! A Christmas thief!" said his conscience. God no longer looked lovingly through the window nor did an angel stand by the bedside. But at Luossavaara the driving snowstorm pounded on a black Lapp statue, a dreadful thing at whose base were reindeer skulls and bird claws, claws of grouse, Christmas grouse. Junnu screamed.

Mother lit a candle and took her boy into her lap. His whole body quivered and shook. Junnu threw his arms about his mother's neck and squeezed her till it seemed her circulation must be cut off. "Mother, I am a thief! The grouse---the Christmas grouse...." He told the story.

Mother stroked her child's forehead and spoke soothingly. "God be praised, that he has not let your conscience grow hard. Believe your sins forgiven. Jesus of Christmas is your saviour. In his name and blood I preach to you, dear child, that sins are forgiven. Tomorrow we will go to Pier to ask for forgiveness."

Pier was alone at home in the Uula hut when Junnu slipped in, led by his mother. He ran at once to Pier and threw arms passionately about his neck, saying, "Pier, forgive me! Yesterday I stole a grouse from your snare!" Pier was baffled; he didn't know just what to do.

"You **will** forgive Junnu, won't you?" inquired his mother beside him.

"It is forgiven," briefly responded Pier, but his face had quite a concerned and serious look. Mother gently tried to tone down the conversation, searching for words, but the boys sat crestfallen.

Afterward, Junnu followed his mother's heels on the road toward home. Slowed by whirling snow, they heard the sound of skis on snow behind them as Pier quickly dashed toward them. "Mother, now he's coming to hit me!" exclaimed the distressed Junnu. They stopped. Pier also stopped and stood looking down at the handles of his poles.

"I just came to say that I have taken a few grouse from your snares too, Junnu."

Junnu's heart leaped warmly in his bosom. "Pier, believe that you too are forgiven in Jesus' name and blood," he proclaimed, his serious face as radiant as Errki Anttis, the one-eyed preacher.

That Christmas night Junnu relished his food and he enjoyed his sleep. God once more looked down so kindly from a brilliant heaven through the window. And an angel again stood near his bed, surely one of the same angels which sang to the shepherds that first Christmas:

"Glory to God in the highest, and on earth peace, good will toward men."

---

[1] Literally, a little over two cubits. A cubit is a measure taken from the length of a man's arm from elbow to fingertip, eighteen to twenty-two inches.

"I'M GOING TO BUY CHRISTMAS!"

First snow that fall did not come until the day before Christmas. When Bridget woke up that morning and looked out at the street through the curtains, everything gleamed white. The porch was white. The roof of the factory was white. The wind had plastered wet snow against the red brick wall so that it was mottled red and white. An old woman trudging past had white flakes on her black bonnet. Some feather-like downy flakes floated in the doorway. "They are like little Christmas angels," thought Bridget. She hurried away from the window to dress, for her room was cold and damp. Her clothes were thin and patched many times, but her slim body had hardened against the cold.

Mother had left for work long before and Bridget found some bread already buttered and a mug of milk left out on the table for her. She folded her hands for grace and then ate quietly. Today she did not have to go to sell Christmas papers. Yesterday the bookstore sold out of Sunday school supplies and settled all the accounts. After breakfast, Bridget admired her twenty bright one mark coins. They were the first real money she ever earned, and with them she could buy her mother a real Christmas present.

She wrapped the money carefully in a piece of paper and thrust her treasure into her pocket, then threw her mother's gray shawl over her shoulders and hurried outside. There the snow pushed into the cracks of her ragged shoes and pinched her toes. Her foot slipped in the gateway and the little hiker tumbled into the snow, but everything still seemed quite joyful. "Christmas, Christmas! I'm going to buy Christmas for Mother, like we had when Daddy was alive! I will buy Christmas!"

In her excitement, Bridget ran right into a gentleman's arms. "Hey, miss, where are **you** going in such a hurry?" he laughed.

"To buy Christmas!"

"Do you need me to carry it for you!"

"I don't think so."

"Well, take this anyway," smiled the stranger and he placed five more shiny coins in her hand. The girl now walked more carefully but her tender thoughts rang more strongly in her ears: "I'll buy Christmas! I'll buy Christmas for my own mother!"

The store was crowded but a salesgirl who knew Bridget noticed her. "What can I do for you?"

"I'm going to buy Christmas for Mother!"

"A whole new Christmas, right now?"

"Entirely!" Customers laughed and the salespeople behind the counters laughed. The old storekeeper emerged from his office with a smile to see who would buy Christmas. He whispered in the ear of the salesgirl, who patted Bridget on the cheek and said, "Come back in a couple hours to get it."

"How much will it cost?" inquired the child shyly and a bit embarrassed.
"We shall see."
"Will this be enough?" Bridget showed her money.
"I'm sure it will," assured the clerk.

The big clock outside the jeweler's store showed eight o'clock and her mother wouldn't get home until one o'clock. Bridget decided to look around and watch the people in the holiday rush until eleven and then hurry home from the market with her Christmas gift. She stopped to gaze at the toy-store window where a whole electric train circled the track and little elves danced and wiggled about. She glanced at the giant fir tree decorated with Christmas lights near the church wall. She saw a Santa with his bushy beard and long knapsack and she saw his elves scurrying briskly and nimbly in and out among the crowd.

She was suddenly startled to hear the big clock striking twelve o'clock. She reached her hand into her pocket to feel for her Christmas money. It wasn't there! Only a hole in the bottom!

Bridget's heart seemed to stop. She stood pale and shivering by the big market square, seeing the tatters and patches as she turned her pocket inside out. Then she tried to recall all of the streets she had walked on. She set out through all the human bustle to retrace her steps. In some places she went back and forth several times. People going the opposite direction bumped into her and she slipped on her freezing toes. Twice she fell into the gutter. The white snow had been trampled into a dirty slush where the bright coins might have been covered up.

People thinned out on the streets and the bulbs in the advertising lights turned on. Little Bridget continued her search. Her feet hurt. The jeweler's clock already showed four o'clock! "Oh, dear Jesus, let me find my money," she sighed as she sat on the jeweler's steps to rest. Downy white flakes floated in the air and Bridget glanced at them wearily. "The littlest Christmas angels," she remembered and then she fell asleep.

"Father, look! A little girl is sleeping on the snowy step!"

"You know, I'm sure she attends the bookstore lady's Sunday school," exclaimed a lady passing by.

"Very likely," answered the man.

"She **must** be awakened, or else she will freeze!"

"You waken her, daughter. And put that doll into her lap. I don't think she has a lot of Christmas joy."

"Oh, Father, you are so kind! I didn't think so, either."

Bridget awakened as someone brushed the snow from her forehead. "Where am I?" she stammered.

"You fell asleep here on the jeweler's steps."

"And what is this pretty thing on my lap?"

"It's the Christmas angel's gift for a nice Sunday school girl."

"But Mother didn't get **Christmas**!" Bridget sobbed.

"No? Why not?"

Bridget sadly related her tale of the day. Father and daughter looked at each other. He said to Bridget, "The stores are already closed, but come with us. We live near you." And so Bridget soon was sitting in a big warm kitchen surrounded by tens of delicious aromas. In her lap were a long silk dress, a lovely doll and a big package which held her Mother's Christmas gift, a bright woolen coat. Her feet had been rubbed with liniment and now they were in nice almost-new shoes and socks. Then she **found** her bright Christmas coins in her worn-out dirty old socks, where they had fallen through the hole in her pocket!

"Don't say a word about what you found or they will take back your gifts!" whispered the evil tormentor. "Don't lie to one another," reminded her conscience from one of her memory verses from Sunday school. And then the girl, tears and laughter mixing on her face, revealed her re-discovered treasure.

The cooks burst into laughter. The kindly uncle laughed. The nice lady laughed and the fat chief cook held his belly and laughed. A big St. Bernard dog yawned happily. "I think you have brought the true Christmas joy into this house," said the uncle.

"May God give you Christmas joy," Bridget answered earnestly. "But now that I have found my money again, I must go to the housewares store to buy my gift for Mother."

"I'll go with you," rejoined the kind lady, smiling. "I want to see just how one buys her mother a completely new Christmas."

Bridget's mother and the housewares store saleslady met them on the street. They showed concern, and then there seemed no end to the embraces and apologizing. Finally Bridget asked timidly, "Can I still go to the store and buy that Christmas?"

"Christmas is already at your home, dear child. That will be payment enough, so you just keep your coins," said the saleslady. "You brought Christmas joy to our store."

At home later, two candles burned on the table. A yellow Christmas pudding steamed in a big pot. All kinds of breads and at least a kilo of butter were in a basket. Sausage and herring were set out and a big bowl of red-cheeked apples. The fragrant, sweet smell of coffee filled the room. In the midst of it all sat a beautiful lady doll, a gift from the Christmas angel. And Mother had a brand new bright red coat.

When Bridget once again told the events of that day before Christmas, her mother cried, lifted her child onto her lap and sobbed. "The Heavenly Father gave Christmas to us orphans since I didn't have the chance to buy it for you," Bridget told her.

Mother cried and laughed too, so the the bowl of Christmas pudding bounced on the table. Christmas joy had been away for two years and now had come once more.

THE CHRISTMAS FISH

Father's earnings were very meager again. He had worked hard all fall. First he was on the crew at the Kourula fisheries where they used large fishing nets with floats at the top and weights at the bottom. However, the catch of whitefish, a very important source of food in Finland, was very poor. Then he was a wood chopper at the Kuspikerran grade school, but preparing firewood did not pay much. So the provisions were scanty at Lintuniemie's small rented farm. The food sufficed but things really were not good.

"There wasn't enough money to buy dried fish," reported Mother. It was two days before Christmas and she had just returned from the little village next to the parish church. "I did get rice for our Christmas pudding, and flour to bake a small dish of salted Baltic herring. We can still be thankful to the Heavenly Father for these. We don't merit even this kind of festive food."

Father, back from work, looked gratefully at his wife and agreed. "Besides, the Kingdom of God isn't meat and drink, but peace and joy in the Holy Spirit. We can miss the true meaning of Christmas even while we enjoy Christmas delicacies, if the Spirit is not in our hearts. I think we will still have a joyous festival."

"We **could** have good food on the table, too. The herring is awfully small for Christmas fish," grumbled fourteen-year-old Jacob. "You should have seen the load of groceries Mrs. Ranta had yesterday."

"It is good to be godly and content with your portion," reproved Father quietly.

"Be content! Be content! Always just content!" exploded the boy. "First it is toil from dawn till dusk until your hands bleed and then be content with salty herring and hard bread!"

"Some don't even have that," said his mother.

"So, should misery bring more misery?" shouted Jacob, losing his temper. He bolted violently out of the house.

"Son, son!" he heard his father calling after him, but his steps carried him furiously down the bank and past the bath-house to the ice.

The gray of the winter day became denser as evening twilight approached. It seemed that the gray sky was lowered over the tops of the spruce near the shore and the world was sinking into a deep sleep. Jacob's pace slowed down and eventually he stopped short at the mouth of the river. His temper had cooled off. Dimly through the dusk he could see the home shore and the pine branch that marked a hole in the ice. The bath-house stood as though it were ashamed of its smallness and greyness in the midst of the now-naked alders. He could make out the boat turned upside-down beside the path; the meadow and the fence; the house against a dark patch of spruce; the well with its hanging bucket. The pump handle looked like an old man's hand raised in blessing. Through the window he could see the flames on the hearth.

Jacob stood still a long time. His recent loss of temper did not fit this peaceful world. Christmas, the festival of peace, "Peace on Earth," was already here. He was ashamed to return home. Jacob circled in the vicinity of the bathhouse for a long time, pretending to examine the weasel tracks. He looked in the out-building where they threshed grain by hand, then followed rabbit tracks along the side of the fish shack and finally peeped in through the door. There hung the nets, the drag nets and the bow nets. On top of the beams was a long line of tackle boxes, hazardous spinning tackle and trawling hooks, winter boots and in the corner an ice-pick. "What if I go fishing tomorrow! I'd have fresh fish for the Christmas table!"

The thought comforted him a lot. He had in mind to do something to cheer Mother and Father, who of course were saddened by what had just happened. Jacob slipped into the living room, ate his supper quietly and then went to bed.

Jacob and his mother rose early on the morning of the day before Christmas. Mother kindled the fire in the baking oven. The boy put on his father's short fur coat and pulled a fur-lined cap over his ears. He looked up an ice-spud and ice-fishing hook and line and went out onto the ice. He chopped a hole in the ice and threw out the ice chips with his skimmer and then he lowered his shiny lure into the water to attract the fish. He jerked and jigged his short rod and watched the lure rock and flash in the dark water.

All was as it should be but there was no sign of a school of perch. Jacob moved to another place, perspiring as he chopped another hole. Then he sat humpbacked for a long time, jerking and waiting in vain. For half a day he chopped ice making ten fishing holes, but did not see a single fish. His feet were cold. He was hungry. Besides all this, he felt exhausted because his bad conscience had kept him awake all through the night.

Silently and sleepily the winter day grew gray and dark as the fisherman walked home, disappointed and crestfallen. "Well, you finally came home!" his mother greeted him cheerfully. "Coffee has just been made and fresh bread is ready, still warm from the oven. Father will be here soon also."

Jacob felt like crying. Mother was certainly cheerful and kind. There was a lot for which he could ask forgiveness. He had a notion to give her a hug as he used to do when he was little, but a young **man** just doesn't do that!

Later, without being asked, Jacob split a pile of firewood and stacked it near the fireplace to dry. He also piled wood for the sauna next to the stove. He hauled water to the bath-house and shoveled the manure from the barn. Even though it looked like there was already a week's supply of hay, he carried a good-sized pile of hay by moonlight to the barn from the meadow. Still, he was depressed at the evening meal and no sleep came when he went to bed.

Once at services Jacob had heard the preacher say that obedience is better than sacrifice.[1] He explained that sometimes a person is willing to do almost anything to avoid the need for obeying the Lord's word and obeying the voice of the conscience that counsels repentance. That thought kept Jacob awake.

The night became endlessly long. There had been baking all day in the kitchen and the house was stifling hot. Jacob's little sisters whimpered in their sleep. Blackie, the dog, growled in his sleep. The clock ticked its even rhythm and struck the hours after what seemed terribly long each time. Finally he heard Mother wake up Father. Jacob could stand it no longer. He jumped out of bed, embraced his father and begged, "Dad, forgive me."

"You are forgiven, son, in Jesus' name and blood. Mother, you come and bless Jacob, too. Didn't I say, 'Christmas will come to us'?"

Jacob cheerfully shoved the ice sled down to the lake. He was going to get the Christmas tree but he decided that on the way he would try his luck at fishing one more time. Stopping at the holes he made yesterday, he skimmed the icy slush out of each one and flashed his bait in the dark water, but his efforts were in vain.

So he went on to get the Christmas tree. He found it almost at once, right at the base of the first point from home. It was only noon when he worked his way back toward the cove near the house. Snowflakes floated in the air. A column of smoke curled up from the bath-house and sleigh bells jingled along the main road. Jacob felt wonderfully light-hearted, as though he were walking on air.

He came once more to the fishing holes. "Why don't I try again? Perhaps the Heavenly Father will send his schools of fish to this part of the lake," thought Jacob. Disentangling his hook and line, he once again lowered the bait that glistened like a tiny whitefish. "Now, I'll give it a couple of light jerks. Now let it rest a moment. Now deeper, now up toward the surface. That motion looks perfect! This hole is right over a well-known dropoff from the shallow bar. I'd expect a lively fellow to be travelling along here now. There! That was a strike! Pull now!" The rod nearly jerked from his hand. "Now, pull it up!"

The fish fell like a black lump on the ice, nearly too big for the hole. It flopped, threw the hook from its lip and again flopped around on the ice for a moment, then gradually stiffened. It was a bass, a true Christmas bass. Jacob guessed it weighed over two kilos!

Now how lightly the sled slid toward the house with its load! Perkko and Mary stood in the yard and shouted with delighted excitement, "Christmas, Christmas!"

Mother came through the door. "Are you bringing Christmas?"

"Christmas and Christmas bass," answered Jacob.

---

[1] See I Samuel 15:22.

SARAH-MARIE RETURNS HOME

How slowly the train rattled along! Sarah-Marie shivered with the excitement inside herself. The conductor had already opened the door and still the journey continued. Now up the last hill, Firewood Hill, and past Chokecherry Cottage. Finally the locomotive whistles and the brakes squeal as the wheels go slower and slower. See the flagman's multi-colored signal flag. The train stops!

"What luck!" she thought. "No one here who knows me. It will be a complete surprise at home. They aren't expecting me for another week. These bags get heavier and heavier, but I'll manage if I keep changing hands." Ice crunched under her feet, although the ground was still bare of snow. But the trees bordering the road were thoroughly covered with frost. Ah, to be at home! To be at home for Christmas!

Near the burned-out clearing, she saw Hilma at the well: "Hi, Sarah-Marie."

"Hi, there!"

"What do you hear in the city?"

"Same old thing."

"There will be a dance at the farmhouse on St. Stephen's day. Fellows will come all the way from Sorjo! You'll come, too, won't you?"

Sarah-Marie flushed. "No. Possibly not. You see...you see, I..." Then she became even more embarrassed.

"Oh, yes, I forgot! We've heard that you have become a believer. Well, pardon me for being a country hick!" said Hilma brusquely, her braids swinging as she started with her pail toward the barn. For a moment, Sarah-Marie stood stock-still. It cut so deeply that a former good friend should act like that!

"But that is how it is to be. 'Blessed are you when people insult you, persecute you and falsely say all kinds of evil against you because of me.' That is what they have always assured us at services." Sarah-Marie spoke half to herself. "On the other hand, it's just as well that the word of my repentance has spread. Perhaps I'll get by easier so far as trials are concerned." Still, Hilma's ridicule hurt deeply inside.

Sarah-Marie's steps gradually became slower. Her cheeks glowed like cranberries and she perspired. As she walked through the woods, the house where the dance was to be appeared at the edge of the village. It seemed distant and foreign, almost like a prison. It had been like a place of slavery for Sarah-Marie.

Sarah-Marie never really wanted to go there, especially not the first time. That time, she sneaked stealthily out through the window at night while Hilma Huhta waited behind the sauna. Going in that fashion made her feel badly, but since she had promised while with a group of girls, it would have been embarrassing to eat her words. In the course of time, it became easier and sometimes she even felt drawn to be there. However, she never felt completely at ease about the matter. Sometimes as she watched the twirling couples, it was like peeking through the window of the insane asylum.

Then, too, she was always aware of her father and mother, first coming from services, then kneeling in prayer for their prodigal daughter. Sighing, they would lie down to rest while still keeping vigil. How she had to steel her heart and harden herself to make herself available in order that someone would take her to that crazy place. First it was the neighbor boys who came and then others from further away.

The last one was her seducer, with whom she soiled her soul and body. When the unclean fun with him was over, he just left town. Then there were times of agony! Her pillow was wet on many nights. On Sunday nights, she had to throw herself into exaggerated whirl and bustle, hoping that her burden would temporarily be eased. **That** was slavery if anything was, straining to be what she was not.

Today the delight of freedom filled Sarah-Marie's innermost being. She almost wondered that believing Christians could still be tempted by such goings-on. It felt good to her that she need never go again. She no longer needed to hear or follow the shouts of the crowd. At night, she could lie down to rest in peace and awaken in morning refreshed! "Old things are passed away, behold all things are new." God is indeed good![1]

In His wisdom, the Heavenly Father directed her to the city. The family could have used her help at home, but Sarah-Marie went anyway. She fled, despite Mother's tears and Father's somber face. But they followed her in their thoughts and prayers.

Everything there was unfamiliar and impersonal. She was alone. In the evening where she worked as one of the kitchen help, she had time to sit down and meditate on the past and future. Twice she tried to kill time at the movies, but her eyes tired there and really, in her inner self, she was sickened and ashamed.

Then her mother wrote, just a few words in seldom-used handwriting: "My child, aren't you lonesome for both your earthly home and your heavenly home?" The letter also included the address where the children of God usually gathered for services in that city. Sarah-Marie had the next Sunday free and she sought out the service at that house. The service had already begun. Uncle Tom, a familiar speaker who had come to her home many times, sat behind the table with a big pulpit Bible open before him. Everything seemed so homelike! People were like old friends. Sarah-Marie felt quite secure in their midst.

It took the speaker some time to get warmed up to his sermon, but then the text was opened to him and the words flowed. He spoke about the lost sheep, the lost coin, the prodigal son. Then he explained how one falls into the way of the prodigal, which is just how Sarah-Marie's life had been. He went on:

"The Lord seeks the lost. The conscience is timid and the soul becomes restless. The Lord speaks by way of the father and mother's mouths, and calls to repentance and faith. Even if Mother no longer has strength to open her lips in reproof and counsel, do not her tear-stained cheeks and furrowed face still speak?

"The Lord continues to call, here, today. How I wish to say to you, stumbling friend on the way of sin, haven't you gathered enought secret sins to your heart? Haven't you been tortured into a painful state of conscience? Wouldn't this be a fitting time to return, in repentance and faith? Behold, the Shepherd seeks the lost, desiring to lift the lost one in his arms and carry him back into the flock. But you only intend to flee! This is the way a person flees from his salvation as long as he is able and has the strength to do so. Perhaps there is one here tonight who no longer has the strength to flee?"

At that, Sarah-Marie burst into tears. "Oh, I am no longer able!" The whole house stirred as though a warm wind had wafted through. "Believe your sins forgiven in Jesus' name and precious blood," echoed from all around.

How the minister's face beamed as he continued his sermon. His eye sparkled. He spoke of the lost being found; how the lost one shyly and fearfully answers the Shepherd's call. He told how the children of God carry the lost into the holy collective body by declaring the gospel of grace, into the fellowship of brothers and sisters who have already come to faith.

Sarah-Marie felt good to be there. It reminded her of when she was a little girl, when the light burned at the ceiling on winter nights. Her mother bounced her on her knee as she sang:

> I am surely a little one, quite little;
> You forgive my sins out of pure grace.
> Precious Father, you won't cast away.

How light her footsteps were on the way to the home where she worked. That night, the kitchen seemed like home to Sarah-Marie. The lady of the house marvelled next morning when she heard ringing out from the kitchen:

> My rejoicing soul
> Won't cease to sing,
> When the poor wearied creature
> Has been relieved of her burden.

Sarah-Marie could already see the cottage home from Heka's clearing. It was just a red speck amid the red berries of the mountain ash and the bright green of the rye field. She saw the pasture from which she fetched the cattle a thousand times. She saw Sarkilampi's tract and finally Father's field and barn and yard.

Children's faces appeared momentarily at the window and then the door burst open. They rushed out, Peter at the head and Marjorie close behind. Both ran straight into the arms of the new arrival. "God's Peace, children! You almost tipped me over and knocked me down!" Sarah-Marie laughed and cried at the same time. Father and Mother also appeared on the porch. For quite some time, they embraced, asking and giving forgiveness.

"It seems to me that Christmas has come!" burst out Marjorie.

"But it's more than a week till Christmas," Peter objected.

"Marjorie is right," Mother agreed. "It seems like Christmas to me, too."

"Christmas indeed," said Father. "Haven't we found a great gift? One who was lost is found!"

"Well, all right, it can be Christmas," assented Peter. "In that way, we can have **two** Christmases.

---

[1] See Rev. 21:4-5.

CHRISTMAS GIFT FOR OLD TEACHER

Everyone in Teal Rapids knew that the elderly lady school teacher was a Christian. Even Perala the shoemaker, who was convincing himself to deny God, admitted: "If there **is** a heaven and if **anyone** gets to go there, this teacher will be among the first."

But nobody talked about it with her! Instead, nearly all the village folk were timid about approaching her. Her very being gave off an impression of unwavering goodness and purity that caused guilty feelings among all who carried hidden sins on their hearts. Of course there were plenty of these in Teal Rapids! The only ones who understood her in their hearts were Liimatta the tailor and Taitta the carpenter. To them she related her trials and griefs. Especially with Grandfather Liimatta, she lamented how poorly she confessed Christ and lived in Christian faith in school and in the village. The old grandpa never argued with her, but only preached the simple gospel of the Saviour of sinners and the forgiveness of sins.

The greatest sorrow in the teacher's heart was that not a single one of her students had found the strength to walk in the path leading to repentance. They all ran wild and partied in godless ways. Even the ones who seemed to comprehend at times in the religious training period fell into sinful ways without guilty conscience. There were those whom she always treated with great kindness who still remained unfeeling. Others were rowdy and bad-mannered, requiring her endless patience. Many times, for the good of the whole class, she spoke privately with these students. Some of these former students, between battles as they fought in the revolution, reported this frail grey-haired lady to the authorities. It seemed that her conscience brought her to warn them, "If you rise against the government you rise against God's decrees." [1]

This was the last year of work for the teacher. The following fall she would retire. The school celebrations of Christmas were over. Elsewhere, days were happy with anticipation and full of bustling preparations for holiday celebrations, but the midwinter days were quiet and gray for a single lady growing older. She did make up gift baskets for the poorest homes in the village. They expected them, almost ordered them, waited ungraciously for the baskets and then criticized the contents while comparing with the neighbors.

Once again the teacher rendered an account before her Lord: "I have been left alone this way because of pride and stubbornness within me. I have just looked on from the side and bewailed the evil of the world. I have not walked in the footsteps of the Master, of whom they said, 'Behold a man gluttonous, and a wine-bibber, a friend of publicans and sinners.'[2] I have been too serious in the midst of my students. I have not learned how to become a child among children, to be joyful among the rejoicing and to cry with the crying. That is why I don't have anything now to my credit to present to God." This thought had often come to her mind. This time it seemed clearly a message from heaven, an almost crushing accounting of her life.

On Christmas Eve the teacher delivered her gift baskets to the appointed homes. The baskets were snatched through the low doorways. "Thank you. I would invite you in but I am still in the middle of Christmas cleaning. Thank you!"

Her last stop was Liimatta's hut. "God's peace. God's peace," she heard from many mouths of children and beloved adults.

"I feel that I am not well with God," she began earnestly. Then she told of the outcome of her inner examination.

The old grandpa encouraged her warmly. "Oh, dear sister, I have experienced the same all through my Christian life. In life we are great sinners and we remain great sinners, which is why moment by moment we need a complete salvation. Isn't it lovely that even with all our faults we may be secure in our Saviour, the Christmas Jesus? Dear sister teacher, sins are forgiven in his name and blood."

On the way home, the mood of the teacher was a bit lighter. But when she was alone again she became disheartened. She tried to refer to the Christmas gospel but it was left as though it were covered under a snowdrift. Finally the message began to echo inside her: "Your place is among the lost!"

Just then someone walked into the courtyard and knocked at the door, timidly at first and then more forcefully. When the lady opened the door, a middle-aged man pushed into the room.

"God's peace, Teacher. I am John Lahtinen, if you remember. The most wicked boy you ever had in your classroom! Can you forgive me for all I did?" The man grasped her wrinkled hand and looked in her eyes. It touched her heart, so that she could hardly stand.

In a weak voice she answered, "Yes, your sins are forgiven, John Lahtinen, in Jesus' name and blood." Sinking into the corner of the sofa, she went on almost rambling: "Yes...yes...John Lahtinen...the school horror...the village terror. Yes, Lahtinen's Jack...my...first...great...Christmas gift!"

"The last sometimes becomes the first," she heard her guest say.

"Right, Jack, publicans and harlots go into the kingdom of God before you! The Lord Jesus be praised!"

Jack Lahtinen then related how in school the teacher's patience, love and tender speaking always touched him painfully. During the frantic race into sinful living he was unable to silence the voice of his conscience. The sharp pain in his chest remained even after he left his school desk. It did not die out when he was drinking or slapping down playing cards or cursing or even denying that God existed. Travelling around the land, he arrived at the Tornio River and remained there after floating logs to their destination. He took a job for the summer as a hired man in a Christian home and there, finally, the Lord took hold of him.

"The people there saw right through me even though I tried to act carefree and be derisive. My employer untiringly spoke to me and glorified the road to heaven, in the field, while fishing, in the sauna, everywhere. The preachers spoke in their services very accurately of my sins. Then I became, how shall I say, uncertain what to do. And so the Christians there were able to bless me with the gospel of forgiveness. Now I've come to visit the home area as a new man, a child of God. There is so much here to ask forgiveness for and make amends. I started with you," smiled the man peacefully and without pride.

John Lahtinen circled the village from house to house and from cottage to cottage. He went to the owner of the lumber mill and confessed that he had cheated the firm in measuring a stack of wood and he offered reimbursement.

"These things happen," he heard. "These things happen to each of us, one thing or another. I can pardon it for my part and I can speak on behalf of my company. It's forgiven. By the way, we have an opening for a foreman at this sawmill."

Bitter tears of repentance were shed in many of the little dwellings. A quiet awakening spread from conscience to conscience. Here and there the awakening swelled to a painful ache of the soul which forced many to ask of the few Christians living in the area: "What must we do to be saved?"

Old Grandpa Liimatta was able to bless a number of the neighbors who lived in a nearby cottage with the tender washing gospel of reconciliation. This was the same gospel which opened the gates of heaven to the thief on the cross on the great day of reconciliation.

Many former students who indeed had much to cry about came to visit the teacher and receive forgiveness. The elder teacher's life became another world. Her happy tears were apt to flow at any time from morn till night. Childlike freedom and joy brightened her face from which the last traces of stiffness disappeared forever.

"Children, dear children! The affairs of bad children are made good before the Father through Jesus!" she repeated in a weak voice of peace.

---

[1] See Romans 13:2
[2] See Matthew 11:19

LITTLE THINGS ARE IMPORTANT

"I want to become a great friend of animals!" said Breta, as she petted a purring kitten. "I'll arrange for a big, well-lighted stable where I'll gather the abused horses of Gypsies and other unkind people. Then I'll care for their wounds and let the hired men include a lot of meal in the scoop."

"**I** will build a real big home for children!" declared Anne with enthusiasm. "Any poor little boy or girl can come there. I'll be a most good-natured Auntie to them. Every day each one will be given a delicious wheat biscuit. And every **other** day all will get pancakes and strawberry jam. In the evenings we will sing songs of Jesus and on Sunday Uncle Karl can come to hold Sunday School."

"Well, **I** shall become a nurse for the sick!" mused Martha. "I will visit poor old ladies free of charge. I will tidy up their tiny houses. I will dress them in snow-white new shirts and give them their medicine. I will read the Bible to them and sing so tenderly that the dear old ladies will weep with emotion."

Evening came and Mother prepared to go milking. "Breta, you can help me in the barn," suggested Mother. The girl raised her head in surprise and asked, "What would I do there?"

"You could give the sheep and calves their hay."

"Okay, I'll come in a minute, after I finish this story." But the story was long and full of suspense. Mother was clattering in the entrance with her pail already full when Breta closed her book. Ashamed, she sneaked quietly into her room.

During the night little Mira became ill. Her worst discomfort soon left her, but during the following day the child was restless. "Anne, please stay with poor Mira a few hours. Entertain her, sing to her and play with her. Change her pants if she wets herself," said Mother as she hurried away to the village on her errands.

Anne really loved little Mira, so to begin with she gladly sat down by the cradle. But Mother was gone a long time. The child began to whimper. Anne noticed that she was wet but thought, "Mother will probably be home soon. She can change her better than I can." The fussing changed to crying. Anne rocked and rocked Mira and she even tried to sing from time to time. Finally she gave up and almost quit trying. When Mother finally arrived, little Mira had screamed herself completely exhausted and Anne was gruff and cross and entirely out of patience. Mother listened for a moment behind the door, then came quietly on into the room, dried the baby and took her into her lap where she fell asleep at once.

"We heard that old Mr. Mikkola is sick," said Mother in the late afternoon. "Martha, would you please go to him and bring this medicine. I think it will help. You could tidy up his place while you're there. Take a song book along and sing some pretty Christian songs. The believing old man would love it."

"But it is such a dreadfully long way there and the blizzard has drifted the road closed. And that grandpa chews tobacco and spits on the floor! How could I clean there! And his house smells so bad and roaches walk on the walls."

Martha looked apprehensively at her mother and then glanced toward Breta and Anne by her side for support. Right then Mother sat herself down before her girls.

"Perhaps I heard wrong yesterday morning. Yesterday I had outstanding children of really great promise. Breta cared for sick abused horses from all over the world in her stables. Anne was the wonderful good-natured auntie for the little children's home she intends to establish. Martha will tenderly care for old people.

"But yesterday this same Martha did not feel like coming to the barn to give even a handful of hay to the sheep and calves. And Anne became impatient with her sick little sister. And Martha did not want to go to bring medicine to a poor sick kindly old neighbor grandpa!"

"Okay, okay, I will go!" mumbled Martha, blushing quite red. She took the package of medicine, found a song-book and slipped out through the door. "May we go too?" begged Breta and Anne.

Mother gave permission. The weather was blustery as the girls walked along the pathway in silence. Finally Breta said, "Well, Mother certainly showed us how we have been selfish and disobedient!"

Old Grandfather Mikkola got his medicine. Martha gave it to him as she had watched it done by the parish nurse. Breta found a juniper brush broom and swept the floor. Anne lit a delightful blaze in the fireplace. Then together they all sang many of their Sunday School songs. They didn't let roaches peeking from the cracks disturb them, either. The old man listened with tears in his eyes and when the children finally prepared to leave he blessed them heartily.

That evening the sheep and calves had three happy chore-girls to feed them. After she returned from the barn, Martha sat quietly like an adult rocking Mira's cradle until she fell asleep.

When Breta, Anne and Martha, the leaves of Mother's very own three-leaf clover, were ready for bed, Mother read the assigned text for the day, which was Judgment Day. She especially emphasized Jesus' words: "Inasmuch as you have done it unto the least of these my brethren, you have done it unto me."

Father listened too. "You see, children," he said very seriously, "the world we live in is full of boastful but lazy talkers who don't want to fulfill the duties of everyday life. It is my hope that my little ones will not become such proud builders of air castles. May God make of you quiet and peaceful servants of Jesus to whom one day it shall be said: "Well done, thou good and faithful servant: thou hast been faithful over a few things, I will make thee ruler over many things!"[1]

---

[1] See Matthew 25:21.

Appendix

A LITTLE FINNISH HISTORY

Those of us who have lived our lives in the United States of America have no experience comparable to that of the Finns. It is appropriate to include a very brief look at Finland itself to add relevance to these stories.

Most will know that Finland is a country of northern Europe, not quite twice as big as the state of Minnesota. Its closest big neighbors are Russia on the east, Sweden on the west, and Germany and Poland to the southwest. The latitude, from 60° to 70° north, is north of all of England and north of most of Alaska.[1] Finland is a relatively low flat country except for a small highland region at the far north. The Gulf Stream to the north, the Baltic Sea on the south and west, and the generally low elevation all contribute to Finland's ability to support temperate-zone agriculture farther north than any other country in the world.

Finland has a long turbulent history, most not of its making. Humans appear to have inhabited Finland at least as early as 7200 B.C. Baltic Finns migrated to Finland beginning about two thousand years ago. Finland has been influenced enormously by Sweden and Russia since as early as 1200 A.D.

The king of Sweden and the Roman Catholic bishop of Uppsala decided in the 12th century that Finland was too resistive to the influence of Sweden and the church and they launched a more forceful influence. Finland was dominated in language and economics and religion by Sweden for three centuries. In 1581 Finland became a Swedish grand duchy (had its own duke) and by 1634 was fully incorporated into the Swedish kingdom.

With the beginning of the Protestant reformation under Martin Luther, young clergymen and seminary students studying at Wittenberg University in Germany brought Lutheran teaching and faith back to Sweden and Finland. In 1527 the Parliament of Sweden declared the king of Sweden to be the head of the church of Sweden, making Sweden and Finland nominally Lutheran. Over ninety per cent of the Finnish population today belongs to the official state Evangelical Lutheran Church.

Sweden declined as a world power as Russia was rising. Part of Finland was ceded to Russia in 1721 after the Great Northern War, and in 1809 all of Finland was ceded to Russia under Alexander I. Russia became a dominating influence on Finland for much of the next two centuries, even at a time of the growth of Finnish nationalism. Russia was defeated in war by Japan in 1905 and experienced its own Bolshevik revolution in 1917 toward the end of World War 1. Finland declared itself an independent republic in 1917.

World War II in 1939 brought an end to Finland's ability to maintain complete neutrality. Finland was consigned to the Soviet sphere of influence by the Hitler-Stalin pact as the Soviet Red Army occupied Poland and the Baltic states. Soviet-Finnish negotiations broke down and Stalin demanded land concessions from Finland. On November 30, 1939, the Soviet Union invaded Finland. The defense of the Mannerheim Line was spirited but the vastly larger Soviet army broke through. The fighting in *Father and Son's Christmas* and *The Return* involved this Soviet intrusion. The 1940 Treaty of Moscow gave Finnish land on the north and east to the U.S.S.R.

When Germany attacked Russia, Finland was willing to join the fight against Russia to get even. Great Britain eventually declared war on Finland. When Germany rebuffed Finnish requests for additional German troops to oppose Russia, a new Finnish government steered a course to withdraw from the war. In 1944 Finland signed an armistice with Great Britain and the Soviet Union and agreed to force the German army to withdraw. Terms of indemnity to the U.S.S.R. were nearly ruinous and strained Finland's resources to the breaking point. Since 1944, relations between Finland and the Soviet Union (which has recently disintegrated) have been non-hostile. Finland still consistently remains non-aligned with the great powers.

This history, of a stubborn little nation of stubborn industrious practical people with great national pride, unavoidably influenced by powers much bigger on all sides, is in the background of the stories in this book. It was in this milieu that the stories in this book took place.

The emergence of Finnish literature is also an interesting history. Three Finns are particularly worthy of our mention. **Mikael Agricola**, one of those contemporaries of Martin Luther studying and teaching at Wittenberg, Germany, deserves the credit for making Finnish literature possible at all. Agricola compiled the Finnish alphabet book so that the people might learn to read in Finnish, particularly to read the Bible for themselves. In 1531 Agricola returned from Germany, eventually becoming rector of the Cathedral School at Turku where young clergy were trained in Lutheran faith. He translated from German into Finnish a catechism of the reformed doctrine and a prayer book. In 1548 he translated the New Testament and in 1552 part of the Old Testament.

Nearly two hundred years passed before further significant Finnish literature emerged. Remember that for all of this time Swedish was the official language, the language of government and the ruling class and economics and education. Finnish, Lappish and Karelian languages and dialects existed but were more often spoken or sung than written.

Finnish nationalism was called forth by Ivar Arwidsson in the first half of the 1800's. He is quoted: "Swedes we are no longer; Russians we can never be; therefore we must be Finns."[2]

A teacher, **Johan Runeberg**, published in 1848 a collection of poems telling the stories of humble Finnish heroes in the wars against Russia. National pride rang in *The Tales of Ensign Stål* in a way not heard before.

At nearly the same time **Elias Lönnrot** created his popular great epic *Kalevala* which proved Finland's right to be recognized as a distinctive nation.

Lönnrot was educated as a medical doctor and practiced throughout his life. Yet his literary contributions cannot be overstated. Lönnrot travelled throughout northern and especially eastern Finland, listening to and gathering and writing down the oral folk poetry and legends told and sung in homes for centuries. He wove these into a poem (our English translation has 335 pages!) reciting the trials and triumphs of the legendary popular heroes, exaggerated at times, in their common daily business of life. Longfellow's *Hiawatha* borrows heavily from this national epic first published in 1835.

Lönnrot accomplished much more. He was a principal in the creation of the official Swedish/German/Finnish dictionary. From his educated background and from his vast collection of sung and spoken materials, he produced a comparative Finnish grammar out of the confusion of Finnish dialects. Lönnrot was an enormously prolific writer throughout his life and was apparently almost revered in his lifetime both for his achievements and for his exemplary lovely relationship to people around him.[3]

---

[1] The Arctic Circle lies at approximately 66.5° north latitude.
[2] *Heroic Finland* by David Hinshaw. G.P.Putnam's Sons, 1952.
[3] *The Kalevala* by Elias Lönnrot, translated by Francis Peabody Magoun, Jr. Harvard University Press, 1963.